The Politics of Enchantment

ROMANTICISM, MEDIA, AND

CULTURAL STUDIES

Cultural Studies Series

Cultural Studies is the multi- and interdisciplinary study of culture, defined anthropologically as a "way of life," performatively as symbolic practice, and ideologically as the collective product of media and cultural industries, i.e., pop culture. Although Cultural Studies is a relative newcomer to the humanities and social sciences, in less than half a century it has taken interdisciplinary scholarship to a new level of sophistication, reinvigorating the liberal arts curriculum with new theories, new topics, and new forms of intellectual partnership.

The Cultural Studies series includes topics such as construction of identities; regionalism/nationalism; cultural citizenship; migration; popular culture; consumer cultures; media and film; the body; postcolonial criticism; cultural policy; sexualities; cultural theory; youth culture; class relations; and gender.

The new Cultural Studies series from Wilfrid Laurier University Press invites submission of manuscripts concerned with critical discussions on power relations concerning gender, class, sexual preference, ethnicity and other macro and micro sites of political struggle.

For further information, please contact the Series Editor:
Jodey Castricano
Department of English
Wilfrid Laurier University Press
75 University Avenue West
Waterloo, Ontario, Canada, N2L 3C5

The Politics of Enchantment

ROMANTICISM, MEDIA, AND

CULTURAL STUDIES

J. David Black

Wilfrid Laurier University Press

This book has been published with the help of a grant from the Humanities and Social Sciences Federation of Canada, using funds provided by the Social Sciences and Humanities Research Council of Canada. We acknowledge the financial support of the Government of Canada through the Book Publishing Industry Development Program for our publishing activities.

National Library of Canada Cataloguing in Publication Data

Black, J. David (John David), 1964–
  The politics of enchantment : romanticism, media, and cultural studies

(Cultural studies series)
Includes bibliographical references and index.
ISBN 0-88920-404-7 (bound)

1. Romanticism.   2. Mass Media—Philosophy.   3. Culture—Philosophy. 4. Mass media criticism.   5. Culture—Study and teaching. I. Title. II. Series.

B836.5.B56 2002   306'.01   C2002-900679-1

© 2002 Wilfrid Laurier University Press
Waterloo, Ontario, Canada   N2L 3C5

Cover design by Leslie Macredie. Image by William Blake, from *For Children: The Gates of Paradise*. The Lessing J. Rosenwald Collection, Library of Congress. © 2001 the William Blake Archive. Used with permission.

Printed in Canada

This book is dedicated to my late father,
John Henry Black,
and to my late graduate supervisor,
Ioan Davies.

Contents

ACKNOWLEDGEMENTS

Writing a book about the romantics and their lessons for contemporary media and cultural criticism has been, appropriately, a labour of love—not to mention the product of the wisdom of my teachers, mentors, and colleagues, the forbearance of my friends, and the support of my family and partner.

Wilfrid Laurier University Press has shown nothing but care and professionalism to this author, even when I missed a deadline. My thanks to director Brian Henderson, who initially read and believed in the manuscript; to Elin Edwards, for her persistence, advice, and paperwork; to Jodey Castricano, the editor of the series in which this book appears; and to Jacqueline Larson for her multiple talents in editing, indexing, and typesetting.

Funding for this project was originally provided by the Social Sciences and Humanities Research Council in the form of a doctoral fellowship. Much later, a grant from the Aid to Scholarly Publications Program at the Humanities and Social Sciences Federation of Canada made publication possible. A further grant from the Faculty of Graduate Studies at Wilfrid Laurier University greatly assisted with the book's preparation.

At Wilfrid Laurier, I would like to thank the late John Chamberlin, Andrew and Harriet Lyons, Paul Tiessen, Iwona Irwin-Zarecka, and my colleagues in the Communication Studies Department; at Chicago, Raymond T. Smith; and at York, Brian Singer, Ian Balfour, Ted Winslow, Janine Marchessault, Gerry Gold, Judith Hawley, and Alan O'Connor.

My friends have offered late-night walks, vegetarian food, and infinite patience. Among them have been Michelle, Elizabeth, Libertad, Theresa, Larry, Cassandra, Xanthe, Florence, Jennifer, Christina, Kathy, and Jenna. Rob, a friend as well as a research and teaching assistant, did such excellent background work on the manuscript that he earned himself a promotion from the ranks of idea junkies.

My family made it possible for me to leave a milltown while ensuring that Cardinal, Ontario, never left me. They gave me my politics, my literacy, and my faith, while sprinkling a liberal amount of corn dust over everything I became. I wish to especially thank my mother, Edna, my brother, Darren, my aunt Ann and late uncle Jack (who came to my graduation at a bad time for us all), and my cousin Peggy (who was first).

My partner, Lynne Hanna, was my eyes when mine were tired. The romantics would agree with Buddha's last words: all things in the world are changeable, and they are not lasting. Though renunciation comes too easily to me, let us be selfish at least in what we have together.

Introduction

THE POLITICS OF ENCHANTMENT

It may have been thought once that those of us who acknowledge our continuing relation to the transformed romantic tradition could simply be read out of the intellectual Left: we belonged somewhere else. But that attempt has failed. We are still here. We do not mean to go.

—E.P. Thompson

At first glance, there seems to be little that is "romantic" about contemporary culture. The word suggests mad poets, swooning lovers, and imaginary ladders to the moon, as suggested by the graphic taken from English romantic poet and artist William Blake's *The Gates of Paradise* featured on this book's cover. If anything, the twenty-first century is all business, surging with the very rationalism that so provoked the founders of the romantic tradition two hundred years ago. Everywhere we look, we witness economic injustice, environmental degradation, Faustian technologies, and a media culture largely oblivious to the new facts of life on Earth. Romantic ideas seem like irrelevant gossamer to a world in which illusions, however beautifully phrased and painted, appear an unaffordable luxury. What then is the point of arguing that romanticism is vital to understanding media and culture today?

Romanticism, originating in Germany during the late eighteenth century, and then passing like a fever to England and beyond in the early nineteenth century, was the first Western philosophical tradition to engage capitalism, to take up culture as a problem for analysis, and to question rationality and how it is implicated in our major political, economic, and social phenomena.

Notes to introduction are on page 171.

These features would be enough to recommend romanticism to our contemporary era, a time when capitalism is remarkable in its unchallenged scope, when culture has emerged as one of the most embattled concepts in both the academy and the crowded world alike, and when postmodernism has again pressed the familiar charges against reason. Reading poetry written by its German forebears, such as Friedrich Schlegel and Friedrich von Hardenberg (known by his pen name, Novalis), or in the Anglo-American intellectual world, more familiar figures like William Blake and John Keats, we forget that romanticism was a *philosophy,* although one often expressed in florid language and pithy epigrams that bear little resemblance to conventional scholarly prose.

This tradition developed during a period when the foundations of our modern, rational, liberal, and capitalist civilization were being established, and the old certainties of medieval Christendom were quickly fading away. It showed precocious sensitivity to the shape of things to come, asking hard questions about this new social order at a time when European society had only just began to separate itself from a pre-modern culture identified with faith and custom. The romantics, with the courage of their own exhilaration, plunged into these catastrophic changes in order to explore topics like the nature of language and reality (which are timeless enough to remain contemporary). In doing so, they inspired much of the vocabulary with which we now discuss issues relating to representation, aesthetics, experience, and the self.

They also identified what social critic Max Weber would later call "the process of disenchantment" that had begun with the very Enlightenment with which the romantics, in their horror at the bloody consequences of the French Revolution, had such an ambivalent relationship (Blechman 1999:2). The Enlightenment brought many good things to Western culture, including the epistemological grounds for critical human intelligence or "reason," skepticism toward religious orthodoxy, and liberal humanism. But the triumph of reason, and its later manifestation in such rational institutions as the market, the modern state, bureaucracy, science, and the public sphere, was in some sense a pyrrhic victory.

Rationalism adopted a scorched earth policy toward anything in culture not definable in strictly logical terms, warring against religion, aesthetics, sentiment, and other non-rational phenomena. Most damaged of all was nature itself, which was regarded by the Enlightenment as dead matter, emptied of its spiritual sublimity. The tragic result was that the world was stripped of its mystery, value, and surprise, and was perceived as something entirely knowable and controllable. For Weber, this "intellectualist rationalization" meant that "there are no mysterious incalculable forces that come into play, but rather that one can, in principle, master all things by calculation" (Blechman 1999:2). Returning art and beauty to a world starved of magic was not some poetic truism among the romantics; rather, aesthetic principles were central to their theories of the state, of ethics, and of history. Theirs, in other words, was a politics of enchantment.

Currently, we encounter a mature modern world where what theorists since have come to call "instrumental" or "technological" rationality has ironically eclipsed our capacity for critical thought. The law of unintended consequences prevails: miraculous new technologies have also produced gridlock, pollution, and profound ethical dilemmas. Rational forms of social and political organization, like the state and the market, answer to neither citizen nor consumer. Yet although modernity and its component parts—utilitarian liberalism, rationalism, and capitalism—seem exhausted, they persist as stubbornly dominant features of everyday life, and indeed, have spread worldwide. Disenchantment, in a time of McWorld, is now a feature of the global human condition.

The humanities and social sciences have, since World War II, expanded to cope with this chronic problem of cultural value—what is the meaning of life under conditions in which meaning itself seems bankrupt and tired? Media and cultural theory have experimented with a bewildering variety of positions in their own attempts to solve the long-standing crisis that was the twentieth century. These interventions include pragmatism, Frankfurt School "critical theory," "media effects," Gramsci and Bakhtin, structuralism, feminism, postmodernism, post-structuralism, and cultural studies. As objects of study, media and culture serve as means to condense and magnify changes in society. When extended to related phenomena like individual and collective identity, or major social institutions like the family, religion, and education, media and culture can be considered the "ground" through which reality itself is organized. Both thus offer a shorthand for addressing cultural change, and bring a reality that's typically far too large to fit onto a screen nonetheless momentarily into view.

Arguably, it is cultural studies (a recent tradition in media and cultural analysis which incorporates elements from a number of these other schools and theorists) that is most comfortable with reading our larger reality through the forms in which that reality is constituted. Bridging the humanities and social sciences, cultural studies is an ambitious field of study that takes high culture (such as art, literature, and performance), popular culture (media and other manufactured cultural products and experiences, including malls and theme parks), and everyday culture (how we work and play, marry and bury) as its subject matter. It understands that such phenomena cannot be studied in isolation, but must be related to larger issues in society, such as class, gender, race, and power.

While sometimes mistaken by critics as a field fecklessly committed to pop cultural trivia, cultural studies involves a remarkable range of material, methods, and perspectives. It first emerged in Britain in the late 1950s, inspired by the writing of Richard Hoggart, Raymond Williams, and the historian E.P. Thompson, then took its original institutional form in the Centre for Contemporary Cultural Studies at the University of Birmingham in 1964. Cultural studies has since become an international project with its own literature, conference circuit, and intellectual celebrities, and must be regarded as one of the most productive and, because it is overtly political, notorious things to happen to intellectual life in some time. Given its wide mandate, cultural studies is inter- and multidisciplinary, borrowing from a number of disciplines such as English, sociology, anthropology, and communication studies. Research in this field has included topics as eclectic as subculture, gender, race, music, visual culture, fashion, urban life, technology, and the global market as a cultural system, though with the understanding that all these items are interrelated.

The choice to use romanticism as an archive of concepts relevant to contemporary media and cultural criticism was inspired by an existential itch that needed scratching, rather than some more high-minded and deliberate intellectual concern. As a theorist teaching in communication studies at a Canadian university, I grew frustrated at the way that recent media and cultural studies literature had come to depend on intellectual sources that were scarcely older than the phenomena that the literature engaged. While there is much that is new about a media culture currently being recast in digital terms, I believe strongly that the issues the latest technologies of simulation confront us with are age-old. To borrow predominantly from sources of post-structuralist and postmodern origin is to limit our repertoire severely. While I am aware of similar efforts by scholars such as Axel Honneth, Jürgen Habermas, and Andrew Feenberg to redeem modern thought in the name of a "critical social theory" that looks back to the Frankfurt School for inspiration, this present argument was not self-consciously drafted with their work in mind. Rather, or so I like to think, its origins were themselves romantic in nature, urged upon me by the romanticism that is wantonly present in our culture, and yet cheated by its half-hearted expression in Top 40 love songs, popular fiction, and soap operas. At the risk of mystifying the romantic, I felt the need for it long before I thought it.

What follows in *The Politics of Enchantment* is a passionate argument in favour of creative anachronism, conjoining a two-hundred-year-old intellectual tradition with one as contemporary as cultural studies. That is, by retrieving eighteenth-century romanticism as an archive of concepts indispensable to understanding twenty-first century media and culture, we equip ourselves with the intellectual tools necessary to a world not altogether different from the one those poetic rebels lived in. While several centuries of science, technology, and other offspring of the Enlightenment have obviously changed the surface of things, the romantics would be entirely comfortable with the deeper questions that today's media and culture generate. Their world, like our own, was one in which the shadow of doubt had fallen over rationality, the status of the true and real had become matters of public concern, and fearsome new technologies had trespassed on fundamental assumptions about human nature. That is, in a world of digital simulation, what is real? Where TV and advertising images are ubiquitous and all-powerful, how do we live with them? And where cultural differences persist despite the homogenizing pressures of globalization, as witnessed so apocalyptically in the attack on the World Trade Center, how do we relate to such differences?

The case for romanticism here is set against a narrative where the legacy of romantic thought is still hotly debated among intellectuals of both the political left and right. This struggle to define romanticism's power to animate and value is what is identified here as the "politics of enchantment." Romantic concepts are applied to some of the more nagging questions in media and cultural criticism, such as the future of ideology critique, the nature of on-line "community," and the relationship of culture and economy, the better to demonstrate in more concrete terms the usefulness of romanticism. Romanticism is here treated as a vital philosophical tradition, and not merely a fondly remembered assortment of poems, essays, and manifestos which, like so many pressed flowers, are beautiful and dead. Such an updated romanticism is also of utmost significance to breathing new life into modern thought after several decades of postmodern challenge, and to persuading the reader that modern thought's best hope is not in merely affirming the Enlightenment heritage, but in bringing romantic thought significantly into contemporary theoretical debates.

Finally, since among the splendid variety of intellectual options available to us, cultural studies has the most promise in reviving romantic concepts for modern theory's purposes, it serves as a vehicle for adapting romanticism in the following pages. That's because, while relatively new, cultural studies is the area of intellectual life most comprehensive in its debt to, and potential for, restoring the romantic critical heritage. What have been attempts thus far scattered in time and among disparate disciplines to revive romantic analysis can be consolidated through cultural studies. This is, after all, cultural studies' unique virtue: its sometimes heretical intellectual range. Throughout the text and taking full advantage of this heterodoxy, core concepts in cultural studies are tested against romantic assumptions. The latent romanticism in cultural studies, a trace element dating to the "big bang" in the late 1950s that brought cultural studies into being, is brought forward and then reintroduced as an active and substantial source for contemporary cultural analysis. The result is a blueprint for a newly "romanticized" body of modern thought, with cultural studies as its appropriate vehicle.

In thus acknowledging "our continuing relation to the transformed romantic tradition," those who believe that poets, lovers, and ladders in the sky might improbably contribute to our understanding of contemporary culture are given much needed encouragement. As Blechman has written of the "heroism of the mind" that romanticism represents: "However one considers it, in light of the human and ecological catastrophes that conformity to social reality will ineluctably deliver, nothing short of such heroism will suffice. Without a cognitive leap into a whole other way of thinking, there is truly nowhere to go, and without making the bet that there *will* be a new future, nothing worth winning can be won" (1999:250).

WIRING BIRMINGHAM

A popular travel guide to English tourist destinations says this of Birmingham:

> England's second largest city may fairly lay claim as the birthplace of the Industrial Revolution. James Watt first hatched in Birmingham the profitable application of the steam engine to mine the country's Black Country. Watt and other famous 18th century members of the Lunar Society regularly met under a full moon in the nearby Soho mansion of manufacturer Matthew Boulton. Together—as Watt, Boulton, and other lunatics such as Joseph Priestly, Charles Darwin and Josiah Wedgewood cheerfully called themselves—launched the revolution that thrust not only England but the world into our modern technological era. (Porter and Prince 1998:514)

Home to the Centre for Contemporary Cultural Studies, Birmingham must have seemed a strange place to imagine the future of media and cultural criticism. Workshop to the world in the nineteenth century, it was a rusting hulk in the post-World War II period, a showcase of economic malaise dreary enough to make travellers wish they were in the Lake District. What then is the value of returning to the theories of media and culture inspired by the Centre for Contemporary Cultural Studies at Birmingham? In other words, why is it necessary to rethink classic and contemporary cultural studies literature, to make it accountable to new media and cultural forms using romanticism as a source of intellectual renewal, and in a phrase, to "wire" Birmingham?

The answer is that there is too little writing on contemporary media culture genuinely in touch with the socialist humanism of the founders of the cultural studies tradition. This absence means that a lot of criticism disregards issues significant to that humanism: the peculiar fate of the material world in a mediated environment; capitalism's deep insinuation into the rhythms of everyday life; the everlasting tension between technology and culture; and the relationship of mind to body in weightless cyberspace. The corollary is that too much of the popular and academic writing on media culture, especially the literature that reflects on new media technologies, borrows from theoretical perspectives that are uncritically flattering to the status quo or, at least, not sensitive to the human costs and the structural significance of media today. The theory wars rage on, and more than egos and tenure are at stake.

In the popular realm, the most influential perspective remains the post-industrial one. Dozens of books from corporate gurus, futurists, and technology mavens argue for a society free of the pollution, labour strife, and inequities of the industrial era. This position is often described as "post-industrial" because it imagines a future of technologically enabled "freedom, democracy, and abundance" where an economy that runs on information and knowledge powers a shift to an unprecedented "information society" (Robins and Webster 1999:9). Among the major post-industrial critics are Daniel Bell, the founder of the tradition, as well as Alvin Toffler and George Gilder, though they have dozens of lesser imitators in the bestseller lists and business sections of major newspapers.

The second position, post-structuralism, is favoured by many academics concerned with contemporary media culture. Born of the disappointment among radical intellectuals with the lack of social change at the end of the 1960s, post-structuralism borrows a number of the concepts and assumptions pioneered by the Swiss linguist Ferdinand de Saussure's structuralist tradition. That is, the world is constituted through language, and can be analyzed in terms of its linguistic components, such as the sign, the referent, and myth. Post-structuralism departs from structuralism (or as it's commonly known when applied to the study of media and culture, semiotics) in arguing that the reality behind our words, images, and other "signs" has effectively disappeared from view, and that language is the only reality we can ever know. While scorned by some for its alleged nihilism, post-structuralism is often employed by scholars in the area of digital media and culture where, for example, its assumption that word and world are synonymous can make it a wonderful source for understanding cyberspace. Important post-structuralist critics of media culture include Jean Baudrillard, Sherry Turkle, and Mark Poster.[1]

Despite their valuable contributions, the central problem these positions pose is that they demand a break with the modern world as the condition of making critical sense of media and culture. That is, they both argue in different ways that new media technologies, such as the personal computer and the Internet, have brought about a radically different reality free of industrialism's agonies and of structuralism's claims that language does point to a "real" world. They are thus *post*-industrial and *post*-structuralist. Because being "post" or *after* industrialism and structuralism figures centrally in their very identity, this matter of the break with the modern past is the pretext for their sweeping claims about the present and future. More to the point, in sharing the assumption that humanity has come to a new phase in history, both positions can be considered "postmodern" in character. That is, they assume that the rational modern world established at the time of the Enlightenment is now obsolete, and that a non-rational postmodern culture of simulation, turbo-capitalism, and spectacle is upon us.

To argue with the postmodern is not to imply that modernity ought to be defended for its own sake, nor is another retrenchment of Enlightenment rationalism against the postmodern scourge intended here. Such defences can actually weaken modernity's case by identifying it too squarely with the rational, ignoring that there is more to modern life than bylaw enforcement and good sanitation. I make the case for modernity because, when romanticism is restored to what we understand the category to be about, the persistence of modern culture even into these supposed postmodern times will be clear. If the world is recognizably modern despite events and phenomena that defy common sense, then romantic ideas remain relevant and, what's more, more sensitive to a strange, shape-shifting culture than the Enlightenment's rationalist legacy. Romanticism compensates for rationality's proven limitations, even as it anticipates much of the best of what postmodern thought has provided, and all without losing historical continuity or resorting to nostalgic inertia.

As this insight is extended to media criticism, we can appreciate that the provocative new technologies characteristic of media culture today are continuous with the "old" media of print, radio, and television. That is, romanticism helps us to see that phenomena such as mutable identities and cyber-community are conceivable in modern terms, and that it is not necessary to jettison modern thought in order to understand them. Moreover, separating new technologies like virtual reality or wireless e-mail from modern categories risks artificially isolating them from media history, leaving them susceptible to agendas that have little to do with media criticism.

In the early stages of this analysis, it became apparent that the obstacle to renewing modern ways of thinking about media and culture might be a matter of the epistemological foundation itself. Modern social theory typically identifies its genealogy with the Enlightenment, flattering the rationalist elements in the Enlightenment philosophers, sociology's classical trio of Marx, Durkheim, and Weber, or where the origins of cultural studies are concerned, structuralism against culturalism. The importance of reconstructing media theory's relationship to the modern has not gone unnoticed by media scholarship. Some media theorists claim the issue is not that the media have suddenly become postmodern and thus out of bounds to modern thought. Rather, the terms by which modern thought are conventionally defined are too limited:

> If the debates sparked off by postmodernism have taught us anything, it is not that the developmental processes characteristic of modern societies have propelled us beyond modernity to some new and as yet undefined age, but rather that our traditional theoretical frameworks for understanding these processes are, in many ways, woefully inadequate. What we need today is not a theory of a new age, but rather a new theory of an age whose broad contours were laid down some while ago, and whose consequences we have yet to fully ascertain. (J. Thompson 1995:9)

Yet an argument is building now in otherwise unrelated literatures within the social sciences and humanities in support of returning romantic ideas to the theoretical agenda. While romanticism has earlier intellectual champions such as Ernst Bloch, Georg Lukács, and Walter Benjamin, the recent literature begins to suggest a synthesis and application not apparent in these important, yet isolated authors. There is an emergent "structure of feeling" or intellectual tendency in favour of a romantic revival that I propose to make more formal and comprehensive than has thus far been articulated. The authors making this case, whether Milner, Blechman, Surin, and Prendergast in cultural studies, Saiedi, Gouldner, and Kumar in sociology, Christensen in literary criticism, or Bowie in philosophy, may be largely unknown to each other. While addressing Raymond Williams, the great romantic conscience of cultural studies, Surin offers a charter statement for those critics who persist in believing romanticism valuable today. "If, as Williams contends [in *Modern Tragedy*], the romantics failed because they were not able to develop an adequate social theory, then it may be that the subsequent development of such a theory will make possible a rereading of romanticism, and not only that, but also reactivation of its 'deepest impulses,' impulses, which as Williams himself points out, have as their 'object' an indubitably revolutionary politics" (Surin 1995:153). If the "subsequent development" and "rereading" of romanticism is to be accomplished, and the "reactivation" of those revolutionary principles pursued, what does it mean to be romantic?

Following Kumar, we can define modernity as a "comprehensive designation of all the changes—intellectual, social and political—that brought into being the modern world." Romanticism represents a dissident and often disparaged tradition in modern social and political thought (1995:67). It is presented here not as a substitute but as a supplement to Enlightenment influence. Juxtaposing Enlightenment and romantic qualities demonstrates how they are not so much opposites as they are complementary powers defining the breadth of human capability. "Reason was opposed by the imagination, artifice by the natural, objectivity by subjectivity, the mundane by the visionary, the world-view of science by the appeal to the uncanny and the supernatural" (Kumar 1995:86). The truth here, as in many things, is in the dialectical convergence. These are not so much opposed traditions as they are projections into cultural history of the left and right hemispheres of the brain.

The general features of early German and (to a lesser extent) English romanticism are suggestive for romantically enriching a new modernism in media and cultural theory.[2] Early German romanticism recognized the centrality of the aesthetic and the discursive, without begging the problem of meaning (as does structuralism) or surrendering the modern (as do post-industrialism and post-structuralism). Early German romantic thought or *Fruhromantik* regarded language as something actively constructive of reality, not a transparent medium for an empirically given referent. Poetry was not just a genre of literature but, because reality was made through language, the very model of life itself. And life was understood as the dynamic play of discourse on a reality that, though never denied its material nature, was believed to derive from the work of the subject upon it. In this, early romanticism embodied not a rejection of the modern, but rather a modernism that rejected dispassionate inquiry. It did so in favour of a model of "praxis"—of critically informed action on the world—which gloried in the self's being deeply embedded in the world it sought to describe, explain, and change.

Romanticism valued the non-rational, the exotic, and the grotesque, believing that difference was the element of social reality most truly human. Knowledge was not characterized by the hermetic categories of Enlightenment scholarship, but by paradox, irony, and contradiction. "Living in a world where received cultural categories and conventional social identities no longer made social reality meaningful," Gouldner claims, the romantics "came to see reality as possessed of intrinsic vagueness. They saw objects as blending into one another, rather than as well-demarcated by clear-cut boundaries" (1973:328). Romantic epistemology (or theories of knowledge), contrary to empiricism, respected that there were both limits on rational knowledge and that knowledge about reality could be gained through non-rational and hermeneutic (i.e., knowledge as gained through textual interpretation) means. Romantic ontology (or theories about the self and its experiences) likewise imagined the subject as an agent in history, but one intimately connected with the object or period acted upon as mediated through language. Lastly, they believed that society was composed of a meaningful and complex pattern, rather than being random and unformed. But they saw society not as a smooth and organic whole, but rather as an incongruous entity in which the individual parts related in uneven and indefinite ways.

USING ROMANTICISM

The Romantic period identified here, and the romanticism adapted for media and cultural theoretical purposes, is neither specifically literary, philosophical, or political, but an expedient compound of the three. The Blake or Shelley specialist may not recognize the poets, nor the intellectual historian the lives and works of the Berlin circle. Primary texts are cited, particularly those of the German romantics, but a large debt is to recent secondary texts and scholars who share my interest in a romantic renaissance in social and political thought. The romanticism here is therefore highly synthesized, filtered through contemporary themes and theoretical preoccupations, and is in every sense of the word *used*.

It must be appreciated that there are as many romanticisms as there are students of the poetry, politics, and philosophy crafted in its name. Romanticism's particular genius may well be its stubborn resistance to a single or unifying interpretation, an intentional ambiguity that makes any definition at best a characterization, little more than a partial and partisan reading of a philosophy often itself literally beyond words. Critical traditions as diverse as phenomenology, New Criticism, and deconstruction, and personalities as diverse as conservative philosopher Carl Schmitt and New Historicist literary critic Jerome McGann, have all claimed romanticism for themselves. This endless difference of opinion reflects not only the refractory nature of romanticism, but as this project presupposes, the fact that it can be reinvented as the times demand.

A brief chapter-by-chapter outline may allow the reader a better understanding of my argument's more wild-eyed and, let me say this once, *romantic* ambitions.

In chapter 1, "The Education of Desire: Romanticizing Cultural Studies," a detailed case is made for "using" romanticism against evidence of its re-emergence in contemporary thought. Here, tribute is paid to Jerome Christensen's pioneering work of applying romantic concepts to the critique of contemporary culture by extending the scope of an essay like his "The Romantic Movement at the End of History" to the task of beginning to build a newly modern and romantic cultural studies.[3] I outline and compare Enlightenment and romantic ideas and canvas literature that argues for a revival of romanticism as a contemporary critical source; I also survey critics who are opposed to romanticism. The chapter closes with a refutation of critics who characterize romanticism as either obsolete or too conservative for analytical purposes, and with some ideas on the redemption of the aesthetic category.

Chapter 2, "The Secret Police at the Disco: Interrogating Cultural Studies," examines important works by major figures in media and cultural studies, and then subjects them to romantic criticism. Raymond Williams on modernity and modernism, Terry Eagleton on ideology and discourse, and Stuart Hall on media theory's responsibility to these concepts are surveyed in detail. David Sholle, a student of Foucault and media, is also addressed as a representative of problems in post-structuralism that are open to romantic critique. In each case, romanticism is shown to be valuable in both criticizing these figures and adapting their work to the cause of a romantic criticism of media. More to the point, romanticism corrects the tendency toward reification—that is, the transformation of human, historical concepts and phenomena into timeless, objective things—in these authors and texts, insofar as romanticism represents an anti-reifying modernism.

Chapter 3, "The Presence of the Past: Some Problems in Media Research," juxtaposes the romantic precedent in interwar media research with the erratic history of media research at the Centre for Contemporary Cultural Studies. In preparation for the romantic theory of new media in chapter 5, a critique of American and British cultural studies and related media research is mounted. This critique is organized around the ways in which certain conceptions of communication and culture undermined media research in both traditions. Where both traditions deemed authentic communications incompatible with the highly mediated conceptions of late modernity, the romantic precedent is invoked to demonstrate how communication is genuine and soulful, although bodies are absent and technologies abundant.

In chapter 4, "The Enemies of Love: Misusing Romanticism," post-industrial and post-structuralist literature on the "information society" is reviewed, with particular attention to Daniel Bell (as the most influential of the post-industrial theorists) and Mark Poster (as the more systematic of the post-structuralist theorists of new media). The chapter demonstrates the inadequacy of conventional "rationalist" critiques of the post-industrial and post-structuralist literatures, particularly as they concentrate on the problem of the "break" with the modern and technological determinism. Then, in light of the "politics of enchantment" theme running throughout the text, the discussion uncovers the appropriation of romanticism by both post-industrial and post-structuralist theories of media.

Chapter 5, "Information Wants To Be Free: A Romantic Approach to Media," develops a romantic theory of contemporary media, with particular application to digital technologies. It outlines a romantic alternative to the post-industrial and post-structuralist media theories, as well as to the neo-Luddite or (loosely characterized) anti-technology position favoured by theorists of a more critical persuasion. This positive romantic alternative in media theory is organized around three issues: the possibility of authentic communications; the nature of identity on-line; and technology as it relates to the critical framework in which it has so often been addressed: instrumental reason.

In chapter 6, "The Market in the Fallen World: Cultural Studies and Political Economy," the contribution that romanticism might make to that holy grail of cultural criticism—a cultural studies of political economy—is elaborated. The discussion makes substantial reference to debates regarding the relationship of economy and culture, and demonstrates a partial solution in a romantic re-evaluation of Williams's "cultural materialism" concept. Romanticism, as the home of a materially sensitive aesthetic criticism, is offered as a platform for cultural studies' critique of political economy as discourse, revitalizing the moribund debate around cultural materialism by romanticizing it. Romantic concepts of the "sublime" (or that quality in experience that is beyond words) and "totality" (society considered as a whole, including the economic, cultural, social, and political factors) help to make sense of political economy in an information-dependent society. I also outline a strategy for an effective means to represent the complexity of a globalizing world.

This book is at best a prologue to the development and application of a full-fledged romantic theory of media. The project can be justly criticized for not doing romantic criticism, for merely demonstrating that it can and should be done. However, with the sad fate of that overreaching romantic hero Dr. Faustus in mind, it seemed safest to establish some guidelines and sign-posts for romantic criticism, develop some extended examples, and leave the unveiling of a full-fledged romantic analysis of media culture to those more certain of their place in heaven. As the popular bumper sticker says, never drive faster than your guardian angel can fly.

Chapter 1

The Education of Desire

ROMANTICIZING CULTURAL STUDIES

He who desires but acts not, breeds pestilence.

—From "Proverbs of Hell" by William Blake, 35

Romanticism presents media and cultural criticism with an ambivalent legacy. This chapter introduces romanticism in greater detail, tables the case for a romantic revival in modern thought, and considers criticism of its value. Given that the work of *using* romanticism may be unsettling for those who identify it with visionary poetry or political reaction, the theme throughout is the timely and progressive nature of these ideas. The contemporary relevance of romanticism is demonstrated by just how contested this legacy remains, a point best captured in two vignettes from a pair of theorists a generation, if not worlds, apart.

ROMANTIC MACHINES

Following the English romantic poets, Matthew Arnold, John Ruskin, William Morris, and F.R. Leavis are important heirs to romantic thought. However, within cultural studies, critic and novelist Raymond Williams remains the principal source of ideas characteristic of German romanticism. In his essay "The Romantic Artist" from *Culture and Society*, the 1958 book most responsible for the formation of cultural studies, Williams argues that the popular view of the English romantic poets as dreamers too busy celebrating daffodils to notice that the meadow had been sold to developers overlooks the radical philosophy and daring activism of the Percy Shelley who wrote

---

Notes to chapter 1 are on pp. 172-74.

political pamphlets, the Lord Byron who died of fever while a volunteer in the Greek war of independence, or the William Blake who brought the wrath of heaven down upon the "Satanic Mills" of industrial England. Important objects of the English poets' critical ire were Jeremy Bentham's utilitarianism and David Ricardo's political economy, which together championed the ideology and structure necessary to elevate the market to the centre of English society. In Williams's opinion, English romanticism, scion of the critical heresies in the Berlin circle, sought to arm the imagination against the cold rationality of liberal capitalism. The romantic movement's political activities were "neither marginal nor incidental, but were essentially related to a large part of the experience from which the poetry itself was made" (Williams 1958:31).

A century and a half after English romanticism's radical turn and forty years since Williams's tribute, digital media critic Sherry Turkle suggests a new appropriation of romanticism's meaning. In the mid-1980s there was what she characterizes as a passionate "romantic" response to the development of computer technology explicitly modelled on human characteristics, such as artificial intelligence (AI). This protest was "romantic" in her view, insofar as critics of AI and similar projects asserted the singularity of the human fact, citing grounds that people "have to be something very different from mere calculating machines" (Turkle 1995:24). Turkle credits romanticism for having developed the original defence, during the Industrial Revolution, of human specialness relative to technology.

However, she argues that such claims must now reckon with technological advances that compel us to take silicon seriously. Computer science has progressed from AI to the creation of experimental biological computers that, using organic components, mimic not merely human intelligence but life itself. Romantic resistance has been made obsolete by the very technology it had long opposed. Once a byword for the assertion of human inviolability, "romantic" has utterly reversed its prior meaning in these rarefied circles, and is now a prefix computer scientists assign to those technologies that actively aspire to imitate human traits, collapsing any ready distinction between machine and humankind:

> These machines were touted not as logical but as biological, not as programmed but as able to learn from experience. The researchers who worked on them said they sought a species of machine that would prove as unpredictable and undetermined as the human mind itself. The cultural presence of these *romantic machines* encouraged a new discourse; both persons and objects were reconfigured, machines as psychological objects, people as living machines. (Turkle 1995:24; emphasis mine)

The appropriation of the romantic represents an etymological twist that might have fascinated the author of *Keywords*. But the migration of the term's meaning, as with Williams's keywords themselves, has more than pedantic interest. It points to a romantic undercurrent in intellectual history that continues to trickle through modern thought as well as cultural studies without general awareness or acknowledgement of its presence.

ROMANTICISM AND CULTURALISM

While there have been several cultural studies texts, especially Janice Radway's classic *Reading the Romance: Women, Patriarchy and Popular Culture* and Eva Illouz's *Consuming the Romantic Utopia: Love and the Cultural Contradictions of Capitalism*, which attend to the problem of the romantic, they take the form of criticism of the popular genres of romance fiction and soap opera, and of romantic love in the culture at large. Romance *as* romanticism has received conspicuously little attention in cultural studies, with the exception of E.P. Thompson's early *William Morris: Romantic to Revolutionary*, sections of Williams's *Culture and Society* and *Modern Tragedy*, and decades later, recent retrospective essays by Surin, Prendergast, and Milner that chasten cultural studies for its indifference to the romantic.

The inattention to romanticism is conspicuous because German and English romanticisms are the primary source of culturalism, the philosophical basis for British cultural studies. Traced to the bourgeois public sphere of the eighteenth century, and the liberal intellectual opinion that the journals of Defoe, Addison, and Steele then fostered, this distinctly British ideology had its first formal incarnation in the "culture and civilization" position articulated by the critics Matthew Arnold and F.R. Leavis in the late nineteenth and early twentieth centuries respectively, its second in the left-culturalism (or left-Leavisism) of Williams, Hoggart, and Thompson in the late 1950s and early 1960s, and its third in the Centre for Contemporary Cultural Studies at the University of Birmingham in 1964.[1]

Culturalism has not been formally codified, except perhaps by its critics, and is more a sensibility than it is a doctrine.[2] Indeed, it is faintly embarrassing to invoke it in the cultural studies literature, as if it were a beloved but dotty old aunt who talked to houseplants. Although diffuse, it has several characteristic features: a view of culture as organic in character, reconciling meanings and practices into one symbiotic whole; a strongly value-centric definition of culture and cultural work, echoing Arnold and Leavis's belief that high culture would quite literally save Western society from barbarism; and an emphasis on experience, rather than aloof observation, as the authentic means to understanding culture. Culturalism constitutes both the ethical core and distinctiveness of British cultural studies, the parent tradition in cultural studies.

The neglect of so influential and home-grown a tradition is not surprising, however, given that culturalism's influence has waned as structuralism and its endless variations in Althusser, Bourdieu, Lacan, and later post-structuralists expanded their influence at the older tradition's expense. In the long-documented tension between culturalism and structuralism in British cultural studies, structuralism has prevailed over its humanist rival. "If some have more recently sought to 'consign the culturalism-structuralist split to the past'...then they have done so nonetheless in terms which privilege the latter" (Milner 1994a:44). Although British cultural studies began in culturalism, the ideology has assumed the status of many a charismatic movement. Its influence today is felt in intellectual features that have survived as anachronisms even as cultural studies has been institutionalized, other less indulgent theories imported, and its founders canonized. Culturalism persists in the experiential and the ethnographic emphasis, in the humanism that survives amid the most astringent structuralisms, and in the strong political agency granted to culture—notably in subculture research.

The decline of romanticism's influence in theory, and especially cultural studies, is a complex story, and will be addressed in various ways throughout this argument. But at least some of the blame must fall to culturalism itself. Culturalism is to romanticism as weak tea is to Guinness, suffering from some of the mawkish sentimentalism into which Matthew Arnold's Victorian culture translated the romantic. Culturalism lacks romanticism's fine edge and iconoclasm, and is weaker for the absence of a defining statement or manifesto. It therefore lasted only as long as cultural studies remained a tradition that was entirely English in its orientation. When structuralism crossed the Channel from France in the 1960s, the ideas of Saussure and Barthes and later Continental philosophies readily consigned culturalism to a fond memory.

E.P. Thompson's intellectual biography of William Morris marks the distance cultural studies needs to travel before romanticism might be returned to its bosom. In Thompson's original dissertation (published in 1955), he makes a familiar case that both the designer and radical, under the influence of the pre-Raphaelite Brotherhood, erred on the side of aestheticism. Met with an ugly capitalist reality, the young Morris is held to have initially retreated under the influence of Gabriel Rossetti to a realm of art-for-art's-sake purity that had to be abandoned before Morris's mature identity as a Marxist was achieved. His socialism, as Thompson originally argued, was the consummation of his romanticism.

This characterization of Morris's progress from romantic to revolutionary, as indicated in Thompson's subtitle, can be contrasted with the Thompson of his postscript to the 1977 second edition. Here, twenty years later, the historian modifies the earlier emphasis on Morris's evolution from aesthete to firebrand, arguing that Marxism disappointed romanticism. Marxism, in abandoning romanticism for the certainties of orthodoxy, lost its credibility as a moral philosophy and its credentials as a source of utopian possibility. Thompson, offering the Cold War culture as cause for his vulgarity and "too tidy" equation of Morris and Marx, grants to Morris's romanticism an autonomy and integrity much greater than his original thesis allowed:

> First, it is more important to understand [Morris] as a (transformed) Romantic than as a (conforming) Marxist. Second, his importance within the Marxist tradition may be seen, today, less in the fact of his adhesion to it than in the Marxist "absences" or failures to meet that adhesion half-way. Morris's "conversion" to Marxism offered a juncture which Marxism failed to reciprocate, and this failure—which is in some sense a *continuing* failure, and not only within the majority Communist tradition—has more to teach us than have homilies as to Morris's great-hearted commitment. (E.P. Thompson 1977:786)

The remedy to this "continuing failure" is being prepared largely outside of cultural studies. Everywhere, there is a rethinking and re-evaluation of its significance in terms highly productive for the field. Literary critic Jerome Christensen believes "in the spirit of Williams, that in the long view cultural populism is romanticism" (1994:470, n35). Alvin Gouldner, an advocate of romantic renewal in the social sciences, argues that early German romanticism pointedly rejected the French Enlightenment identification of modernity with reason, science, and technology, preferring to read modernity from cultural issues: "In the Romantic view...the 'modern' was not marked by the eruption of science and rationalism but, rather, by certain innovations in the arts and especially in literary culture" (1973:325). Philosopher Andrew Bowie credits early German romanticism as the source of many current debates in theory, suggesting that it made a "descent into discourse" well before the contemporary obsession with language attributed to postmodern and post-structuralist positions. "The 'linguistic turn,' the turn towards language, rather than the mind, as the primary object of philosophical investigation, which is usually seen as the product of the twentieth century, is a consequence of central aspects of Romantic philosophy" (Bowie 1997:22).

Elsewhere a critic of romanticism, Eagleton acknowledges that "many of the notions thought to be peculiar to post-structuralism—discursive indeterminacy, the play of difference, the subject as non-self-identical, an infinity of signification and the rest—are the common currency of Novalis, Schelling and Schleirmacher" (1991b:38). Eagleton credits this theoretical anachronism with the fact that "the French don't read the German Romantics, or indeed very much at all but themselves" (1991b:38). Ironic as that explanation is, Eagleton's quip doesn't do justice to what seem strong parallels between economic and cultural developments at the turn of the eighteenth and twentieth centuries. A case can be made for what appear to be "significant and determining continuities" between the romantic period and contemporary debates among modern and postmodern positions, appreciating that "the debate of the 1790s, in other words, does not give us all the terms required for an understanding of the 1980s, but it remains relevant to its composition and articulation" (Simpson 1993:15-16).

Both periods witnessed the rise of crudely effective arguments in favour of the vast expansion of market forces. In the 1820s and '30s, there was David Ricardo's political economy, which gave a rationale for the end of mercantile protectionism and the beginning of free-trade capitalism later in the nineteenth century. Since the 1980s, we have lived through a period of resurgent neo-liberalism reminiscent of Ricardo's creed; coupling this creed with the "authoritarian populism" of Thatcher and Reagan, the cultural primacy of media and technology, and globalization, cultural studies has christened our period "New Times." Both periods also fostered strong countervailing movements dedicated to fighting the market's hegemony: early German romanticism and its sympathizers among the English and other romantics, and cultural studies today in its likewise several national variants. And both these movements themselves demonstrated an early commitment to criticizing the philosophical positions dominant in their respective eras: namely utilitarianism in the first case, and the neo-conservatism that has served to enforce social disciplines, such as antagonism toward the state and the criminalization of the poor and unemployed, necessary to supporting the market's new power in our post-Keynesian era.

Yet early German romanticism and its love child, English romanticism, are generally neglected in the social sciences. "What is usually ignored...is the profound impact Romanticism had on the categories, concepts, and methodology of sociohistorical studies" (Saiedi 1993:59). Romanticism is responsible for many of the most important concepts in sociology. "The categories of history, social totality, community, tradition, meaning, hermeneutics, and alienation which made sociology possible are all Romantic concepts," as are "concepts of agency, the unity of culture, social totality, historical reason, normative orientation, the moral foundation of social order, the autonomy of language, and interpretation" (Saiedi 1993:59, 107). Perversely, despite the fact that many of the major concepts in social theory have a romantic prove-nance, within the sociological literature "there is a virtual absence of sub-stantive analysis of Romanticism" (Saiedi 1993:61).[3]

Romanticism's ill-deserved obscurity is not for lack of self-promotion or scandal, as the many bold manifestos and love affairs among the German and English romantics demonstrate, not least to their outraged contemporaries. The marginalization of romanticism follows from its sometimes deep conser-vatism, from the romantic habit of expressing ideas in a poetic idiom "hardly compatible with the conceptual and systematic language of social theory" (Saiedi 1993:107), and the strong identification of the social sciences with the Enlightenment project. To know just what we're talking about, some explanation of Enlightenment and romantic thought is now in order.

ENLIGHTENMENT AND ROMANTIC THOUGHT COMPARED

By "Enlightenment" we principally refer to the French Enlightenment, that remarkable period dating roughly from the 1710s to the revolutionary year of 1789, when the acknowledged philosophical tenets of the social sciences were founded.[4] Strongly influenced by Greek and Roman texts discovered in the preceding Renaissance period (roughly spanning the fourteenth to sixteenth centuries), French *philosophes* like Rousseau, Voltaire, and Diderot began their demolition of feudal institutions and ideas. Their heavy equipment was impressive: reason, above all; the formal equality of individuals and the rule of law, both indebted to an emergent liberalism traceable to Locke; the intellec-tual and political priority of order, consensus, and progress; a utopian belief in human betterment against the pessimistic anti-humanism of the medieval Church; and lastly, among other features, the power of both natural and social science to support social reform. The social sciences are so identified with Enlightenment values that "according to the conventional view, sociology was born when the scientific method and the rationalistic categories of the Enlightenment were applied to the realm of social and cultural studies" (Saiedi 1993:107). This dramatically underplays the influence of Romanticism upon social, cultural, and media theory, since "such a genealogy of sociological the-ory is one-sided" (Saiedi 1993:107).

Romanticism, like the Enlightenment, manifested differently within France, Great Britain, Germany, and the United States. However, as the French Enlightenment tradition might be thought parent to British Enlightenment figures like Adam Smith and David Hume or the American revolutionaries, "Romanticism was a predominantly German phenomenon"

(Saiedi: 1993:65). Romanticism owes its radioactive core to the cadre of radicalized artists and philosophers who congregated in Jena, a German intellectual centre for centuries, and then Berlin between 1797 and 1801, the early romantic period. The late romantic period, as conservative as the early period was radical, lasted from the turn of the century until the late 1820s.[5] But among the German romantics, notably in their turn-of-the-century prime, rank some of the spectacular sensibilities of the age.

Chief among these radical aesthetes were the Schlegel brothers, Friedrich and August (co-editors of the early German romantic house organ, *Athenaeum*), the theologian Friedrich Schleirmacher, Friedrich Hardenburg (better known by his pen name, Novalis), and the poet Friedrich Hölderlin. Key transitional personalities were Kant, for his devastating critique of empiricism; Herder, for his original definition of culture in its ethnographic sense as a complex "way of life" of which all humans were capable (the philosophical basis for cultural relativism); and Goethe, whose enormous influence over German culture, through Faust and other romantic themes, prepared the European imagination for romanticism's emergence. Germany was late to develop the capitalism that had given rise to a politically powerful and self-conscious bourgeoisie in England, and so the early romantics sought revolution in the only sector permitted by Germany's Prussian feudalism: culture. On terms similar to the British "left-culturalists" who saw in Cold War-era culture one of the few remaining avenues for political dissent, the Berlin circle turned to "the sphere of culture, to the achievements of intellect and art that were more individually controllable: they fostered a movement for cultural revitalization instead of a political revolution" (Gouldner 1973:324).

What were the main themes of early German romanticism, as written on the hearts of these philosopher kings? The seven theses of the 1796 romantic manifesto, "The System Program of German Idealism," (Surin 1995:153-54) provide an outline through which early romantic principles can be explained in detail.[6]

1. The highest form of reason is the aesthetic, and truth and goodness are united in beauty. Philosophy must perforce become an aesthetic philosophy.

Like cultural studies, early German romanticism defined language and culture as active and dynamic phenomena, capable of shaping material reality without, it is important to qualify, reducing or subjecting it to determination by language and culture. Language, synonymous with reality itself in the romantic perspective, "should mix and fuse poetry and prose, inspiration and criticism, the poetry of art and the poetry of nature; and make poetry lively and sociable, and life and society poetical" writes Friedrich Schlegel in the *Athenaeum Fragments* (1988:192). In their acknowledgement of a material world not to be assimilated to culture or epistemological categories, the romantics differ importantly from their philosophical compatriots in Germany, the idealists Hegel, Fichte, Schelling, and Kant.

Kant's formative influence on early German romanticism is universally acknowledged. It was Kant who mitigated the prior influence of Locke's empiricist epistemology, particularly his model of the mind as a thing passively impressed upon by objectively available stimulus in reality. Against the Lockean "tabula rasa," Kant proposed a theory of knowledge whereby the mind actively generates its own categories, which are (to reverse the Lockean associationist sequence) then used to mold the raw data of the senses. The world for Kant is something we might know only subjectively, since a permanent gap exists between the world as it appears to the mind (phenomena) and the external "real" world of things-in-themselves (noumena) beyond our senses.

Objective knowledge of the noumenal realm is thus not possible, since the phenomenal world of experience is the product of the categorizing work of human intelligence. Hence the tremendous importance of the aesthetic for Kant and the romantics, since our images of the world are our best guesses about its nature. Kant's vision of reality as contingent and human-made makes him the point of transition from the Enlightenment to romanticism, though the early romantics rejected his idealist belief in the dualistic, Cartesian separation of consciousness and reality. Romanticism preferred a model of reality where self and social world are intermingled, and physical objects are thought to incarnate aspects of consciousness, emotion, and spirit. The world was genuinely alive for them. As Friedrich Schlegel believed: "Just as there is, despite all the senses, no external world without the imagination, so too there is no spiritual world without feeling, no matter how much sense there is" (Blechman 1999:23).

The rejection of Kant's dualism did not imply wholesale rejection of Kant's epistemological revolution—his recognition that the world, intellectually speaking, is what we make of it. Rather, the early romantics recognized a perpetually contingent relationship between mind and matter that was captured in their delight in irony and disorder. The relationship between agency (i.e., the power of the individual to act) and reality is fraught with ambiguity, and action itself is consequently characterized as a form of play. Late romanticism would overturn the Kantian break with empiricism, after the Terror and the Napoleonic wars had caused them to regret their previous enthusiasm for the French Revolution. Late romantics like Adam Müller favoured a more medieval epistemology where language was immediately and mystically bound to the real, a determinacy sanctioned by God.

In the romantic universe, the aesthetic function of communication is the highest human faculty. By this "aesthetic" model of communication, the romantics meant the ability to create words and pictures that represent the mind's own subjective experience of reality, rather than seek the mere mimetic duplicate of that reality which empiricism prefers. In an empirically unknowable world, words and images assume the condition of art. It was the aesthetic that offered the only hope of reconciling a subject with an objective world torn apart by modernity. Art was essential to *Bildung*, or cultural formation, by which the romantics meant the development of a person's creative and spiritual powers. A community devoted to such actualization through art was restored to the autonomy and human potential it had lost as rationality pervaded life.

"Truth" was therefore not the product of reason or dialectical process. Rather, truth was both real and yet existed outside of language in the indeterminate noumenal realm of the "not yet said," where it might be revealed (though not captured) in aesthetic terms. The form of truth we normally ascribe to art—the capacity to disclose hitherto unknown glimpses of reality—was the condition of *all* truth as far as the early romantics were concerned. Truth manifested itself in "truths"; there are many truths, defined by difference and exception rather than conforming to some single unitary rationale for truth. This unknowable world did not inspire fear, but rather love, in the romantics. Love was a serious philosophical premise for them, the primary cause of action and movement in the social world, and related by analogy to the forces of attraction and repulsion in the universe. It was the mysterious force that motivated the individual's relations with community, and the community's with nature.

The belief that life cannot be adequately understood through rational means led the romantics to greatly prize and to seek knowledge through the non-rational, including as their subject matter such human intangibles as the imagination, spirituality, and play. Friedrich Schlegel gives voice to this in his meditation, "On Incomprehensibility," arguing that much of the substance of humanity must be left, as far as rational apprehension is concerned, in the dark for fear that rationality would bleed it of life-giving power. "It would fare badly with you if, as you demand, the whole world were ever to become wholly comprehensible in earnest. And isn't this entire, unending world constructed by the understanding out of incomprehensibility and chaos?" (F. Schlegel 1988:185).

2. All metaphysics will eventually be replaced by ethics. The ruling idea of this ethics is "the representation of myself as an absolutely free being."

3. A new "physics" will have to be devised to deal with the question: How must a world for moral being be constituted?

The romantics rejected metaphysics on the grounds of language's, and frequently, the world's own uncertainty. For example, Novalis claims in the "Monologue" that "it is the same with language as it is with mathematical formulae—they constitute a world in itself—their play is self-sufficient, they express nothing but their own marvellous nature, and this is the very reason why they are so expressive, why they are the mirror to the strange play of relationships among things" (Novalis 1988:274). In other words, there is no final and definite truth that logic can appeal to, but rather meaning is uncannily free-floating and without foundation.

In the absence of an epistemological bottom line, the romantics turned to their favourite theme, the subject, and the moral dimension in which the individual self lives: ethics and praxis. Such a position requires a high degree of tolerance for difference, because experience is radically relativized among the separate members of society, and the search for meaning is the individual's responsibility—not reflected in some sacred script or timeless code. This required a conception of society's nature and dimensions that was generous enough to accommodate such a world of difference, and it was one the romantics delivered.

The romantic model of society taken as a whole or "social totality" (that is, including all the known elements in experience, including economy, politics, social relations, culture, etc.) was not dialectical in nature. That is, they rejected the idea that discrete elements in the social totality related with each other in patterned, predictable ways. They also refused to accept that the myriad elements that make up a given society were subject to some superordinate unifying logic, or that social process tended toward a synthesis or ultimate goal. Theirs was a view of society comfortable with the randomness of experience and the open-endedness of history.

The romantics reconciled totality and difference, arguing that any vision of society must be complex enough to accommodate the fact of difference and the limits of human understanding. Society's intelligibility, moreover, is not merely a given or an *a priori* phenomenon, mystically invested in nature or God, but rather must be constantly reinvented in everyday practice. That is, it falls to us to make the world make sense, even as we must cope with its often opaque nature. Despite the uncertainty, the presence of beauty is proof that humanity is capable of rising above the mundanely rational. Beauty—

whether in art or nature—is the sign of a species struggling toward freedom and the realization of its potential.

One result of this romantic epiphany is a view of the material world that respects the interlacing of the social and the natural, the ideal and the real, allowing that these two halves of human experience are in dynamic tension. This tension ensures that the world can never be wholly transparent to us, yet enables language and culture to meaningfully contribute to its making. Not for them the economic determinism of some of the more orthodox Marxisms. Rather, for the romantics the imagination is taken to be "the complement of any materialism, since it is the imagination that enables materialism to retain its constructive power in the very moment that materialism has lost its hope" (Surin 1995:158).

Enlightenment thought sought the creation of universal categories for the subject, culture, and humanity generally, valuing inclusive criteria for determining these fundamental things as necessary to realizing a common global community. Romantic thought, by contrast, revelled in the grotesque, the absurd, and the exotic. Bearing comparison to both Foucault and Bakhtin in their love of the irregular, the romantics showed a degree of regard for "difference" that would not be repeated until the social movements of the 1960s. For example, in his *Lectures on Dramatic Art and Literature,* August Schlegel, with a critical eye on Enlightenment impulses toward classification and order, commits romanticism to the cause of difference: "The groundwork of human nature is no doubt everywhere the same; but in all our investigations, we may observe that, throughout the whole range of nature, there is no elementary power so simple, but that it is capable of dividing and diverging into opposite directions. The whole play of vital motion hinges on harmony and contrast" (A. Schlegel 1988:256).

4. The state has to be destroyed because it cannot be what it is without curtailing the freedom of human beings.

5. Neither God nor immortality must be sought outside of humanity.

Romanticism is well-known for its cultish acclaim of the subject, as evidenced in the Byronic or Faustian hero. However, the positive side of its individualism is its impressive confidence in human agency vis-à-vis structure, and of labour and other forms of action as the source of culture. Of equal value is romanticism's fidelity to parts of the human repertoire that go unsung in the rationalism of the social sciences, including emotion, the body, imagination, and experience.

Romanticism resisted mightily the tendency of Enlightenment thought to "reify" its object—to change historical phenomena into timeless objects. But its resistance did not assert an essentialist humanism that provided some historical basis for culture, since the romantic subject is constituted in relationship with others. Rather, it argued for the deep implication of the subject with the objective world, of the imagination with the obstinate fact of material nature, refusing the Cartesian dichotomies endorsed by the Enlightenment. Most important among these forms of interaction were play and art, given that, for the romantics, aesthetic behaviour was the gold standard for other forms of practice. The rational Enlightenment subject, everywhere equal but everywhere the same, is met with romanticism's advocacy of the unique and original "qualitative" individual. The romantic self is impelled by love, inspired by beauty, and realizes his or her individuality by participating in community.

The romantic revolution in culture was not about artistic self-indulgence. Art was life because culture was the means to directly fashion a conscious world within which one lived. The romantic subject was often represented as a poet-magician conjuring new realities through discourse. Schlegel, for example, says of this erratic romantic hero that "for a man who has achieved a certain height and universality of creation, his inner being is an ongoing chain of the most enormous revolutions" (in White 1999:4). This subject always trembled on the edge of madness, and irrational and passionate states of being were generally regarded as the condition of the self escaping from the "iron cage" of rationality. Social action, moreover, was understood to be symbolic in nature, and thus open to be "read" in the same way a text is interpretable.

Early romantic politics were revolutionary, and the protagonists identified themselves with the French Revolution's emancipatory goals. But the romantics opposed the asocial contractual models of politics organized around a state that were favoured by Enlightenment icons like Hobbes and Montesquieu. Their ideal polity was communitarian, rather than exclusively invested in the rights and freedoms of the individual, and favoured more radical forms of democracy than those offered by liberal theorists. Every citizen was, metaphorically speaking, an artist, insofar as the very essence of being human and the basis of social good was creativity in all things. Art was the primary means to re-enchant the world; it restored a world that was damaged by instrumental rationality to itself.

Their theology was similarly humane and flexible. Although God's existence could not be empirically proven, the romantic concept of divinity took as a given the reality of God, as well as other intangibles (e.g., good and evil). They paid tribute to the power of the imagination; God had already made an appearance in the history of human thought, and so following their aesthetic logic, God must *be*. The romantics also attributed God-like features to humanity, since it was the unique responsibility of human beings to create reality; their image of the human being was of a creative divinity shaping the world in its image. Against the Enlightenment's skepticism toward religion, the romantics believed passionately in the possibility of a spiritual renaissance. Religion was optimally the highest form of culture, a realm where the romantic ideals of freedom, love, and creativity were realized in their fullness. They were "pantheistic humanists," believing that God was in every one and in all things.[7]

6. A "religion of the senses" is needed by "the masses" and the philosopher alike.

7. A "new mythology," one that is a "mythology of reason" at the service of "the ideas," will also be needed.

The romantics did not see reality as a series of bounded classifications, such as thought to separate human from non-human, organic from inorganic, etc. Rather, the world greeted them in terms that exceeded their rational need for order, and all its vital categories were mixed together. This could amount to a kind of animism: the belief that all elements in the universe are mystically connected and alive. This romantic "religion of the senses" may seem at first too vaporous to be of value to theory. Yet, considered as a critique of dualism, the all-too-human habit of splitting the universe into pairs of two (e.g., male/female, subject/object, etc.), romantic spirituality offers a powerful hedge against the post-structuralist tendency to identify the modern with a dispassionate dualism.

Romanticism mounted a critique of dualism well before the emergence of French theories that were critical of structuralism. The critique of dualism is a romantic speciality, and germane to understanding a media culture where our cultural categories are daily more permeable and in play. Living through the final days of the feudal order, the early romantics saw themselves as witnesses to a world where "received cultural categories and conventional social identities no longer made social reality meaningful" (Gouldner 1973:328).

Although the notion of metanarratives came about almost two centuries after the romantics, the anti-empirical romantics were already critical of what today we would call metanarratives. The concept is associated with the work of postmodern theorist Jean-François Lyotard. Metanarratives are the large explanatory frameworks that proliferated in modern history, and were used to make comprehensive sense of reality. Important modern metanarratives include Christianity, Marxism, liberalism, and other major ideologies of the period. Postmodern critics believe metanarratives to be evidence of the arrogance of modern culture, notably since they unrealistically reduce the world's complexity to a series of premises. Lyotard, arguing that the world is not comprehensible on such grandiose terms, favours understanding it on far humbler terms and from the perspective of individual biography, scraps of meaning, and other more modest narratives.

The romantic critique of metanarrative did not then resign itself to the local and the personal, as does Lyotard. Rather, romanticism assumed from the outset that our frameworks were fictional and that there were limits on their power to explain. Yet the romantics did not reject these fictions or surrender the possibility of knowing something meaningful of the world. To live as a modern was to forever rewrite these stories, without reducing reality to a single narrative or teleological pattern. However fictional and limited, modern metanarratives were necessary because conventional religion was no longer adequate, and the strange complexity of modern life demanded that we develop a better mythology.

Characteristically, romanticism refused to spell out just what a mythology appropriate to modern life should be. It would reconcile the ideal and the real; it would complement, not replace, reason; it would support freedom and autonomy, opposing the mechanistic world view suggested by the Enlightenment; and it would identify reason in such a way that it was detached from instrumental goals like efficiency and control, and realigned with a fuller conception of what human life is about. Though the romantics' concern to rethink modern culture on such terms might seem hopelessly unrealistic, themes such as they espoused are as contemporary as today's headlines. Some of the most ingenious political movements of the last several decades, such as the Mexican Zapatistas and the anti-globalization protests, reflect a similar desire for a new and improved modern metanarrative.[8]

Although its infectious idealism ought to win it friends everywhere, romanticism has met with fierce resistance from scholars across the ideological spectrum. Marxist and liberal theorists have either believed romanticism a conservative philosophy, or worse, a postmodern one. A key concern among them, despite their differences in outlook, is the romantic attachment to the aesthetic—the human capacity for recognizing and creating beauty. Indeed, their various criticisms of the aesthetic are significant in determining their evaluation of the romantic, as the two are so often joined in the scholarly imagination.

THE TROUBLE WITH BEAUTY

The category of human experience known as the "aesthetic" has a checkered history, not least within cultural studies. The conventional history of the aesthetic argues that the aesthetic faculty (i.e., that part of us that's dedicated to the imaginary representation of the world in art and culture) was, until the modern era, an integral part of a human sensibility. It featured moral judgement and logical-scientific reason as its second and third parts. Synthesizing the power to distinguish good from evil, to see beauty, and to think logically, the mind was once a garden variously overgrown and cultivated, but nonetheless whole and integrated. For example, the German idealist Schiller, in his essay *On the Aesthetic Education of Man,* speaks of an Edenic unified sensibility shattered by a "civilization...which inflicted this wound upon modern man," one where "the inner unity of human nature was severed too, and a disastrous conflict set its harmonious powers at variance" (Simpson 1988:130). Just as Christianity has the Fall from the Garden of Eden to explain the origins of sin, or Islam the idealized purity of Bedouin values among the followers of Mohammed in seventh century Medina to chasten contemporary Muslims, the myth of humanity's tragic separation from an organic culture identified with the pre-modern past has been used to explain much that is wrong in modernity.

This apocalyptic history of the aesthetic has romantic origins, but has ironically since been used as a rhetorical weapon against romanticism. As the story is told, the calamitous pressures of modern life acted to separate the aesthetic, moral, and logical faculties from each other, meaning that beauty, goodness, and truth no longer enjoyed their customary harmonious balance. According to this mythology of mind, once the aesthetic became a separate category, it came readily to be understood as the most powerful and untrustworthy of the three faculties. Not surprisingly in a Christian civilization that has burned books, destroyed graven images, and sermonized on the virtues of plainness, beauty is made to be the serpent.

Long cast as the id to the modern ego, and in contact with dark and turbulent parts of human experience, the fortunes of the aesthetic rose while capitalism's "creative destruction" changed the face of Europe and the New World. New image-making technologies like photography, film, and television, and a world so confusing it no longer seemed accessible via rational words, made conditions highly favourable for the triumph of the aesthetic. Cultural workers and critics alike began to retreat from experience, confronted by an emergent society of the spectacle, where images proliferated in vast numbers outside of conventional contexts that once afforded moral and rational control. Persuaded of the unrepresentability of complex modern experience, the avant-garde laid down its pens and paintbrushes, and surrendered control of the aesthetic to advertising executives and special effects.

Once abandoned by modern artists and intellectuals, the aesthetic category then became the special preserve of postmodernism. Postmodernism, the body of art, theory, and practice that arose to explain the so-called postmodern era (alleged to have begun with the end of modernity in the 1960s), gave up entirely on trying to represent the world. Postmodern artists like Andy Warhol and David Lynch famously made overexposed celebrities and the surreal subtext of ordinary suburban life their subject matter; postmodern showplaces like Disney's planned community, "Celebration," constructed a heartwarming small-town past that never actually existed. Utterly divorced from the real, postmodernism abandoned any pretense that aesthetics would or could be responsible to reality. Images became ever more beautiful and fantastic, and ever more amorally indifferent to experience.

But the received history of the aesthetic as a paradise lost has prevented a more constructive relationship between cultural studies and the aesthetic from developing, and at great cost to the ability of cultural critics to explain the spectacle. Out of concern to salvage this most romantic of concepts and restore it to its modern pedigree, it is necessary to examine arguments opposed to romanticism and the aesthetic, and recommend changes to how we relate the history of the aesthetic. This is because the fates of both romanticism and the aesthetic are significantly intertwined, and because criticisms of one are often displaced antagonisms toward the other. The subject matter is abstract, but its global significance is as real as CNN. It is in our day-to-day struggle to make sense in a world of images that the romantic is condensed and lived, where its vagaries becomes real to us and its issues of compelling importance.

Criticism of romanticism as it relates to the aesthetic tends to be twofold. Either romanticism is an antiquated and reactionary movement rooted in medieval values and mystifying rhetoric, a rearguard action against the Enlightenment tangentially responsible for the Nazis. (The Nazis made remarkable use of images, art, and pageant to convey their ideology, operating from what critic Walter Benjamin so perceptively identified as the "fascist aesthetic," and both the romantic and aesthetic have been stigmatized since the Nuremberg rallies and the mass burnings of "decadent" modern art.) Or romanticism is the precursor to the postmodern, which is seen as an overextended version of romanticism that runs amok in a world with little rational constraint. The fluid and foundationless culture of postmodernity is alleged to be the result, that is, of a romanticism that has overwhelmed the Enlightenment values that held it in check, and now rules over an empire of signs.

Karl Mannheim's is the classic liberal indictment of German romanticism's reactionary tendencies. He argues that the early radical energies of the Berlin circle became conservative due to the countervailing pressure of Prussian conservatism in early eighteenth-century Germany. Where Enlightenment philosophers wrote in the context of a bourgeois revolution and an emergent scientific and industrial complex, German romantics had no such home for their more progressive side. The homeless nature of these intellectuals made their convergence with Catholic conservatism inevitable, since once adrift they sought the certainty of an absolute faith. Mannheim dramatizes the plight of the early romantics as if they had been prodigal youths who, in a pique of guilty remorse, became conservative. Testifying to their religious turn, he writes that "just as romantic thought failed to find its political aims within itself, so it took over, at a certain stage of its development, certain fundamental ideas opposed to the Enlightenment from the inventory of ideas from feudalistic conservatism" (1953:130).

While German romanticism became unmistakably conservative in the early nineteenth century, this does not justify ignoring the extraordinary vision of radical democracy evident in the early texts. It is also a common view that "political romanticism," in its regard for organic community, was a precursor to Nazism. The romantic view that art was political has often been regarded as the inspiration for the infamous fusion of aesthetics and politics the Nazi propagandists practised, as evident in the party's love of spectacle, highly choreographed rallies, and use of design and colour to advance National Socialist ideals. While it is impossible to do justice here to the polemics over the Nazi appropriation of romanticism (a debate centered in the work of German philosopher Carl Schmitt), several things are clear.

But the early romantics were anything but racist. They believed deeply in cultural authenticity: they extended tolerance and pluralism to all cultures, and are regarded as a major source of contemporary multiculturalism. The romantics were severe critics of the state, and believed that the best political system was one where political domination itself was rendered obsolete. They were ahead of their time in their criticism of science and technology. (Yet technology became central to the Nazi's glorification of German achievements.) And unlike the Nazis, the romantics were not against reason—they were merely its best critics. Blechman reminds us that

> A fresh look at the spirit motivating early romantic political thought can thus show in what ways we would be making a serious historical and intellectual error to consider romanticism a purely regressive or reactionary tendency of German culture....Early German romanticism was an essentially utopian movement that aspired to give greater depth and meaning to the cosmopolitan ideal of universal freedom and equality. (1999:11)

Marxist literary theorist Terry Eagleton is equally condemning of the English romantics, claiming that they saw the symbol as "the panacea for all problems," part of a conservative function which had them offering fanciful symbolic resolution of real social problems (1983:21). The symbol or literary artifact was an ideological tool promoting the specious unity of diverse interests, classes, and otherwise. Eagleton parodies: "If only the lower orders were to forget their grievances and pull together for the good of all, much tedious turmoil could be avoided" (1983:22). But again, more so than Mannheim, Eagleton overlooks the radical content of English romantic thought.

What's interesting about Eagleton as a critic of the romantic are his charges against the aesthetic. He argues that it has been incorporated into ideology, its image-making powers stripped of any autonomy and subordinated to power's dictate. Where this is a potential recognized famously in Marcuse's work on Marxist aesthetics, it is a process of corruption much more advanced in Eagleton's work. Though Eagleton is conscientious in granting the aesthetic category its political promise—"it offers a generous utopian image of reconciliation between men and women at present divided from one another"—the aesthetic is similarly that which "blocks and mystifies the real political movement towards such historical community" (1990:9).

Yet as Andrew Bowie (a frequent debating partner of Eagleton's in the periodical literature) argues, Eagleton's magisterial *The Ideology of the Aesthetic* is all too typical in this narrative of ideology's reduction. Rather than giving the aesthetic its due, Eagleton is too hasty in defining it as an ideological problem. "In some ways Eagleton repeats, in relation to philosophy, the major fault of his earlier work on literature, which too hastily reduced [the aesthetic] to the ideological circumstances of its production, without being able to account for its specific power or its radical potential" (Bowie 1991:37). The problem remains that "Eagleton is too concerned with the unmasking of the ideology of the aesthetic really to understand the philosophical actuality of the aesthetic" (1991:37), at obvious cost to our appreciation of the romantics.

The critique of romanticism by theorists writing on the postmodern is no more satisfying, implying as it does a ready continuity between romanticism and the worst excesses of this notorious phase in cultural history. For example, Marxist geographer and theorist David Harvey offhandedly associates (without actually naming) the romantic with nihilism, speculating that postmodernism's secret history is probably a romantic one: "To the degree that it does try to legitimate itself by reference to the past, therefore, postmodernism typically harks back to that wing of thought, Nietzsche in particular, that emphasizes the deep chaos of modern life and its intractability toward rational thought" (1989:44). Literary critic Fredric Jameson's response is still more curious, acknowledging the importance of romanticism to the modern/postmodern issue while relegating the point to a casual aside. "I must here omit yet another series of debates, largely academic, in which the very continuity of modernism as it is here reaffirmed is itself called into question by some vaster sense of the profound continuity of romanticism, from the late eighteenth century on, of which both the modern and the postmodern will be seen as mere organic stages" (Jameson 1991:59).

These dismissals and oversights ignore attempts, albeit by admitted partisans of the romantic in social theory, to demonstrate the credibility of the romantic position. There is the argument that Marx's emphasis on praxis (i.e., that reason or theory alone cannot emancipate), the impulse to end alienation, his stress on the concrete circumstances of material life (defying Enlightenment abstraction), his love of the grotesque as represented in contradiction, and his arguments against capitalism's reifying powers, have romantic origins (Gouldner 1973:336). Moreover, critics often confuse romanticism's rejection of a firm foundation to truth—their allowance for the possibility of truth through hermeneutic disclosure—with postmodernism's rejection of truth in any form (Bowie 1997:87). All things considered, the rush to judge romanticism and the aesthetic suggests a long-standing "tendency of the Left to hand over cultural resources to the enemy without a fight," and an unwise aversion to the aesthetic which leaves many critics feeling that romanticism is "too dangerous to be let fully into 'real politics'" (Bowie 1991:36).

What is the benefit for cultural studies of this exercise in deprogramming? If romanticism retains an edgy vision of modernity sensitive to discourse, truth, and the aesthetic, cultural studies largely does not. Driven by endless micro-analyses of cultural phenomena without a proven means to relate culture satisfactorily to the material world, cultural studies surrenders the aesthetic all too freely. Yet the very aesthetic category that liberal critics like Mannheim and neo-Marxist critics like Eagleton, Jameson, and Harvey dishonour may offer a new foundation for cultural studies. That is, as Ioan Davies writes, to reclaim the aesthetic is to give cultural studies a long-lost platform for restoring its relevance and honing its analysis in an image-saturated world: "The cultural turn in Marxism, shorn of a politico-social foundation, was therefore bound to become yet one more manifestation of the *avant-garde*, a glittery gad-fly on the wall of history. Its success (or its doom—depending on how we read our place in history) is therefore, up to now, largely aesthetic. But that aesthetic, *pace* Marcuse, might yet be the moment on which a new political economy will be built" (Davies 1991:341).

The nostalgia for the lost holism of a unified sensibility, or as it is more commonly phrased in Williams, the "common culture," has worked a powerful magic upon cultural studies. Cultural critics from Right to Left—from Arnold, Leavis, and Eliot to Thompson and Williams—have founded their theoretical and political hopes on this romantic vision, and just as surely been disappointed in their ambitions.[9] What is genuinely ironic, and instructive as far as utopian longing is open to learning anything, is that the aestheticization of society has indeed arrived, but on capitalism's gaudy terms. We are surrounded by the most impressive and gorgeous imagery, but often of the most boring things: products, celebrities, simulations of nature, the market, and war. This is all the more reason why cultural studies should reclaim the aesthetic category, and thereby, the romantic as its own. As subculture critic Dick Hebdige argues, "the reappraisal of political and intellectual priorities which has been forced upon us by a whole series of cultural, political and epistemological crises" has fostered "a renewal of interest in the origin and meaning of the aesthetic experience" (Hebdige 1996:66).

What should be abandoned is the mythology of a lost holism, a mythology that has been more than anything an easy target for its critics and which has obscured romanticism's value. An alternate perspective that separates the aesthetic from this narrative, and asserts its timely and critical nature, is evident in the work of Ian Hunter. In his essay "Aesthetics and Cultural Studies" (Grossberg, Nelson, and Treichler 1992), Hunter argues that the aesthetic dimension is both more continual (it did not become hopelessly corrupted when modernity arrived) and more limited in its potential (it will not summarily heal a shattered world). The function of the aesthetic is to be found "not in the structural relations that divide society into incomplete fragments, but in the entirely contingent and circumstantial relations through which an ethic has been incorporated in the social sphere" (Hunter in Grossberg et al. 1992:364).[10] Arguing that cultural studies retains the nostalgic vision of the aesthetic at its critical peril, Hunter suggests that the aesthetic is very much more with us than the precedent of Schiller provides.

What is necessary is a view of the aesthetic that rightly rejects the nostalgia for a lost holism, while making room for the irregular relationship between the aesthetic and the rest of reality that Hunter calls for. Beauty, in other words, happens, but when and where we cannot expect. The solution may well lie in reclaiming rather than reifying the aesthetic by giving it a "politico-social foundation" predicated on a refurbished romanticism. A romanticism rid of the mythology of unified sensibility is a romanticism better adapted to use in contemporary reality. Located between the tragic narrative and the ideological tool is a conception of the aesthetic as a form of knowledge that persists in a society, and as a form of sensibility that never knew life before the Fall. In this light, a romanticism re-engineered for contemporary challenges is worth having, with its strong advocacy of the aesthetic intact.

Chapter 2

The Secret Police at the Disco

INTERROGATING CULTURAL STUDIES

> We've got an entire academic pedagogy devoted to the notion
> that symbolic dissent—imagining, say, that the secret police
> don't want us to go to the disco, but that we're doing it anyway—
> is as real and as meaningful, or, better yet, *more* real and *more*
> meaningful than the humdrum business of organizing and
> movement-building.
>
> —Tom Frank, "When Class Disappears," 7

Tom Frank is perhaps the best critic cultural studies ever had. As editor of *The Baffler*, a Chicago-based magazine of crankily brilliant cultural criticism, he is impatient with cultural studies' elaborate semiotic analyses of *Sex Pistols* lyrics while, a world away, wars rage and children die for lack of vitamins or clean water. His criticism of cultural studies' radical chic is a helpful place to begin a more finely grained romantic revision, because it argues that theory needs to radicalize itself anew. But contrary to Frank's view, the problem is not that symbolic dissent is useless, but that cultural criticism is too often developed in ways that are neither worldly nor relevant.

Frank is correct in arguing that a lot of the scholarship done in the name of cultural studies sullies that good name, especially when it allows that everything—from disco dancing to shopping—is potentially revolutionary. Such a cavalier approach to political change has drawn criticism from within the ranks of cultural studies scholars too, notably in Jim McGuigan's argument that this tendency amounts to "cultural populism."[1] But Frank's caution is especially appropriate in this chapter devoted to some detailed theoretical work that brings romanticism to bear on key concepts in media and cultural studies. However hair-splitting the analysis, the point is to use romanticism to make theory worldly again by demonstrating how sensitive romanticism is to a reality that theory at its best makes momentarily transparent.

I now turn to romanticism's value in rethinking what may be (after "culture") the two cardinal concepts in media and cultural criticism: modernity (including modernism) and ideology. This exercise in "romanticizing" fundamental concepts in media and cultural criticism, notably as reflected in cultural studies literature on the topics, appropriately centres on several personalities whose work symbolizes the schizoid personality of the field: Raymond Williams on the problem of modernity and modernism, and Terry Eagleton and Stuart Hall on ideology. Comparative reference is also made to David Sholle's argument for a Foucauldian alternative to the ideology concept.

The purpose here is to "use" romanticism on these key concepts prior to taking on larger areas of interest. An updated romanticism offers, first, a perspective on the modern that may improve on Williams's influential and idiosyncratic reading of modernity and modernism; and second, an aesthetic mode of representation superior in some ways to both ideology and the competing Foucauldian notion of "discourse." Because modernity and ideology are almost universally used as concepts in media and cultural studies, and are intellectually prior to media and cultural criticism in general, it seemed appropriate to begin the work of romanticizing theory here. The theme that unites the two concepts, and that relates so productively to the use of romanticism, is the concept and phenomenon of "reification." Romanticism has, after all, been described as that species of modern thought that is uniquely "anti-reifying."

ROMANTICISM AS "NON-REIFYING" MODERNISM

Reification comes from the Latin *res* (thing) and *facere* (to make), and means literally "to make a thing." In Marxist terminology, reification is a particular form or effect of alienation, the process by which the worker is separated from the fruits of his or her labour. As outlined in his 1922 essay, "Reification and the Consciousness of the Proletariat," Georg Lukács defined reification as the suppression of the sensuous and subjective nature of human life under capitalism, and once suppressed, the terms by which we, our concepts, and institutions, become objectified "things." Capitalism, working through the alienation process, erases the human presence from our social worlds, reducing sentient beings to static and functional entities wholly defined by their role in production, and turning our material and intellectual products against us. Alienation is, in some sense, the act of being separated.

In turn, reification is the awful social condition in which we are compelled to live once that separation has occurred, and humanity is humbled before the majestic power of capital.

As reification deepens, strange things begin to happen. Reality becomes ethereal and ghostly as it is filtered through the logic of capital, resulting in a barren, airless social moonscape. That is, we find ourselves as human beings living in a world where traces of our humanity are systematically erased, yet our products, institutions, and concepts have become animate and powerful. Something of this is experienced now in the era of globalization, as workers, investors, and consumers alike must struggle to coexist with an intangible global market that can nonetheless motivate mass layoffs or price hikes with impunity. "The transformation of the commodity relation into a thing of 'ghostly objectivity' cannot therefore content itself with the reduction of all objects for the gratification of human needs to commodities," but also "stamps its imprint on the whole consciousness of man" (Lukács 1971:100). Reification moves well beyond commodity fetishism (the process whereby we impute subjective human qualities to objects—we give names to products like "Joy," "Cavalier," or "Mr. Clean" at the cost of becoming object-like ourselves), and enters into the very tissue of thought and practice. In airbrushing humanity from the world, reification renders it flat, featureless, and without wonder—in a word, reification disenchants the world.

As indicated, the reification process also addresses "the whole consciousness of man," and more specifically, theory. We create complex systems of thought, calling these taxonomies, disciplines, or theories, yet over time they can become arbitrary and escape our control. All theories are socially generated and organized bodies of knowledge, of course, and necessarily bear significant traces of their time and place of origin. But the tendency of thought, as Lukács believed, is that it loses its moorings in history and society, erases evidence of its human origins, and then confronts us as an invisible yet palpably dangerous force.

Out of this process, anti-dialectical in the extreme, emerge monstrous theoretical systems like scientific racism, Marxism-Leninism, or laissez-faire economics. But even at the mildest level, far from this worst-case sketch, reification turns living ideas into dead formulas and catchphrases. Concepts become objects, thoughts become things, and theory consequently becomes an ideology in its own right, rather than something that can help us "hack" society's master codes. The terrible irony here is that theory, devoted to understanding and perhaps then changing reality, actually acts to make reality disappear. Anticipating the concepts of "discourse" and "power/knowledge" that Foucault would develop decades later, Lukács warns that:

the more intricate a modern science becomes and the better it understands itself methodologically, the more resolutely it will turn its back on the onto-logical problems of its own sphere of influence and eliminate them from the realm where it has achieved some insight. The more highly developed it becomes and the more scientific, the more it will become a formally closed system of partial laws. It will then find that the world lying beyond its confines, and in particular the material base which it is its task to under-stand, *its own concrete underlying reality,* lies, methodologically and in principle, *beyond its grasp.* (1971:104)

The infinite layers of bureaucracy, technology, and other forms of com-plexity that suffocate our lives are the signs of reification. In a digital age, reification is magnified by the endless strata of codes, networks, and other abstract structures that originate in technology and bureaucracy, and are lay-ered upon our lives like so much sediment. Although reification is invisible and engenders endless abstractions, its consequences for life and thought are anything but ephemeral. Canadian political scientist Thomas Homer-Dixon has recently recast this problem as the "ingenuity gap," arguing that our social, technological, and economic systems have become so complex that they dan-gerously exceed our ability to comprehend and repair them (Homer-Dixon 2001). Even as we create technological and other means to solve these prob-lems, the solutions end up adding to the aggregate complexity of the world, and overwhelm whatever ingenuity we might bring to bear.

This same plague of reification applies to several of the most important fig-ures and the conceptual contributions under their influence in cultural stud-ies, namely Williams's idea of the modern, and Eagleton's and Hall's separate reflections on ideology. Where Williams is concerned, reification has corre-sponding disastrous effects for his thinking about modernism, particularly as far as accommodating anti-realist modernisms (e.g., surrealism, Dada) and the emergence of electronic media in the early twentieth century are concerned. Eagleton and Hall, on the other hand, commit themselves to strong theories of ideology that override other elements, such as the concept of discourse, which have a more vital attachment to the romantic tradition. All three par-ties inadvertently reify the concepts they have helped shape due to the nature of their relationship to intellectual history. Although as theorists they have very different and even competing relationships to cultural studies, Williams, Eagleton, and Hall are alike in adding to the very problems they would find answers for, making for a vicious and self-defeating circular logic.

As a body of cultural theory committed to re-enchanting the world on modern terms, romanticism brings its anti-reifying powers to bear on a reality that daily sinks deeper under the weight of its own categories. Romanticism reintroduces the supple and sensuous human qualities that reification removes. The anti-reifying power of romanticism lies in its early critique of reason, particularly as reason is deformed into the instrumental rationality that Max Weber, the Frankfurt School, Habermas, and others have identified as a core problem in modernity. As Gouldner explains: "Above all, romanticism rejected bourgeois, vulgar materialism's tendency to 'deaden' the universe and men with it. In the words of Georg Lukács, "Romanticism was a rejection of 'reification' and, we might add, it expressed a refusal to equate modernity with reification. Romanticism sought a path to a *non*-reifying modernism" (Gouldner 1973:331).

Closer examination of Williams and the modern, then Eagleton and Hall, and that most modern of concepts, ideology, reveals in a more intimate scale just how romanticism can rid them of their reification, and provide a model of modernity and of representation adequate to the condition of being digital.

CULTURAL STUDIES AND MODERNITY

Modernity and modernism are easily the most ambitious concepts in the critical vocabulary, condensing between them many of the features of life in the West. Modernity is the complex series of changes to Western culture, such as the emergence of the nation-state, capitalism, science, the triumph of reason, the bureaucratic state, secularization, and other phenomena that emerged during the eighteenth century in Europe in opposition to the medieval past, then spread throughout the world. Modernism, considered a little later in this chapter, is the term given to those various human attempts to talk about and represent this revolutionary transformation, most conventionally captured in a rapid-fire series of aesthetic and political movements that arose in the late nineteenth and early twentieth centuries, including Impressionism, surrealism, Dada, etc. A more elastic definition of modernism would expand it beyond the work of Dali or Brecht, however, and allow that traditions in media and cultural theory, such as the Frankfurt School or "media effects," as well as political movements like fascism, liberal democracy, and feminism, can also be understood as modernisms of a different kind. These broader modernisms, as much as the paintings of Paul Klee or the novels of Virginia Woolf, make it possible to see and act upon the elusive modern condition.

The great conscience of British cultural history, the Welsh-born critic Raymond Williams, had special responsibility for formulating the reading of modernity and modernism most influential in cultural studies.[2] From the early cultural histories to the millennium-minded *The Year 2000*, Williams represented the super-ego of an intellectual project all too willing at times to forget the Chartists for the sake of the Spice Girls. Characteristic of Williams's outlook, as was proper to the author of the "long revolution" concept, was an abiding patience and critical reserve in evaluating historical process.[3]

Unfortunately, in the case of his reading of modernity and modernism, Williams's historical imagination has proved faulty. The "extremely weighty matter of Williams's attitude to the famous 'project of modernity'" has been noted, as has his "barely concealed hostility, informed by what, at its worst, we have to call prejudice" regarding modernism (Prendergast 1995:17, 19). As we'll see, Williams's view of the modern is too indebted to organicism and realism, and too uncomfortable with contradiction, to be compatible with a modern world marked by differentiation and crisis. In contrast, the romantic defines the challenge of modernity as the task of living meaningfully within just such a crisis-ridden modern culture. The romantic awareness of modernity's contradictory nature was evident in the emphasis they granted to the irony in the juxtaposition of the ideals they venerated and the shortcomings of actual experience. Friedrich Schlegel suggests aphoristically that "irony is the clear consciousness of eternal agility, of an infinitely teeming chaos" (Simpson 1988:198). Without resort to romanticism's more sophisticated comprehension of modernity, Williams lacks the theoretical resources necessary to theorize modernity and modernism satisfactorily. After first understanding Williams's reading of romanticism, a better understanding of his awkwardness with respect to this pair of conceptual totems is possible.

Consideration of Williams's relationship to romanticism begins with the anti-theoretical tendency of English intellectual culture—the context for his particular lineage within those related currents in cultural criticism known as "culture and civilization" and culturalism. The early Williams shared the general disregard of the English intelligentsia for theory, notably their "monotonous contempt for 'Grand Theory,' for a model that is seen (unconvincingly) as trying to 'swallow reality in one gulp'"—a phrase coined by E.P. Thompson in his famous attack on the high-theory stylings of Louis Althusser published as *The Poverty of Theory* (Simpson 1993:176). In a later statement in *Politics and Letters,* a collection of interviews with the editorial board of the *New Left Review,* Williams speaks of his decision to get "into theory" at a relatively advanced stage in his career. It is therefore clear that his affiliation with romanticism, as announced in the opening pages of his first book *Culture and Society,* would have been made in a context unreceptive to theory.

Though Williams was certainly aware of German romanticism (as evident from his discussion in *Modern Tragedy,* the book in which he directly considers it), his adaptation of romanticism is problematic. Williams conflated the various romanticisms into the sentimental form of English romanticism, eliminating much of the German theoretical sophistication, a pattern which would act "to assimilate the several (some would say the many) romanticisms to one particular manifestation—the English—of this always quite diverse movement" (Surin 1995:152). The unfortunate result is that the very tradition that moved Marx and Weber to explore the relationship between self and shattered world is effectively absent from Williams's work. As Surin sees it:

> Williams insisted that we are today still confronted...by the question, the question posed quintessentially for tragedy, of the necessity and possibility of reconciling freedom and nature (or necessity). And it is precisely this question that was central for German idealism and theoretical romanticism; it was this question that this movement addressed so uncompromisingly under the rubric of tragedy. Williams, however, gave no indication in *Modern Tragedy* that romanticism, and especially German romanticism, addressed this question more powerfully and productively than any other intellectual movement. (Surin 1995:151)

Confronted by this question of culture's relationship to social and natural constraint, Williams grants culture undue power by opting for an organic model of society, one where culture has unearned deterministic tendencies. Just how he comes by this decision can be illustrated by some speculative intellectual history. The probability of anti-theoreticism aside, how did English romanticism relate to the German? The fact that the British and French romantics were strongly influenced by their romantic counterparts in Germany is universally acknowledged. For instance, the poet-philosophers Samuel Taylor Coleridge and William Wordsworth visited Germany, and the conservative Coleridge and later Thomas Carlyle both published works devoted to systematically introducing German romantic thought in England. As Saiedi finds, in revolt against their own indigenous experience of the Enlightenment, French and British romantics were "receptive to German ideas of life, society and religion" (Saiedi 1993:65).[4]

What is likely, however, given Williams's relationship to the "culture and civilization" position developed by Victorian critic Matthew Arnold, and early twentieth-century literary lion F.R. Leavis, is that the conservative late rather than the radical early German romanticism was more influential on Williams. The possibility of this particular lineage is strengthened in part by the conservative nature of Coleridge's and Carlyle's work and the equally conservative inclinations of Arnold and Leavis. Moreover, Williams's view of culture's organic nature and its relationship to social structure, apart from being deeply indebted to Arnold and Leavis, also strongly resembles late German romantic opinions on the same issues. This may be seen in a brief comparison of "culture and civilization," culturalism, and late German romantic conservative ideas.

Arnold and Leavis believed that there was a permanent contradiction between (to use Leavis's famous slogan) "mass civilization and minority culture." High culture, argued Arnold (1869:49), "is at variance with the mechanical and material civilization in esteem with us," and "the best that has been thought and said" was to offer a high-minded palliative to those suffering through the wrenching social transformation of the Industrial Revolution. Culture was identified as the deeply naturalized and idealized integration of morality and meaning, preserving through time the essential features of British national character. This "organic" view of culture, so-called because it suggests a complex, non-dialectical, and almost ecological relationship between elements in a culture, was set against "civilization," meaning here modern, urban industrial society with its class warfare and other social ills. Society was the source of change, contradiction, and chaotic energies that culture would check and direct. Rather than draw our attention to the problems in society, then, culture was to magically resolve them by pointing to a transcendent set of values safely above the factory apprentice's fatigue and the choking air of London.

The most immediate sources for Williams's allegiance to organicism, and his intolerance for the fractious and fragmentary nature of modern life, are Arnold and Leavis, themselves deeply representative of certain aspects of English romanticism.[5] Long after their ideas were no longer in vogue in British cultural studies, Williams remained beholden to Arnold and Leavis's view that culture and modern society are irreconcilably opposed, a fact which limited his ability to explain the contemporary world. Williams's reluctance to breach the culture and society dichotomy persisted through his long and brilliant career. Grossberg elaborates:

> For those authors Williams located in the "culture and society tradition," the separation is taken for granted; culture is simply appropriated and transformed into a position from which that very separation can be described and judged. But Williams refused such a separation. Cultural studies had to reinsert culture into the practical everyday life of people, into the totality of a whole way of life. *Yet Williams was never able to actually escape this separation*—both in his privileging of certain forms of culture (literature) and in his desire to equate culture with some sort of totality and/or ethical standard. (Grossberg 1997:16; my emphasis)

The distinctions between the older theorists and Williams are nonetheless important. Where for Arnold and Leavis an organic vision of social order required a backward glance toward a conservative cultural authority invested in canonical hierarchy, self-evident values, and elite cultural leadership, Williams believed the organic culture to be viable on socialist terms. And it is because of these politics that the difference between these two pillars of "culture and civilization" and Williams can be appreciated, notably as the former tradition is reinvented by Williams as culturalism. Williams has an irreproachable fidelity to human praxis, to righting economic wrongs, and to a socialist future that accepts the presence of technology and mass-produced popular culture. Not for him is Arnold's wish for a culture beyond machinery or Leavis's apocalyptic view of mass culture as a place where "the landmarks have shifted, multiplied and crowded upon one another, the distinctions and dividing lines...blurred away" (Leavis 1930:19). Yet culturalism, the particular form of cultural theory with which Williams is eternally identified, has serious problems that might be seen to at least resemble, if not derive from, late romantic sources.

Culturalism, to reprise Hall's slightly embarrassed account in "Cultural Studies: Two Paradigms," is a form of socialist humanism that concedes to culture the considerable power to shape society, power which acts to ground cultural production in sensuous human reality. Credited with breaking from economically deterministic base/superstructure models of society by dint of what Williams called "cultural materialism," culturalism values experience and agency (whereas orthodox Marxism devalued these as forms of false consciousness and structurally determined behaviour). In other words, Williams follows the Italian Communist Antonio Gramsci in granting culture a power to direct human affairs on terms roughly comparable to the economy, thereby reclaiming the vivacious fact of experience as a source for human thought and action. Yet unlike Gramsci, Williams removes this shaping power from people themselves, and ultimately relocates it at the ontological foundations of the culture.

In Williams's intimate acquaintance with the concept, culture is defined both as something people produce in conversation and other forms of symbolic exchange, and as a value-laden wholeness by which such interaction is sanctified. However, in wanting culture to be as alive and supple as something produced in conversation, yet as enduring as traditional values and practices, Williams enters into what Hall believes a significant contradiction. The problem is not that Williams values tradition. It's that tradition is enshrined as a metaphysical principle which binds everything in society into a morally cohesive whole. The underlying metaphysic is prior to any form of symbolic interaction that would otherwise create meaning in the moment, and therefore makes cultural practices (e.g., artistic creation, conversation, custom) into derivative phenomena with little bearing on society. This paradoxical view of culture—superficially dynamic, yet ultimately static—is captured in Williams's famous "structure of feeling" concept.

By the "structure of feeling," Williams meant the phenomenon whereby culture in a given historical period has a particular character or signature through which can be read the deeper patterns active at the time. This deep structure binds and makes distinctive the diffuse experience of living at a given time and place, resolving the chaos and complexity of experience into an intelligible pattern. As Williams said of the "structure of feeling": "All that is lived and made, by a given community in a given period, is, we now commonly believe, essentially related, although in practice, and in detail, this is not always easy to see" (Williams 1968:17).

Hall believes that given the tendency of culturalists like Richard Hoggart, E.P. Thompson, and Williams to find underlying patterns and unities underlying the most disparate of phenomena, the culturalist position is essentializing (1986:39). That is, culture is a constellation of unchanging, timeless properties or "essences" that then exert undue influence on other variables in society. Such organicism and essentialism is captured in the "structure of feeling" concept. The two definitions of culture that Hall identified—as the discursive product of everyday, interactional experience and as a foundational metaphysic giving surface phenomena their particular character—are never entirely reconciled in Williams's work, moving Hall to argue that the balance is decidedly tipped in favour of the transcendental whole. Hall insists that "this sense of cultural totality—of the whole historical process—overrides any effort to keep the instances and elements distinct" (1986:39).

With concepts such as "structure of feeling," Williams tilts away from agency and the early German premises comfortable with contradiction, and toward the totalizing and mystifying definition favoured by both Arnold and Leavis and late German romanticism. Culturalism therefore limits cultural studies' effectiveness in analysis of phenomena—as novel as new media and as pressing as the future of modernity in light of the postmodern critique— that would benefit from "romanticizing." This tension between subject-centred and materialist compared to essentialist and organic conceptions of culture lies at the generous heart of German romanticism. Romanticism "is simultaneously the most radical theory of individual uniqueness, freedom and subjectivity," where the subject's creative practice is the very centre of cultural production, and "at the same time, an extreme theory of cultural unity, sociological realism, and historical reason" (Saiedi 1993:107).

The problem is not necessarily that late German romanticism favoured an organic conception of social totality *per se*, but the *kind* of organicism it favoured. Where in early German romanticism, organic or natural models of reality are invoked as antidotes to the Enlightenment preference for mechanistic language that defined reality as a machine, in the later phase "the same metaphor implies the idea of totality, functional interdependence, priority of the whole to the parts, structural unity and order" (Saiedi 1993:157). Clearly then there are organicisms such as that favoured by the early German romantics which, although not favouring a dialectical conception of social process, maintain a dynamic and progressive outlook. But later German romanticism's organicism is a much more petrified form, suggesting an unreal coherence and equilibrium typical of Williams's own work. The late Romantic view of organicism is, arguably, the same that manifests in Arnold and Leavis, and thereby, in Williams's concept of culture, as crystallized in the "structure of feeling" concept.

Williams can be criticized for both positing a wholeness thought to exist prior to the crises that come with modernity—an awkward socialist version of the Eden myth—and for identifying that wholeness with a set of transcendent values, such as the authenticity of working class experience or community, which Williams himself selected. Culture then becomes a matter of faith. Whatever threatens that belief system is denied status as "culture," consigned to the large and amorphous category that is the "social," an analytical separation that acts ultimately to reify Williams's model of society by simultaneously naturalizing culture (as organic) and isolating the social. Phenomena such as technology that confront us with their inherent ambiguity are banished to the hinterland of the social so that they do not violate the integrity of the culture concept. Culture conceived in such organic terms thus loses its contact with history, with the contradictions that would help culture grow, and with the political movements Williams championed throughout his career. Without a more worldly model of culture, Williams leaves cultural studies ill-prepared to address modernity and the many mutations it has undergone in the later twentieth century.

CULTURAL STUDIES AND MODERNISM

The modern aesthetic and political movements collectively known as "modernism" that emerged in the mid-nineteenth century, causing riots and consternation everywhere, have always provoked (and indeed, encouraged) strong reactions from the general public and intellectuals alike. The Nazis burned the modern, the Italian fascists and Stalinist communists made it into propaganda, and even more democratically minded societies and citizens had to make peace with these dangerous visions in art, architecture, literature, theatre, and many other forms. Modernism would have it no other way, since the politicization of our aesthetic response is very much the point. Williams's own response to modernism, given his vast interpretive gifts and political sophistication, is therefore instructive in thinking about his relationship to romanticism and the modern.

Williams believed in modernism, but of a particular kind and only to a point: the point of the late nineteenth century. The modernism of this period, he argues in his essay "When Was Modernism?" (Williams 1989), citing social realists like Charles Dickens and Gustave Flaubert, and the aesthetic movement known as Impressionism, retained its critical edge regarding bourgeois aesthetics. But the modernism of the 1890s-1920s period, a period coincident with both anti-realist modernisms such as Dada, surrealism, and futurism that broke with the attempt to represent the world objectively, and the emergence of new media technologies like radio, film, and television, does not qualify as having the same critical, anti-bourgeois content. Arguing that the erratic energy of these later modernisms was spent as they split between progressive (he names Pablo Picasso and Bertolt Brecht) and reactionary factions (he names Ezra Pound, Wyndham Lewis and F.T. Marinetti), Williams proposes that the modernism of the *fin de siècle* was deeply compromised: "What has quite rapidly happened is that Modernism quickly lost its anti-bourgeois stance, and achieved comfortable integration into the new international capitalism. Its attempt at a universal market, transfrontier and transclass, turned out to be spurious. Its forms lent themselves to cultural competition and the commercial interplay of obsolescence, with its shifts of schools, styles and fashion so essential to the market" (Williams 1989:35).

Even a sympathetic account of Williams's modernism (Pinkney 1989:23) allows that the Welsh academic and novelist was inconsistent in his reckoning of modernism. Williams unaccountably passed from the above-noted recognition of modernism's radicalism (as he saw it, one tragically neutralized by the assimilation of modernist forms into the design of consumer goods, advertising, etc.) to a position where twentieth-century, anti-realist modernism itself is written off as a complicit, reactionary, and bourgeois phenomenon with no radical past. Referring to Williams's book *The Year 2000*, Pinkney argues "this most recent account tends to neglect the role of 'consumer modernism' and to paint the modernisms of the turn of the century as homogeneously doom-laden and angst-ridden" (1989:23). While successfully demonstrating that Williams was no bumpkin with artistic pretensions—a "British Lukács" clinging to realism due to an allergy to experiment—Pinkney admits that modernism and traditionalism are at war for Williams's soul. "The *modernism* that is Williams's almost by instinct is locked in combat, in one phase of his work, with a politico-intellectual decision in favour of a realism that thwarts many of his own deepest political energies" (Pinkney 1989:28).

The implication here is that modernity as an authentic form of culture ended with the introduction of the new modernisms. Modernity ceases to qualify as a legitimate and resistant "structure of feeling" at the moment that it passes through modernisms that don't respect the organic conception of culture. Modernity and modernism alike are thereby denied any autonomy, a fact Williams underlines when he writes in *The Country and the City* (1973:295) that, like rural and urban life themselves, "the total character of what we know as modern society has been similarly determined" by capitalism. Indeed, culture itself in the early twentieth-century modern is made to seem what Williams in his early work, *Communications*, called "anti-culture"; that is, "alien to almost everybody, persistently hostile to art and intellectual activity," the culture not of the "ordinary man" but of the "disinherited" (1962:115).[6]

In Williams's opinion, twentieth-century modernists had also wrought an inauthentic culture best rendered in terms of the "global village" concept he so hated, a Potemkin village where this rootless intelligentsia had honorary citizenship. Against the settled and self-perpetuating organic conception of culture favoured by Williams, the modern was by contrast negatively identified with a restless mobility—a quality memorably captured in his concept of "mobile privatization."[7] Mobile privatization, the keystone of Williams's book *Television: Technology and Cultural Form*, was a phenomenon defining modern society as a vast number of human satellites in orbit, endlessly moving in their private envelopes of mass-media experience and without benefit of a shared public sphere. As such, Williams's conception of modernism is of a cultural sensibility and practice uncomfortable with aesthetic principles that part with realism, and slow to accommodate the vexed nature of contemporary life. Such a definition of modernity as mobility is a staple of cultural studies' analysis of the modern, as Grossberg argues: "Unlike many other theories of the emergence of the modern (including the 'culture and society tradition'), cultural studies is driven less by a vision of a total qualitative transformation of society (e.g., from the traditional to the modern or from community to mass society)—cultural studies was never about the destruction of community—than by a concern for the consequences of new forms and degrees of mobility" (1997:16).

All this is to say that whatever one might think of the desirability of an organic notion of culture, twentieth-century modernity and its modernisms should be allowed some measure of autonomy. If that is allowed, then a nonorganic (or alternatively, a variation reflecting a more sophisticated organicism) conception of culture is appropriate to the period culminating in the horrors of the Great War and the death of late-nineteenth century liberal ideals, and is not some abomination born of a monstrous capitalism. The fact that the modern aesthetic entered the marketplace by being built into appliances, cars, and office towers does not dissolve the truth-telling power of the Bauhaus or Le Corbusier. Early German romanticism supports a realistic and necessary reading of modernity as compatible with such contradictions; late German romanticism, closer in spirit and substance to Williams's more immediate sources in Arnold and Leavis, does not.

If Williams's goal of developing something other than "a narrowly urban-industrial imagination of modernity" (Pinkney 1989:31) is to be achieved, then romanticism needs to be revisited. There is enormous value in arguing for a view of society that respects complex connections, whether as an antidote to the niche markets into which theory has too often located itself, or as a basis for defence against capital. But Williams's prejudice against a complexity that is incompatible with a rather conservative variant of the organic conception of culture is not the best means to revive the hopes of an unashamedly modern cultural theory. Williams's views are reifying to the extent that the age-old separation of culture and society is maintained in his work, a separation enforced by Williams's identification of the social with contradiction, change, and false community. Cultural studies needs and deserves a better model of the modern.

The reintroduction of romanticism offers a non-reifying alternative to cultural studies. What is more, romanticism makes the ideology concept more sensitive to the texture and dynamism characteristic of the reality that is, after all, the concept's unique burden to explain. Romanticism offers a model of representation that refuses the fossilization of the ideology concept by finding a happy medium between ideology and discourse, thereby remaining sensitive to the real, if relative, indeterminacy of the contemporary world.

IDEOLOGY AND THE ENLIGHTENMENT

Ideology may be succinctly defined as a systematic and comprehensive image of reality, one typically experienced uncritically as the common-sense terms by which a person lives in and knows the world. For example, the dominant ideology in the West has been liberalism, complicated as it is by its relationship with modernity, industrial capitalism, and Western culture's earlier ideological basis in Greek and Roman Antiquity and Christian doctrine. Ideologies may be attached to and authorized by a society's elite, in which case they may be regarded as "dominant" ideologies; or they may arise from other institutions or social groups as competing reality principles. Following

Gramsci's hegemony concept, his reinterpretation of ideology, ideologies are not simply imposed from above by a conniving ruling class upon the unsuspecting, passive masses, but are rather negotiated between groups and interests at various social strata, reflecting both elite ambitions, and popular wishes and needs. And after Althusser, we understand that ideology is a permanent fixture of life, not a temporary illusion that might be dissipated once we know the truth. Ideology is "always already" with us, in that the limitations of human consciousness mean that we can never know the world as it truly is, but only through the filter of these mental fabrications manufactured by various "institutional state apparatuses" like education, religion, and media.

After culture, the concept of ideology may be the most important in cultural studies. From French *philosophe* Destutt de Tracy's original 1796 definition of ideology as the "systematic study of ideas and sensations" to the most advanced rethinking of the concept in light of Gramsci and Althusser, the concept comes down to cultural studies being freighted with the Enlightenment values it absorbed from de Tracy's era (Cormack 1992). Ideology is ultimately the idea that authorizes all media and cultural criticism, in that it describes how various phenomena—from fashion to fitness clubs—can be seen to contribute to a common picture of reality. Without the concept of ideology, a systematic view of media and culture is difficult to achieve, because each message is encountered in isolation. Ideology appreciates that all messages, no matter how trivial, can be taken as supporting a comprehensive world view. I'll be arguing that ideology's Enlightenment past represents a liability, and romanticism a means to correct, redefine, and save this most valuable of intellectual properties from overextension.

Whether in its classic or contemporary form, the concept of ideology is infused with rationalism, retaining to this day a residue of Enlightenment confidence in the sheer transparency of reality. "However far the concept of ideology has travelled since the days of the *Institut National*, however varied its uses have become, nevertheless it remains tied to the ideals of the Enlightenment, in particular to the ideals of the rational understanding of the world and of the rational self-determination of human beings" (Thompson 1990:32-33). While recent work by John Thompson and Terry Eagleton is self-conscious of ideology's overweening identification with rationality— Eagleton calling for a theory of ideology that welcomes "the affective, unconscious, mythical or symbolic dimensions" (Eagleton 1991a:221)—neither theorist seriously questions its Enlightenment pedigree.

The acknowledged challenge to the ideology concept's validity and, by extension, ideology critique's practical efficacy, has come from post-structuralism and its contention that reality (or, speaking semiotically, the referent) has disappeared beyond the limits of language. Hence the real is unreach-able, and the "truth" is merely a rhetorical construct—the invention of whom or whatever controls representation at a particular time. But the more serious if less explicit challenge to ideology comes from inside its own conceptual universe, whereby it may be seen as the victim of its own success. The prob-lem is that ideology critique's *own* ideology, the Enlightenment values of which it was made, have disposed it to a self-defeating process of reification. That is, the ideology concept has itself become ideological, greatly reducing its power to explain reality.

Even critics sympathetic to a modernist criticism—for example, editors of a book optimistically subtitled "reconstructing ideology critique"—have recently raised similar concerns. Canvassing the various ways in which radi-cal criticism has confronted the Enlightenment heritage, from the Frankfurt School's charge that reason was hijacked by narrowly bureaucratic "instru-mental" rationality under capitalism, to feminist and post-structuralist argu-ments that ideology critique appeals to masculine forms of reason or an unten-able foundationalism, Billig and Simons (1994:2) state that "the suspicion is raised that Marx and Engels's project of 'enlightenment' was itself in the grip of an ideology, one which put an innocent trust in the power of reason and an optimistic faith in modernity." Although theory has time and again had to reinvent itself to answer to postcolonial studies, queer theory, and other argu-ments for reality's stubborn refusal to fit into models prepared for it, ideology critique boldly assumes that ideology can ultimately be traced from its origins in social structure to the text where it's manifested in an image or an argu-ment. Such overreaching can ironically invite despair, as confident theory meets with a reality that seems daily more complex and intractable, forcing criticism either to grand Althusserian vagaries or the smallness of vision which generates endless analyses of Madonna or *X-Files:* "The growth of cul-tural studies also expresses, often indirectly, an increasing political pessimism, at least as compared with the bright optimism of the early pages of *The German Ideology.* No longer do cultural critics believe that a sudden ray of illumination will, like a laser beam, remove the cancer of ideological illusion. Each work of cultural analysis emphasizes the depth and breadth of the ideo-logical processes in the age of the mass media. In so doing, each reveals the enormity of the task of emancipation" (Billig and Simons 1994:4).

IDEOLOGY AND LANGUAGE

The most naive understanding of language assumes that language is a simple mirror of our thoughts, feelings, or the impressions our senses take of the

world. Yet the ideology concept is built upon this sort of understanding of representation—of how we "re-present" reality back to ourselves when we talk
about it. The ideology concept is disposed to reification due to its reliance on
a model of representation—of how we *re*-present reality to ourselves in mediated form—that denies to language the power to deflect ideology or shape
society in a significant way.[8] Language, in other words, is not allowed to
"mean" very much at all, since it is allowed very little influence on the nature
and direction of ideology, or its social implications.

These limitations are made possible by the presence of the Enlightenment
heritage in social theory, which prefers the realist and rationalist values supported by ideology to the ungovernable properties of language better appreciated by romanticism. Ideology critique thus relies on a model of language,
imported from the Russian theorist Valentin Volosinov's *Marxism and the
Philosophy of Language*, that reduces language to a transparent and neutral
medium or carrier, rather than seeing language as a social force in its own
right.[9] Language is therefore reified at the source, its social content and character suppressed in favour of a model of language that assumes language's
transparency, thus making possible ideology critique's grand claims to peer
deeply into reality. Overcome, the prevalent theory of representation in cultural studies is defined almost exclusively in ideological terms, an uncomfortable choice for an intellectual project dedicated to the study of culture.

Volosinov's influential model underwrites the self-reifying nature of ideology critique by defining the sign as the sum total of meanings imparted to it
by social interests contending for its control in society. Eagleton (1991a),
deriving much of his essay on "Ideology and Discourse" in *Ideology: An
Introduction* from Volosinov's book, approvingly characterizes the Russian
theorist's view of this competition: "A particular social sign is pulled this way
and that by competing social interests, inscribed from within by a multiplicity of ideological 'accents'; and it is in this way that it sustains its dynamism
and vitality" (195). The work of giving ideology a meaningful social and
material context, of course, is recognized as this Bakhtin circle member's great
contribution; but it represents also a problem where language is concerned. In
being defined as the product of ideological struggle, language is forbidden its
autonomy, meaning that a variable of huge importance is reduced to an
insignificant ingredient in reality.

Volosinov's great achievement was to break with psychological theories of
ideology that—like the near mystical concept of "ether," which pre-atomic
physics thought to be the medium connecting matter and energy in the universe—made ideology into an invisible, if insidious, process magically capable
of clouding the minds of millions. Volosinov defined ideology as a phenome-

non bound up with language; he bumped the metaphysics from the concept and replaced it with a thoroughly materialist interpretation of how ideology works. The material nature of what semioticians call the "sign" or basic unit of meaning was invested in the actual physical form or manifestation it took (e.g., the chalk dust on the blackboard, the fleshy fact of the hand waving "hello"). Because it was material in this sense, language was recognized as a complement to the larger social forces of labour and capital, and not altogether different from other means of production.

However, although it's defined in contrast to a simple notion of language as merely reflective of consciousness, Volosinov's model remains reflective in nature. That is, though Volosinov acknowledges the sign's autonomy—its "refracting" power—this autonomy is merely the dynamism imputed to it by social struggle. Language in and of itself is denied the capacity to resist its determination because its material and social identity is defined in terms that favour Volosinov's model of ideology. The sign is material, but Volosinov surrenders its formal properties the better to bury it in dialectical process all the more securely. The sign is social, but only insofar as it is the object and instrument of social contest. Put simply, because the sign is the product of the various interests contending to give it meaning, it is nothing in and of itself.

Beyond the fact of our imperfect ability to articulate experience or the inherent ambiguity of meaning, words and pictures have a material nature. They are artifacts in themselves. They exist in sound and radio waves; they have weight, colour, and other formal properties as signifiers. And however driven by social interests language may be, the objective identity of these media makes them not entirely susceptible to anyone's control. It is because we don't recognize words and images *as objects* that we condemn them to being mere reified objects. Medium theory, notably as espoused by the great "Toronto School" theorists like Harold Innis and Marshall McLuhan, made a case for media as independent variables that cannot be ignored.

Moreover, because of their social nature, words and pictures have a history. Over time, they are shaped and selected by processes other than exclusively ideological ones, and their meanings are multiplied through use to the point of (at least potential) indeterminacy, before their appearance in a given ideological contest. We wear out words and images, and seek new meanings; novel experiences demand that our means of expression expand likewise; and the sheer fact of use encourages some words and images to prosper, while others perish in a kind of linguistic Darwinism. Much of this sociolinguistic process occurs at a level that is arguably pre-ideological, and part of the life cycle of language itself.

In creditably separating himself and improving upon Ferdinand de Saussure's formalism, and thereby giving the sign a material identity and a social context, Volosinov ironically acted to deny the social origins and significance of form. "Language," he claims, "acquires life and historically evolves precisely here, in concrete verbal communication, and not in the abstract linguistic system of language forms, nor in the individual psyche of speakers" (1929:95). Yet, there is no such thing as abstract "form": the formal properties of language are necessarily themselves social in nature, and in their discursive guise, contain meaningful possibilities—even new worlds—that are neither captured nor exhausted by ideological contest. Williams, in an otherwise approving review of Volosinov's breakthrough, allows that the Russian scholar (believed by some to have been Mikhail Bakhtin wearing a Stalin-era pseudonym) may have obscured the internal dynamic between form and content in the sign itself: "Volosinov, even after these fundamental restatements, continues to speak of the 'sign-system': the formulation that had been decisively made in Saussurean linguistics. But if we follow his arguments we find how difficult and misleading this formulation can be. 'Sign' itself—the mark or token; the formal element— has to be revalued to emphasize its variability and internally active elements, indicating not only an internal structure but an internal dynamic" (1977:42).

Eagleton (1991a:195) admits that Volosinov overplays the role of ideology in the sign's constitution—"language and ideology are in one sense identical to Volosinov, they are not in another"—but argues (again, following Volosinov's lead) that social interests struggling over the sign define its relative autonomy. But though the sound and fury of ideological combat certainly bring signs new life, as we have seen in the culture wars around the literary canon or the teaching of media literacy in high schools, the signs are valuable to those interests only because they have a past that can be exploited, one which is not exhausted in the moment of use. This "dumbing down" of the sign is evident in Eagleton's account of ideology, which acts to intensify Volosinov's conflation of ideology and sign: "If ideology cannot be divorced from the sign, then neither can the sign be isolated from concrete forms of social intercourse. It is within these alone that the sign 'lives'; and these forms of intercourse must in turn be related to the material basis of social life. The sign and its social situation are inextricably fused together, and this situation determines from within the form and structure of an utterance" (1991a:195).

It's one thing to acknowledge that the sign cannot be isolated from context, and quite another to argue that the sign is "inextricably fused" to social structure. This reductive definition of the sign is made all the more vexatiously complete by Eagleton's treatment of the problem of indeterminacy— the empirically unknowable and uncontrollable nature of language and reality. He is correct to argue that "textuality, ambiguity, indeterminacy lie often enough on the sign of dominant ideological discourses themselves" (1991a:198). But instead of recovering these things on behalf of a critical perspective, he concedes the point by consigning them to post-structuralism. "Post-structuralist thought often enough sets up ideology in this 'straw target' style, only to go on to confront it with the creative ambiguities of `textuality' or the sliding of the signifier" (1991a:198).

With the "creative ambiguities" of textuality and signifier safely out of the way, then ideology, sign, and structure may by all rights be "fused." But Eagleton's consistency, as noted in a review of his *The Ideology of the Aesthetic*, has historically come at the expense of the aesthetic, a fact which will return to haunt his analysis. "[Eagleton] reads the philosophical tradition of modernity in such a way that he takes too little account of the fact that there always has been, especially in relation to the aesthetic, a vital subversive element in that tradition's conception of subjectivity, which resists assimilation into conceptuality and forces philosophy to admit its own failure to achieve full transparency" (Bowie 1991:37). There are modern, romantic ways of honouring the contrariness of language, without writing the matter off as a desperate post-structuralist gambit.

But Eagleton ignores the pertinent sociolinguistic fact via Volosinov. That is, language's formal properties do impress themselves on communication in ways that are not reducible to the material location nor strategic ploys of its users. Although ideology itself plays a part in the historical sifting and selection of linguistic resources, so does the formal and material existence of language, as do the everyday exigencies of communicative practice, accident, and innovation. Given its weak theory of representation, ideology critique's power is flattered and inflated beyond its means, but at the expense of denying the material form and social content of language. The consequences of this weak concept of language, and hence the potential for a romantic revision of stock concepts of ideology and discourse in cultural studies, also register in instructive ways in the media theory of Stuart Hall.

IDEOLOGY AND AUDIENCE

Audiences are significant in ways not always revealed by the extensive analyses of viewing behaviour done by major critics of audience, such as David Morley and Ien Ang. The importance of audience lies in the fact that in a highly mediated culture, the family in the living room, or the billion watching a World Cup soccer final, are our stand-in for democracy itself. That is, whenever we research audience, we are also thereby researching the parameters for meaningful public participation in a society where North Americans spend an average 10 years of their lives watching television.[10] Images of passive audiences overwhelmed and mesmerized by media spectacles have had metaphorical value as ways for theorists to express their concern for, or in some cases, opposition to democracy. But more recent models of active audiences, like those represented most famously in Stuart Hall's work, reclaim viewing as an activity compatible with more conventional forms of democratic expression, such as voting, protests, and debate.

Hall, a contemporary of Raymond Williams and other founders of British cultural studies, is the field's best-known living theorist of audience. Director of the Centre for Contemporary Cultural Studies from 1969 to 1979, Hall was sufficiently influential to represent the core contribution to media scholarship there (Dworkin 1997:169). Hall's media theoretical *tour de force* is "Encoding/Decoding in Television Discourse," originally published as a booklet through the Centre, then endlessly anthologized. In "Encoding/Decoding," Hall broke the monopoly of the long-dominant "media effects" school on the study of audience, and offered a platform for much subsequent work in media reception and cultural practice generally within cultural studies.[11] Where the "media effects" model had argued that audiences were largely passive in the face of powerful media messages, Hall conjured a viewing public that was much more active in interpreting content. This was a brave and liberating position, especially given a long-standing tendency in criticism dating to the late nineteenth-century "crowd theory" of Gustave Le Bon which construed audiences as victims stupefied by media power.

Encoding/decoding is a model of audience behaviour that has been enormously influential, and yet for reasons largely out of Hall's control, equally troublesome. As the encoding/decoding model was assimilated into cultural studies, notably in the United States, it became *the* model for imagining how audiences and publics related to textual phenomena, and as a result was remarkably overextended. Its success is as much ideological as it is a reflection of the model's productivity, because it appealed to liberal norms in American cultural studies that insisted on theories compatible with individual freedom and free will. Originating as a model to explain how audiences related to ideology, it ironically became an alibi for explaining away the very existence of coercive frameworks through which common-sense reality is defined.

In his essay, a characteristic Hall blend of Volosinov, Althussser, and Gramsci, Hall provides not only an alternate model of reception as filtered through the usual structuralist premises of how meaning is socially produced, but also an influential metaphor for agency (i.e., for how people take action and are thus "agents") in cultural studies. Hall's genius was to use structuralism to break down the mediation process into distinct moments, and then to privilege those moments when the ideological content of a given message was most in flux. For Hall, the meaning of a particular media message was most open to negotiation at the point where it was first encoded, for example, by media workers in a TV production unit; and second, when it was decoded by the people viewing the program. Once the referent or real world event being mediated at the sending end (e.g., a news story about an imminent war) had passed under the sign of discourse, it was largely free of determination until it had been consumed and reproduced in the minds and lives of the viewers.

For a message to have any consequence, rational meaning had to be taken from it. Slyly appropriating the effects model's language for the occasion, particularly notions of "effect" and the "uses and gratifications" that supposedly motivated viewers to watch in the first place, Hall argued that "before this message can have an 'effect' (however defined), satisfy a 'need' or be put to a 'use,' it must first be appropriated as a meaningful discourse and be meaningfully decoded. It is this set of decoded meanings which 'have an effect,' influence, entertain, instruct or persuade, with very complex perceptual, cognitive, emotional, ideological or behavioural consequences" (1980a:130).

Audience members then, according to their own relationship to the program's messages, either irresistibly believed the ideological content of the message (what Hall called a dominant or hegemonic reading), generally believed the message but thought it didn't necessarily apply to their own personal or local circumstances (negotiated reading), or interpreted the message as ideological and resisted it (oppositional reading). That much is now legendary in cultural studies. However, Hall's model, and his advocacy for returning the "repressed" concept of ideology to media studies, invites a romantic indictment on several counts.

That is, the problems in "Encoding/Decoding" have been reproduced in much subsequent media scholarship influenced by the Centre. These problems are the weakness of language in his analysis relative to ideology; the related problem of his inattention to "affect" or the non-rational realm of experience and emotion; and ultimately, structuralism's responsibility to the problem of meaning. The issue here is not that Hall intended the encoding/decoding model to become a theoretical formula used to capture textual activity of all kinds, or that he hasn't grown beyond this in his later work. But the influence of the model continues, out of all proportion to its originality or intended scope when first published in 1980, and is a force that can be reckoned with romantically.

In "Encoding/Decoding," Hall defines language's role in a way that reduces it to just another synonym for ideology. Though there is token acknowledgement of the fact that other discourses (e.g., professional and technical communications among media workers producing a given show) have some influence on the content of a given message, Hall's sensitivity to issues of language, as opposed to ideology, ends there. What's missing in Hall's analysis is recognition of the fact that the conditions of representation extend well beyond the particular moments of encoding and decoding he has outlined. That is, both media producers and consumers are themselves implicated in discourses of various kinds (e.g., gender, class, race and ethnicity, religion, taste, understandings of particular issues derived from education, life experience, etc.) which do not reduce to a simple notion of ideology. The contingency, the relative autonomy, and the lack of necessary symmetry between encoding and decoding moments which Hall argues are found in the interval between encoding and decoding, are also found outside the mere parameters of mediation, in the strictest sense.

The message does not simply enter its discursive form once it's been encoded, as Hall's model suggests: *it is never outside of discourse.* Hall's use of "interpellation"—the Althusserian concept whereby an individual's identity is constructed for him or her by the linguistic structures of which culture is made—dematerializes Hall's idea of audience to the point where the three-part grid of dominant, negotiated, and oppositional responses is cast into doubt. There really is no existential purchase, and therefore no guarantee of contradiction, from which his decoders might challenge the ideology in a given message. The result is that Hall's presumably "active" model of audience is made into an ironically passive construct of how audiences operate. Grossberg seconds this critique of Hall's model:

> Surprisingly, in the end, this seems to leave no space for the power of either the text itself or the historical actor to excite and incite historical struggles around particular discourses. While Hall argues that the audience cannot be seen as passive cultural dopes, he cannot elaborate its positivity. Neither aspect of the relation [i.e., the encoding and decoding moments] can be understood as merely a matter of tendential structures that have, historically, already articulated a particular discourse or subject into powerful ideological positions. (Grossberg 1996a:167)

John Fiske, in his friendly critique of Hall's model, attempts to much more fully socialize encoding and decoding, allowing the people at either end all the texture and contradiction that life inside multiple, intersecting discourses allows. Citing Morley's ethnographic audience studies as an exemplary correction of Hall, Fiske argues that accounting for the discourse in which the decoding party is situated means that the critical moment for analysis is not when the viewer interprets the text, but when her or his discourses meet the discourses in which the text is located. Fiske claims that "reading becomes a negotiation between the social sense inscribed in the program and the meanings of social experience made by its wide variety of viewers; this negotiation is a discursive one" (Fiske 1987:269). The media text, rather than possessing a single ideological point by which the receiver's critical powers are tried and tested, is then no longer a delimited and homogeneous thing, but a site for the production of multiple meanings and subject positions.

These criticisms of Hall's media theory aside, his more recent work on "articulation" demonstrates the same reification seen in "Encoding/ Decoding." By "articulation," Hall describes how the structural relationship of larger moments, such as the relationship of market liberalism to anti-corporate globalization protests, can unfold. "Articulation" is a means to imagine how the convergence of two phenomena may occur outside of some notion of necessary or determined historical change. Hall explains it this way: "An articulation is thus the form of the connection that *can* make a unity of two different elements," "under certain conditions," and according to a dialectical relationship which is "not necessary, determined, absolute and essential for all time" (Grossberg 1996b:141). In other words, "articulation" is Hall's way of explaining why certain events or phenomena emerge without his having to resort to a doctrinaire formula.

Articulation, according to Hall, grants an elective and contingent quality to historical change. It explains why and why not certain changes may occur (e.g., the "failed revolution" among the Western working class), how particular relations endure over time to the point where they are deeply naturalized and exert a powerful force on other structures (e.g., the Roman Catholic Church's hegemony in medieval Europe), and how human agents can take advantage of moments of structural opportunity to make constructive changes. Yet criticism of "articulation" acknowledges Hall's failure to effectively distinguish ideology from discourse, suggesting a single-mindedness that limits much of Hall's analysis largely to the level of individual acts of signification. Grossberg, for example, describes Hall's lack of attention to the role of socially organized language—"discourse"—with respect to the fashioning of ideological representations of the world:

> The failure of cultural studies is not that it continues to hold to the importance of signifying and ideological practices but rather, that it always limits its sense of discursive effectivity to this plane. It fails to recognize that discourses may not only have contradictory effects within the ideological, but that those ideological effects may themselves be placed within complex networks of other sorts of effects. Consequently, the particular model of articulation falls back into a structuralism of empty spaces in which

every place in the ideological web is equally weighted, equally charged so to speak. The cultural field remains a product of oddly autonomous, indeterminate struggles, an amorphous field of equal differences and hence of equivalences. (Grossberg1996a:167)

Even after Hall's break with Althusserianism, signalled in his "The Rediscovery of 'Ideology': Return of the Repressed in Media Studies," he never successfully recovered a working and effective concept of representation. Schiller argues that "although Hall also cautiously suggested that ideology and language should not be treated as identical, and even conceded in 1980 that there existed an 'immensely powerful pull towards idealism in Cultural Studies,' the hold exercised over theory by structuralist conceptions of language was such that Hall could arrive at no thoroughgoing alternative formulation" (1996:154). The reduction of language to a mere reflex of ideology reflects what is for Schiller an endemic problem in communication studies as a discipline. It has an unfortunate preference for a model of communication that is disastrously abstracted and repeatedly reified. That is, the discipline defines communication itself as a spectral and immaterial phenomenon quite divorced from what Schiller believes is its actual identity: communication is labour (1996:157).

Affect—the emotional, sensory, and experiential fact of human life—is also unhappily compromised by the strong ideology concept in Hall's work. The ideology concept on which Hall depends is thoroughly rationalist in nature, depicting the moment of reception as a matter of good or bad interpretive choices made in relation to a media text. But rational comprehension and choice are but a small part of how we experience information, when emotions, the unconscious mind, and even the body are also directly addressed by media messages. All these elements are registered on romanticism's more sensitive filters, yet emotions or the body are largely absent in ideology critique. No one examining a music video, an infomercial, or even a lot of ordinary contemporary programming (given action sequences, representation of sexuality, etc.) should assume that media can alone be critically defined as messages rationally decoded by the receiver. The result of such a definition of media is a textualism that locates excessive determining power in the media text (not unlike the media effects model), even as it supposedly argues for the relative autonomy of the audience. The ultimate irony is that Hall is not really able to transcend the passivity of the behaviouristic effects model, nor its view of media reception as largely cognitive in nature, although he certainly provided audience research a way out of the wilderness.

Hall's structuralism is also impaired by the "pessimism" that follows on cultural theory's insensitivity to affect, such as those structuralisms conceptually incapable of dealing well with history and the subject. That is, when theory doesn't make room for the naturally resilient and better parts of ourselves, such as feeling, pleasure, experience, etc., it is vulnerable to a fatalism that follows on such overweening rationalism. (Pessimism is the logical response to depictions of the human subject essentially overruled by the power of ideology.) Hall himself has spoken to the need to address "sensibility" in popular culture, but just what this sensibility is and on what terms it is recognizably human are unexplained (Grossberg 1996a:168). It remains that the overuse of ideology and the absence of affect leads to a kind of despair about the human prospect, an efficient minimalization of the subject which leaves the critic wondering just who she or he is supposed to defend. As James Carey says of the dangers: "When ideology becomes a term to describe an entire way of life or just another name for what is going on, then the rich phenomenological diversity of modern societies becomes reduced to a flattened analysis of conflict between classes and factions. Economics may have been the original dismal science; cultural/ideological studies now threaten to displace it" (1988:105).

The last romantic problem with Hall's work addresses its theoretical debt to structural linguistics, and structuralism's ultimate origins in Enlightenment thought: the problem of meaning. Structuralism can act to compress the sensuous elements of a given text to the point where its texture and complexity are reduced to an orderly system that quite belies the text's autonomy (McRobbie 1994:14). In this pursuit of a certain epistemological purity, structuralism signals its intention to leave issues of content behind in favour of underlying form. For Hall this move "from content to structure or from manifest meaning to the level of code is an absolutely characteristic one in the critical approach" (1982:71). This is fine for the analyst, but leaves serious questions wide open for the layperson who must inhabit a reality which, as Hall puts it in his own "Return of the Repressed" essay, is really only a "reality effect"—a deeply naturalized complex of representations.

It is one thing to plead for a hermeneutic solution to structuralism's formality (and such an appeal to the traces of human consciousness in a text leads to different problems). But it is another to ask that the irregularity of human-made meaning be recognized in light of the structuralist preference for elegant, orderly objects of analysis. This is a self-critical and unconventional humanism that romanticism can deliver. Denied such a capacity for dimension and depth, structuralism exposed itself to reification, as did other objectivist conceptions of language like Russian formalism. The work of Saussure and subsequent structuralists, as Williams himself wrote, represents "the major theoretical expression of this reified understanding of language" (Williams

1977:27). Structuralism's inability to sincerely address meaning's many sides left it open to the euphoric celebration of meaninglessness that followed in the more extreme post-structuralisms.

DISCOURSE AND MEDIA STUDIES

The grand ambition to find a concept to explain just how reality works did not end with ideology. The obvious alternative to the ideological model of representation developed by Volosinov and passed down through Eagleton and Hall is the model of discourse adapted from Foucault. David Sholle's article, "Critical Studies: From the Theory of Ideology to Power/Knowledge" discusses the possibilities inherent in Foucault's special understanding of what discourse is, and how it applies to media. Sholle's post-structuralist analysis is as valuable for its criticism of the ideology concept as it is illustrative of the shortcomings of a strong "discourse" position. Moreover, it shows how the Foucauldian concept of discourse presents an immediate contrast with ideology, since it was developed in part as a replacement for the ideology concept. The discourse concept is an implicit criticism of ideology's claims to point to truth or reality, and therefore together they suggest a continuum of sorts in which these world-beating, all-powerful notions provide parameters for discussion.

Reading Foucault, Sholle argues that the concept of ideology represents a misunderstanding of social totality; the concept assumes a separation between discursive practices (e.g., media, writing, speaking) and non-discursive or material practices (e.g., labour) that do not really exist. Acknowledging Raymond Williams's own discomfort with "ideology" (it serves as a stop-gap or analytical alibi when the work of tracing what causes what in society falters—when the theorist condemns as "ideology" that which she or he cannot discern as part of the chain of determination [Sholle 1988:29; see also Williams 1980:245]), Sholle argues that the ideology concept does not respect the autonomy of discourse. Citing Mark Poster, Sholle notes that "discourses are already powers and do not need to find their material force somewhere else, as in the mode of production" (Sholle 1988:28). The ideology concept's failing, after whatever protocols and permutations Marxist cultural theory requires, is that it must ultimately return to the economic base as a means of explanation.

In adhering to a theory of ideology that yokes base to superstructure—or non-discursive to discursive, to use the Foucauldian lexicon—Sholle argues that Marxism avoids confronting the "double problematic" at its core. That is, Marxism claims empirical knowledge of the conditions under which consciousness is produced, cinching this claim by use of the ideology concept. Yet,

Marxism's hubris is necessarily qualified by the fact that language interposes itself between student and studied. Marxism cannot make claims in the name of ideology critique without acknowledging the fact that "the continual presence of conditions of language, communication and signification, conditions that act as limits on knowledge, forces Marxism to recognize the tenuous nature of its project to find the instance of determination" (Sholle 1988:25).

Sholle's solution to the "double problematic" is to collapse the distinction between what is language and what (like the material world) is not, and argue that "discursive and non-discursive practices should be examined at the same level, as material practices" (Sholle 1988:29). That is, both the things we say and the things we do should be considered as having real, objective, and "material" consequences for the world. Although this Foucauldian solution raises as many problems at it solves, Sholle poses a question by which the romantic alternative might also be judged:

> At the theoretical level, the concept of ideology, as tied in with the double problematic of the human sciences, inevitably duplicates that dichotomy. The concept of ideology is found wanting if it is inserted into a totalizing discourse, a discourse that attempts to show how objects are determined....But can this area of ideology critique be articulated in another discursive space, one that does not separate discourse and practice, one that reconceptualizes discourse as itself a material practice? (1988:29-30)

Sholle's answer to the rhetorical question he poses bears examining. That is, can the concept of ideology find a new epistemological home where it doesn't definitively separate the discursive and non-discursive and thus, it might be said, end up reifying the object of analysis? First, just as the ideology concept pretends to an overweening rationalism, the power/knowledge theme on which Foucault's alternative rests makes no more room for affect, experience, and imagination, especially since knowledge is narrowly defined as cognitive in nature. Reason may play the villain in the Foucauldian model as much as it retains heroic stature in ideology critique; but reason remains the central character in both dramatizations of the real.

Moreover, as in the strong ideology thesis, indeterminacy is also suppressed in Sholle's argument, being subject to the totalizing panoptic power implicit in discourse. But this is a model of discourse which, like Eagleton's and Hall's Volosinovian models, depends on a simple and unresistant theory of language, and therefore makes indeterminacy a theoretical straw target. Discourse may be granted equal status with non-discursive practices, insofar as both are recognized for their material effects on the world. But the source of discourse's new power derives from sources external to itself. Its materiality has nothing to do with the intrinsic properties of language in its pure or applied discursive form, but rather has everything to do with the "will to power" motivating language to obscure and dangerous ends.

This strong motivation suggests a resemblance between Sholle's discourse concept and ideology, borne out by his ready appropriation of ideology within a Foucauldian framework. Ideology becomes the means to name the presence of power in discourse. As Sholle argues: "No longer is ideology a false consciousness or a reflection of class interests or an imaginary relation or a production of obfuscating ideas. Rather, ideology is that condition of all discourse that is present as the embodiment or articulation of power, as the maintenance of control over definition itself" (1988:37). The reifying nature of Sholle's model of (non)-representation is thus revealed as more profound than Eagleton's and Hall's, and just as self-serving. While scolding Marxists for their determinism, Sholle just as crudely appropriates the material world to itself through an intellectual sleight of hand. Denying that the referent is in any way meaningfully discernible due to the "double problematic," Sholle assimilates the material into the condition of discourse by crediting discourse with status as "material practice."

Discourse therefore enjoys the benefits of having direct effect upon reality, without having to actually answer to that reality, or to the sensuous and formal properties of language that remind us of its presence in every act of communication. Unchecked and unaccountable, discourse's overextension is parallel to that suffered by ideology. Eagleton is useful here, for his argument that the "category of discourse is inflated to the point where it imperializes the whole world, eliding the distinction between thought and material reality" (Eagleton 1991a:219). With the social and material world thus conveniently dissolved into discourse, neither it nor the forms in which it resides, such as language or culture, can offer any point of resistance.

Ironically, then, a theory that seeks to restore to discourse a power lost to it in ideology critique persists in a reifying form of intellectual practice. The major difference is that where the ideological sign reflects the sum total of social interests contending for it, the "discursive sign" (to coin an awkward phrase) endlessly reflects the play of power and knowledge internal to itself— a one-way mirror, if you like. The relational nature of reality is mocked then with the endless play of signification within discourse itself. Ideology critique reifies by isolating textual meaning from context (followed by equally implausible claims to connection between text and social structure). Sholle's poststructuralism does the same, but asks us to accept the largely pointless relationship of signs within discourse and in a manner undisciplined by the material world.

The discourse model, in relentlessly separating what is within language from what is outside it and thus not speakable, acts to consign anything that troubles its perfection to the silent and non-discursive void. The "unspeakable" is an analytical convenience for post-structuralism, a memory hole where things that might conflict with the Foucauldian narrative can be disposed of through "exclusion." (A similarity to Williams's use of the social might be noted.) Sholle believes that "the media create a way of seeing, a method of ordering and judging, or a means of selection and preference that constitutes the domain of that which is discussable (stable)" (1988:34-35). But discourse can act to *include* as well, with a relative autonomy that is not supported by Sholle's position. The truth may not be "out there" in the uncomplicated way that ideology critique often implies, but neither is it merely an effect of language. Rather, as will be seen in discussion of the romantic "aesthetic" theory of representation, truth can both have an existence outside of discourse in the realm of the "unsaid," yet not be humbly reduced to something that can be rationally captured.

Sholle's question is worth repeating. Can ideology critique find a place where discursive and non-discursive phenomena—such as culture and the economy—can coexist in the theoretical imagination without being reduced to each other? In other words, is there a happy medium in our consideration of how reality works? Romanticism represents an intermediate position between the strong ideology thesis of Eagleton and Hall, and the strong discourse position taken by Sholle. The "aesthetic" model of representation that romanticism favours is at once more sensitive to the indeterminate reality in which we live, while inspiring confidence that meaningful things might be said of it.

A ROMANTIC MODEL OF REPRESENTATION

Representation is a topic endlessly debated in contemporary theory. Many current debates about the status of truth and the politics of representation have their origins in romantic thought. Central for the present discussion is the romantic interest in the autonomy of language, compared to the fate it suffered within the "strong" models of ideology and discourse. In addressing what is termed here the romantic "aesthetic" model of representation, some constructive way out of the unproductive dualism of ideology versus discourse might be found. Once out of this impasse, what becomes apparent is that some fresh insight into the utopian function of culture—a bit of daylight through the cracks in this pair of monolithic concepts—becomes possible.

For the romantic, the fact that language cannot be reduced to anything else is a function of its separate identity in nature. That is, language is an "other" to the speaker, and exists apart from direct control by self, structure, power, or what have you. For the romantic, the materiality of the sign derives from the fact that "language is, in one sense, manifested like any other thing in the world" (Bowie 1997:73). It is independent from its users, possessing a social nature that cannot be merely co-opted or denied, as it is in both ideology critique inspired by Volosinov's linguistic theory, and in work motivated by Foucault's "discourse" concept. Language is "both determinable as a natural phenomenon and beyond such law-bound determination when the resources it offers are recombined to remake our ways of understanding the world" (Bowie 1997:73).

The romantics did not see language's representational function primarily in empirical or rational terms, as if we were merely taking a photograph with our words and images. Rather, language was significantly defined in terms of its aesthetic role. The truth of communication was the truth of art: it gives us glimpses of the real revealed through the creative ingenuity of the speaker, cameraperson, or journalist. The romantics did not reject reason, but allowed that defining knowledge in terms of rationality alone squandered the richness of sensory experience. The "aesthetic" mode of representation opts for a middle way between ideology critique's insistence on the correspondence of sign and referent, and post-structuralism's preference for non-correspondence.

In favouring this intermediate position, romanticism took what has come to be familiarly defined as a "hermeneutic" reading of the relationship between word and world. Knowledge consists in the disclosure or revelation of what was, prior to utterance, not yet said, the defamiliarization of a hitherto unknown or ineffable reality. By contrast, ideology critique allows little surprise or discovery in its epistemology, since new information is further evidence of a ruling class's conspiracy (or resistance thereto). And post-structuralism writes off the unrepresented as a permanent unknown excluded from the sealed envelope of discourse, a discourse authorized by the relentless machinations of power/knowledge. Both concepts, in thus limiting opportunity for novelty and wonder, contribute to greater disenchantment. As Bowie argues:

> In the modern period the world becomes more and more knowable, and more and more meaningless....Although they do not regressively reject advances in scientific knowledge...the Romantics look for a conception of truth which does not simply equate truth with conceptual determination, at the same time as regarding the natural sciences as a vital part of the new picture of the world. The crucial aim was a new *integration* of the elements of the world: hence the idea that aesthetic forms give a higher kind of meaning than assertions of a determinate nature, whose meaning is anyway dependent upon their contexts. (Bowie 1997:80)

Romanticism doesn't dismiss the stability of the everyday signs and state-ments on which life and sanity depend. We can still order an egg salad sand-wich at a lunch counter, and expect to be understood. But the metaphoric or allegorical character of the aesthetic or romantic sign—the fact that, given the limitations of language, signs can only approximate their referents in real-ity by drawing analogies—means that even the most conventional of signs is vulnerable to change. Given the relational nature of romantic epistemology and ontology, context is always changing, as relations that draw into question previous models of reality are discovered and incorporated into knowledge. Where for ideology critique, context is an ultimately knowable and rather homogeneous totality, and where for post-structuralism, context is irrelevant due to the unbounded textuality of experience, romanticism supports a con-tinuous process of reinvention through contextual redefinition. We take action without knowing for certain what the consequences will be. But as the romantic social universe depends on just such action taking place, in its vision of a wantonly dynamic world, inaction is unthinkable.

Romanticism seeks to salvage the ideology concept by limiting its applica-tion, notably by making it answer to the indeterminate and reflexive nature of language honoured by the aesthetic. To this end, romantic theory defines ideology as a particular function of the sign or text alone, and not something that consummately traces the whole of social totality from superstructural text to economic base, and back again. "In the Romantic conception, art can be regarded as reconciling in the realm of appearance what is unreconciled in reality, and thus as a form of ideology" (Bowie 1997:14). Such a conception, fulfilling a "utopian" role for culture, would not be out of place in the Frankfurt School's musings. But with the exception of Williams's call for a "systematic" utopian vision in *The Year 2000* (1983a:12-15), epic statements on behalf of a more perfect future have largely been embarrassed into silence in cultural studies. A politically progressive tendency remains in the defence of the oppositional value of popular culture, but comprehensive visions wor-thy of a manifesto are hard to find. That's why the romantic tradition's deep feeling for the power of appearance redeems the utopian function of culture by engineering the relationship between appearance and the real in novel terms.

These terms are best appreciated in comparison with the Marxist and post-structuralist alternatives. Marxists have often preferred to define the aesthetic as one more instance of ideology's ubiquity, a beautiful lie that culture tells with devastating consequences. Any aspiration to close the gap between appearance and reality is suspected as an ideological *coup de grâce* and false utopia, since truth begins in an objective apprehension of the real. Theorists in the Foucauldian tradition, on the other hand, believe the gap was never open in the first place, that appearance is all we have. Romanticism, however, does not prejudge the attempt to reconcile the world as it is and as it might be, but argues we must continue to travel the distance between appearance and reality, and reserve our evaluation for the final product, if it should ever come.

What is exceptional about the romantic aesthetic theory of representation here is its refusal to accept the brute conversion of language, our primary cultural resource, into ideological values. Culture is allowed the latitude necessary to realize and work out its own potential in human life. The romantic utopia is less prescriptive—a plot in the collective farm, manna from the sky—and argues rather that the good society lies in revealing the relatedness of all things as they are manifested between the aesthetically apparent realm of art, culture, and discourse, and the real.

Romanticism is inherently non-reifying because it understands the making of utopia as the making of relationships, using the finite and recombinant elements of language to explore a near infinite social totality. "Language's internal relationships make an articulated world possible, but even if the world of things is also essentially a web of relations one cannot finally articulate a way of mapping, in language, one set of relations on to the other, because that would entail a further web of relations, and so on" (Bowie 1997:69). The fate of many utopias to become self-parodies or nightmarish tyrannies (once the dogma and the reality are fused and the new world reified) is thus avoided by the romantic. Utopia becomes a process, not a product, and each manifestation of the good points to another and another.

Romanticism offers an epistemology not unlike that implied by Williams's "structure of feeling" concept, with the important difference that the connectivity of elements in the romantic vision of totality is never given, but must always be worked for, since the context itself is ever changing. Romanticism lives for the work of making connections in a world where phenomena are ideologically isolated beyond redemption or reduced to a homogeneous power/knowledge equation. As much as ideology and discourse seek to convert culture into themselves, the romantic aesthetic model of representation constantly reminds us of the incommensurate nature of word and world, self and other, even as it celebrates our efforts to cross these divides. In this doomed effort to cross between fundamental categories, the romantics find us at our most human, taking advantage of the power of the imagination, so endlessly and fruitfully frustrated, to picture new worlds for the making.

Chapter 3

The Presence of the Past

SOME PROBLEMS IN MEDIA RESEARCH

> As for romance, what does romance mean? I have heard peo-
> ple miscalled for being romantic, but what romance means is the
> capacity for a true conception of history, a power of making the
> past part of the present.
>
> —Victorian critic and designer William Morris,
> in a letter to his daughter May
> (E.P. Thompson 1977:148)

MEDIA THEORY AND MODERNITY

Media criticism has been called a "displaced critique of modern life" (Jentzen 1990:64) in which we address our unresolved concerns about this anxious epoch in human culture. That is, whenever we talk about media, we are in a subtler sense also speaking about the modern world. Whether the topic is screen violence or declining literacy, there is an underlying acknowledgement of the surprising nature of modernity and its features in the question implicit in every righteous letter to the editor or desperate call to a radio talk show. It is the question, often appalled and sometimes afraid, that asks: what is this world where such strange and shocking things happen, and what is it coming to? With the arrival of Johannes Gutenberg's press in the mid-1450s, it was clear that something uncanny had entered the world.

The relationship between media and modernity has been central to most twentieth-century traditions in media and cultural theory. These include John Dewey's pragmatism and its concern to recapture Jeffersonian ideals against

---

Notes to chapter 3 are on pp. 176-78.

the hulking backdrop of mass society; the Frankfurt School and instrumental rationality; the media effects school and its use of high-modernist, quasi-scientific method to take the measure of media's relationship to liberal democracy; Jürgen Habermas and his ambition to recover the eighteenth-century public sphere for use in the twentieth century; Marshall McLuhan and the contradictions between modern print discourse and the holistic, "audile-tactile" electronic media; and even post-structuralism, if only to argue that the first task of digital technology has been to advertise in all its multimedia glory the end of the modern age.

But one of the most important if overlooked opportunities for media theory is that most modern of all eras, the interwar period. The 1920s and 1930s brought us the speakeasy, the breadline, and the "It" girl. But they also fostered a unique set of cultural conditions, as mass audiences experienced radio for the first time. This encounter produced both a popular intelligence in the general public, and a sympathetic theoretical response among American pragmatists, which surpassed in quality and insight the dominant media paradigm of the day, the propaganda theory of Edward Bernays, Harold Lasswell, and Walter Lippmann.

The new sensibility was also significantly romantic in nature, and provides the basis for a contrast between the media research done at the Centre for Contemporary Cultural Studies and the interwar media culture that is the substance of the first half of this chapter. The romantic character of the interwar period provides an unacknowledged precedent for how media and modernity relate—one which media and cultural studies in the Birmingham style can learn from. It is a "past" that, upon being made part of theory's present, provides a superior foundation for thinking about contemporary media as modern phenomena and, of course, on romantic terms.

MEDIA RESEARCH AT THE CENTRE FOR CONTEMPORARY CULTURAL STUDIES

If, as deconstruction has it, we can learn much about a given discourse by reading deeply into the marked absences and silences in its development, then the intellectual history of media and cultural theory at Birmingham is something of an open book. The evidence is admittedly circumstantial, but the circumstances of theory's development at the Centre, and the Birmingham media group's own reception to those theories, are telling enough. Noteworthy here is the media group's inflexibility to new theories, especially those such as post-structuralism, which would later lead the academic imagination into areas like digital technology, subjectivity and media, and the cultural implications of globalization.

Hall's canonical account of the history of the Centre, "Cultural Studies and the Centre: Some Problematics and Problems," surprisingly demonstrates how awkward and incomplete the media group's response is to post-structuralism, and how partial and inconclusive its relationship is to other major theoretical currents. The media group is on record as refusing serious engagement with post-structuralism, whose roster includes Jacques Derrida, Michel Foucault, Julia Kristeva, the later Roland Barthes, and Jacques Lacan. As Hall explains it, "the media group has been critical of the 'autonomy' it saw implied in those positions and the universalism entailed by the revisions of psychoanalysis advanced by Lacan" (1980b:37). The media group's account of its engagement with post-structuralism effectively ends there, as it reflects on the implications of French post-structuralism associated with the 1960s and '70s journal, *Tel Quel.*

The rather unadaptive nature of Birmingham media research, which might account for its antipathy to learning from post-structuralism, is confirmed in Dworkin's history of the Centre. Dworkin offers an instructive comparison between the severe limitations on human agency implicit in the Centre's media research, and the generous room given to action in the subculture research done there by Dick Hebdige, Angela McRobbie, and others. Subculture theory stressed, in a noticeably romantic key, the relative freedom of angry punks and working-class youth to creatively decode and defy their circumstances. But in comparison, the Centre's media group stressed limits on communication. Audience behaviour was seen as contained by ideology and class, and the range of human agency was conservatively drawn (Dworkin 1997:168).

Though the media group was successful in rejecting the American "effects" model of mediation which, building on propaganda theory, offered a more sophisticated rationale for how media messages were alleged to directly affect human behaviour, it failed to come to terms with the theoretical tradition that now dominates the interpretation of new media: post-structuralism. Much of post-structuralism's value has been in theorizing the textual nature of human experience, work assisted by the introduction of Foucault's concept of discourse. While post-structuralism deserves criticism on many counts, its view of meaning as intertextual, "floating," and free of an immediate relationship to place and history is an appropriate challenge to British cultural studies's overidentification of communication, with a definition of culture that is antagonistic to mass and new media conditions.

The case for the Centre's rather eccentric intellectual history is strengthened by the infelicitous history of theory there, apart from media questions. Gramsci is the most influential of the long-lost relatives whom Birmingham restored to the cultural Marxist family tree. But his concept of hegemony is infamously overextended to the point where cultural studies is often accused of seeing revolutionary potential in comic books and couch potatoes. Moreover, there have been numerous omissions in Birmingham's past which only recently have been corrected—and which have obvious bearing on the development of media theory there. Long after Williams and Hall wrote their seminal works, forgotten authors were being added to the canon. As Davies says, "certain theorists, until the late 1980s, were largely ignored (Mikhail Bakhtin, Pierre Bourdieu, Alain Touraine, the Frankfurt School)" (1995:3).

Add to this the fact that most of the major primers (as of the late 1990s) written to explain cultural studies to undergraduate and graduate students (Davies, Brantlinger, Fiske, Inglis, Kellner, Turner, Storey, Milner) say very little about mass media and almost nothing about new media, so the circumstantial evidence of these gaps begins to be persuasive. Media theorist Roger Silverstone argues that "even those theories that do address the role of media...also fail to do justice to the complexity of mass communication in modern societies" (1994:136-37). The neo-marxist legacy on which Birmingham draws has been criticized for ignoring the formative relationship of media to modern society, and for failing to respect the limits of ideology's power (Silverstone 1994:137).[1] Too often, cultural studies has defined media and audience as secondary phenomena, as vehicles for the superior power of ideology.

The decades of the 1920s and '30s offer an instructive example. It was a period in which culture at every level—high culture, manufactured popular culture, and everyday experience—saw spectacular changes. In the paranoid days of what is now called "propaganda theory," there is evidence from public discourse, scholarship, and the deeper structure of life of a romantic corrective to Birmingham's inconsistency. As media theory seeks a new mythology, one as open to a romantic reading of modernity as it is to rationalism, it need look no further than the world between the wars.

THE INTERWAR PERIOD AS A ROMANTIC PRECEDENT IN MEDIA THEORY

The conventional histories of media theory and research typically characterize the interwar period, marking the beginning of formal media research in the United States, as a brave if benighted era. Confronted by the sheer novelty of radio and cinema at a time of great cultural experiment, economic uncertainty, and apocalyptic politics, media research in the 1920s and 1930s is often depicted as crudely fascinated with the sheer power of media messages, the defining crisis being the famous 1938 "War of the Worlds" broadcast. Theorists often define this period as one preoccupied with the "magic bullet" model, in which media confront naive publics with a brute force strongly reminiscent of World War I propaganda, their messages shooting directly into collective consciousness and behaviour. As Crisell (1986) puts it in his semiotic analysis of radio: "When the question 'What effect do the media have upon their audiences?' was first put during the interwar years it was assumed to be a simple one with an obvious answer: they exerted a persuasive and pervasive effect, transmitting simple and deliberate messages to which their audiences reacted in direct, predictable, uniform and often dramatic ways" (196).

However, a recent revisionist account suggests that students of the interwar period must answer to a new version, one identified with a very different understanding of the decades of flappers, avant-gardes, and jazz. Media historian John Durham Peters argues against the conventional image of a decade of masses without conversation and messages without resistance (Peters 1996).[2] Looking deeper than the present day caricatures of propaganda theory, Peters demonstrates how radio research of the period saw the mighty "empire of the air" as a humane if uncanny place where communication of warmth and authenticity was sustained—a quality of connection usually reserved for direct interpersonal exchange. Against the long-standing view, favoured by propaganda theory and common sense, that twentieth-century media culture was a bleak landscape of manipulated millions, the radio-loving public demonstrated that communication of the quality normally associated with face-to-face immediacy was possible in mass-mediated conditions. Peters believes that "many were fascinated and alarmed by radio's apparent intimacy, its penetration of private spaces, and its ability to stage dialogues and personal relationships with listeners" (1996:109).

Media historian Susan Douglas (1999) describes a 1920s radio culture of DX-ing ham-radio operators and listeners who countered the growth in the scale of society with a technology that crossed boundaries and created an early form of cyberspace through the airwaves (DX-ing was the practice of seeking out and logging distant transmitting stations). Radio magazines of the era enthused about the fabulous potential for social good in the fragile crystal set, as strangers living at great distances shared ideas or transmitted live music from their garages. Yet, even period radio's homely rhetorical touches could not replace the missing bodies, making for an "uncanny surplus" that haunted radio listeners— the sensation of being near and far, among friends and alone at one's radio set, all at once. This anxiety did not preclude the possibility of authentic communication among radio listeners, but it did give broadcaster and listener an ambiguity much richer than the determinism of propaganda theory ever allowed.

The best scholarly witnesses to this haunted, romantic media-scape were John Dewey and other American intellectuals associated with pragmatism. Ranging from William James's writings on religion to C.S. Pierce's linguistic theories, pragmatism was heir to the mid-nineteenth-century transcendentalism of Emerson, Thoreau, and Whitman. True to its name, it sought pragmatic solutions to the problems of the age, applying the lever of some of the best ideas in the twentieth century to its most crippling problems. A central concern was maintaining a meaningful moral and humane culture within modernity, especially at a time when its terrible costs were showing themselves. Dewey, the author of many books such as *The Public and Its Problems* and *Liberalism and Social Action* over a long, productive lifetime, famously called this culture the "Great Community," and its alienated antithesis, the "Great Society." The Great Community was where citizens came together and, despite the impossibility of perfect understanding between communicating minds, sought to craft a culture born of the hard work of coordinating their separate visions. Peters says of Dewey: "Communication meant taking part in a collective world, not sharing the secrets of consciousness" (1999:18).

Dewey's rejection of metaphysics, his belief in language's part in social construction, and the profoundly moral content of his analysis, all qualify him and his fellow pragmatists as part of a romantic continuum. Dewey was "steeped in romanticism," and to a degree that his book, *Art as Experience,* "is as nearly a systematization of romantic insights into art and aesthetics as we have available" (Wheeler 1993:147). What is apparent here, despite propaganda theory's images of shell-shocked audiences bombarded into mental submission, is that a counter-tradition with a romantic provenance was at work in the interwar period. The work of reclaiming this period has just begun, as is evident in media historians like James Carey and Hanno Hardt who look to the neglected pragmatists rather than mid-century media effects as a point of origin for American media and cultural studies.

The pragmatists were articulating an ethos that already existed, and in response to a public captivated by the electromagnetic magic of the first decade of radio. But the interwar period's romanticism was still deeper than what was manifested in radio culture or theory. It was present also in the pre- and interwar critique of Cartesian and Newtonian conventions regarding subjectivity, time, and space. Einstein and Bergson, as well as artist-activists from the impressionists through the Weimar period, contributed to a new view of culture that posited a greater fluidity, relativism, and multiplicity than had seemed possible in modern intellectual history since the romantic era. A series of sweeping changes in technology and culture, as well as the stream-of-consciousness novel, psychoanalysis, and cubism, "created distinctive new modes of thinking about and experiencing time and space" in the 1880-1918 period (Kern 1983:1). These developments gave form to a comprehensive anti-rationalist and arguably romantic position celebrating emotion, imagination, and experience. As historian Modris Eksteins says, "the romantic rebellion, which, with its distrust of mechanistic systems, extended back over a century, coincided at the *fin de siècle* with the rapidly advancing scientific demolition of the Newtonian universe" (1989:31).

While intellectual history is far too uncertain a science to claim that German and English romanticism resurfaced in the interwar period whole and unaltered after a century, the evidence from radio, pragmatism, and the larger culture persuade us of the diffuse romantic personality of the times. This revisionist overview of "romantic" interwar media research can be turned into a productive analogy for rethinking media today. Peters argues encouragingly: "Historic ideas on radio's curious status between what a later generation would call mass and interpersonal communication may prove useful in our attempts to study a social order in which the personal and the political, the erotic and the social, and the dialogic and the broadcast are hopelessly intertwined" (1996:121).

The "convergence" of digital technologies is an issue of such compelling interest in high-tech circles that it represents a kind of holy grail. That is, building upon the fact that binary code allows any two machines to talk to and cooperate with each other, the amassing of any number of separate technologies (e.g., telephone, television, Internet) in a single device is hypothetically possible. While the culture industries devote research dollars and justify mergers that would otherwise be halted on anti-trust grounds, there is another kind of confluence already developing. The really interesting convergence, apart from whether we can soon surf the web through our toasters, is occurring between those areas thought historically divided in media research: mass and interpersonal communication. This is the relationship that interwar radio culture was precociously sensitive to, and one we rediscover today when, for example, short message (SMS) devices such as the Blackberry allow us to send wireless e-mail to a close friend or a number of strangers from almost anywhere.

After World War II, the commercialization of radio that had begun in the 1930s was completed, and the media system was rebuilt using the authoritarian architecture of centralized broadcast and passive terminals we are familiar with today. The romantic frontier that early radio opened up, with its DX-ing and homemade programming, was turned over to chain ownership and standardized formats. Television followed soon after in the early 1950s, adopting a similar platform. With this change in the corporate structure of the media system came the definitive separation of mass and interpersonal communication. Senders gained in range and power as networks formed and advertising became the primary source of revenue—while receivers lost the power of speech, and became consumers instead of creative partners.

This was a separation enshrined in the media effects research that came to prominence in the USA at the time, and later in some of the more important works of media criticism from Birmingham, such as Raymond Williams's *Communications* and *Television: Technology and Cultural Form* and Stuart Hall's essay, "Encoding and Decoding in Television Discourse." But the romantic structure of media experience has never disappeared; it's only been forgotten as its infrastructure was defined in top-down terms. Peters's observations about the period underscore its romantic character and the cost to criticism of indifference to this ethos: "The postwar divorce between mass and interpersonal...amounts to an evasion...of the more uncanny and difficult fact that our face-to-face relationships, no less than our media lives, are populated by imaginary characters, fantasy projections, and voices and images from afar" (1996:110). It is to the nature of this post-war faithlessness to the romantic precedent, and the ways in which media theory contributed to this lack of fidelity, that this argument now turns.

MASS COMMUNICATION VERSUS MASS MEDIA

British cultural studies is by no means exclusively devoted to problems in mass media; it takes the whole of culture as its preserve. Yet, much of the impetus for its development derives from its early productive antagonism with the variously labelled "effects," "administrative research," or "mass communications" model of media criticism identified with major American communication theorists Paul Lazarsfeld, Robert Merton, and Wilbur Schramm. In relatively early key texts, such as Williams's *Communications* (1962) and *Television: Technology and Cultural Form* (1974), and Hall's later "Encoding/Decoding" (1980) and "The Rediscovery of Ideology" (1982) essays, Williams and Hall established the argument for a definitive break between British cultural studies and the "effects" tradition that had been dominant in media criticism since World War II.

Williams refutes the effects model on the grounds that it assumes media work in a vacuum, improbably addressing human consciousness without reference to institutions, class, or other social variables. This frees the media effects tradition from having to account for the complex pattern of relationships in which media are invested, ones more subtle and dangerous than the simple linear model of causation (e.g., see a killing on TV, and copy the act in real life) the effects model implied. As Williams argues, "much otherwise sophisticated work in information and communication theory rests on and frequently conceals this first, deeply bourgeois, ideological position" (1980:51). Hall confirms how much media research in the Birmingham tradition depended on this rejection. He writes: "Media studies broke with the models of 'direct influence'—using a sort of stimulus-response model with heavy behaviourist overtones, media content serving as a trigger—into a framework which drew much more on what can broadly be defined as the 'ideological' role of the media" (Hall 1980c:117). Conventionally, this separation of British media research from American "mass communications" is defined in terms of the critique of "effects," the passive audience, and media's mission as the means to coordinate other social institutions for the good of the whole society. British cultural studies instead favoured a critical view of media, with a concept of ideology, an active audience capable of interpreting and acting on messages beyond ideology's dictation, and an appreciation of media's role as a means to sustaining political and economic inequality.

Yet the effects school and British cultural studies probably agree as much as they disagree where the possibility of authentic communication in modern "mass" society is concerned. Both British cultural studies and the "effects" positions isolated their models of communication in highly delimited forms, be they Williams's "knowable community" within the "common culture," or Lazarsfeld's vision of the audience as one who needed protection from media influence (protection in the form of Jeffersonian confines of their local democratic traditions of debate and consensus). Once these audiences were snugly located in their various interpersonal and particular contexts, the social world surrounding them would appear huge, incomprehensible, and threatening.

Meaningful communication was therefore seen as impossible within mass society, and the mass media were defined as the principal agents of alienation. Real communication happened despite, rather than within "mass" conditions, whether the emphasis was on media or society at large. The work of Williams and Lazarsfeld, who regarded authentic communication and mass media as incompatible and antagonistic, represents a theoretical impasse with which media theory has had to contend. Peters summarizes their legacy like this:

> The defining project of media studies since, both in cultural studies following Raymond Williams and in empirical research following Lazarsfeld, has been to separate mass media from mass society. The task has been to show that people retained their dignity or their wits before a massive persuasion apparatus, and that despite the one-way, anonymous messages, people still conversed, took pleasure, or fought back. With all the emphasis on complicating the social, the idea of mass communication has been left largely unexamined. (1996:109)

Of course, the alienation of communication in a society dependent on indirect social relationships (as conducted through media and other institutions in modern society) did not stop with Williams or Lazarsfeld. It continues into the present in the form of recent cultural studies research on both sides of the Atlantic, a time when the hitherto largely separate development of British cultural studies and American media effects has been eased by the emergence of an American cultural studies tradition, and some convergence between British and American approaches to media.[3] In the American case, the isolation of communication can be defined, using Grossberg's pregnant phrase, as the problem of "communicational cultural studies." In the British case, it might be captured conversely as the problem of "cultural communication studies," if the neologism can be pardoned for the sake of highlighting the complementary British error.

AMERICAN "COMMUNICATIONAL CULTURAL STUDIES"

The fate of communication in British and American cultural studies media research is best appreciated in the context of their shared and incongruent history. Until the mid-1980s, British cultural studies largely favoured textual analysis centred on the analysis of all forms of communication as cultural artifacts, while American mass communications research preferred empirical studies and largely ignored the problem of culture (Kellner 1995:30).[4] The dichotomy of British and American research during the effects hegemony that lasted for decades after World War II was followed by a *rapprochement* in the mid-1980s that was as revealing as the original split. Even as the media effects tradition's dominance passed, the renascent American cultural studies tradition of the mid-1980s, borrowing heartily from 1920s pragmatism and Chicago School sociology to return "culture" to the centre of analysis, failed to learn from the effects school's mistakes. The unfortunate result was that the American cultural studies tradition, just as media functionalism before it, isolated communication from the social conditions in which media and their audiences actually operated.

Even as American scholars began to read Williams and Hall in the hopes of bringing culture back into American media analysis, they tended to read the British project in a way that installed communication as the primary principle. This conflated communication and culture at culture's expense, and made for a model of communication as idealized as the previous effects model was positivist (Grossberg 1997). The result in the US was the deracination of Williams's model of communications as culture. That is, culture (in the emphatically materialist and dialectical sense Williams had envisioned) was replaced with a neo-pragmatist emphasis on symbolic interaction. Culture lost its earthiness, its connection with person and place, and was reduced to value-laden signs transacted among individuals. This ironically resulted in the reproduction of the social vacuum and the unlikely directness of mediation assumed in the effects tradition (Hardt 1992:184).

Furthermore, the Americans overextended Hall's encoding/decoding model to the point where "what was originally offered as a theoretical-semiotic solution to a particular contextually defined set of empirical problems has become instead *the* general model of cultural studies" (Grossberg 1997:283). American cultural studies also borrowed from an unrepresentative small selection of influential British writings—the early Williams, Hall's encoding/decoding model, and Hebdige's *Subculture*—to create a scholarship where "the sense of culture as practice, form and institution has been lost" (O'Connor 1989b:408). The unfortunate outcome was a liberal incorporation of the more radical British material. American cultural studies took the subject Williams and Hall rescued from the condescension of Frankfurt School critical theory—a person credited with praxis and agency—and made that actor into an over-theorized symbol of liberal individualism.

The absorption and neutralization of Williams and Hall by American communication studies has made for a "communicational cultural studies," an analysis that reifies communication and culture to the point where "communicational cultural studies can never actually confront the question of effects, because it cannot theorize the relationship of meaning to anything else" (Grossberg 1997:284). The incorporation of Williams and Hall acts to dehistoricize cultural production, and to define it as individual practice rather than a collective phenomenon coextensive with the social structures it informs, criticizes, and revises. Although the "communicational cultural studies" project was intended to replace the "passive audience" model with which the effects tradition had long dominated American debates about culture, the communicating individual imagined by American cultural studies, when his or her significance to the social world at large is considered, is made into something just as impotent. Questions about the nature, form, and shape of power, and how domination and subordination are actually experienced, go unanswered in the idealized American research (Grossberg 1997:285).

BRITISH "CULTURAL COMMUNICATION STUDIES"

The British experience of communications, of course, cannot pretend to the same isolation and belated discovery of culture as American "communicational cultural studies." British cultural studies was aware of American functionalist media criticism almost from its inception, and after some early and eclectic borrowing from their colonial cousins, sharply diverged from functionalist models and methods alike. However, the idiosyncratic character of media studies stemming from the Centre does go some way to explain how British cultural studies failed to make its models of communication adequate to the real world of late modernity.

Williams and Hall both develop their media theory in a way that limits its value in a media culture where communication is increasingly neither face-to-face nor identified with any conventional sense of the local. This might be regarded as a problem, to coin an awkward phrase, of "cultural communication studies." That is, where the American absorption of culture into communication idealizes culture in neo-pragmatist terms that recall the errors of the media effects school, British cultural studies identifies communication with the maintenance of a spatially grounded and historically particular concept of culture.[5] In other words, where American cultural studies posits a model of communication "relatively autonomous of the real material and economic conditions of the world and people's lives" (Grossberg 1997:284), British cultural studies conversely identifies communication so strongly with a fixed sense of space and place that Birmingham's theoretical relevance is inhibited.

There is tremendous value in what O'Connor terms Birmingham's "sense of the rootedness of communication processes in social reproduction and politics" (1989b:408). Born of the rich sense of place that any visitor to Britain finds, where every tiny village seems to house a historic national treasure, British cultural studies brought to theory a sensitivity to the grain of experience. But the value of rootedness may be overstated in a Western world that is restlessly mobile and wired, and in a majority world where economic migration or political refugee status is too often necessary. There must be other ways of imagining culture that respect these realities. However, where the Americans reify culture within a too idealist view of communication, the British overly privilege the local and the concrete, materializing culture too much. Both positions limit the utility of the concept of "communication" when contexts are as liquid as cyberspace, or as porous as countries subject to international capital, both far removed from the venerable localism of British cultural studies. This localism is evident, in quite different ways, in Williams and Hall.

WILLIAMS AND "KNOWABLE COMMUNITY"

Williams, in his oddly neglected *Television: Technology and Cultural Form*, argues that television was developed as a means by which capitalism might maintain the minimal amount of social integration necessary to allow the economy to function, particularly as the influence of traditional institutions like church, school, and neighbourhood had faded.[6] Television provides a kind of instant community for itinerant moderns, a community that is fundamentally implicated in the market's health via advertising. As modern viewers turn their televisions on in their business hotels and suburban living rooms, they join a community of celebrities, familiar stories, and nationally advertised products. They experience television as "flow," as an endless series of programs, ads, and promotional spots without the formal boundaries of conventional narratives. This flow trains viewers to see the real world as a similarly constant stream of images which, after years of watching news of famine or war followed by commercials for deodorant and candy bars, leaves them unable to recognize contradiction.

Television for Williams is the medium of modernity. Given the ambivalence with which he approaches the modern, the book sets out to kill the messenger as well as those theorists, notably the "effects" tradition and Marshall McLuhan, who are taken to uncritically endorsing television's presence. The character of this technologically mediated form of social order, that Williams argues is strategically engineered by elites at the point of maximum advantage to the status quo, is defined by what he calls "mobile privatization." "Mobile privatization" meant that the public was simultaneously resigned to the private consumption of events and personalities produced for television, while the lack of local connection made these populations more amenable to the rapid mobility of labour required by capital (and the need to purchase a ready-made, homogeneous culture that could not be had in one's backyard). Williams writes: "Socially, this complex is characterized by the two apparently paradoxical yet deeply connected tendencies of modern urban industrial living: on the one hand mobility, on the other hand the more apparently self-sufficient family home" (1974:26).

The success of "mobile privatization" in Williams's mind may account for the pessimism in his *Television* book (and that pessimism for the book's neglect in media theory), because Williams barely gestures to the resistant possibilities in television reception, and so consigns this resistance to avant-garde production techniques rather than to viewing practices.[7] Local and direct relations were therefore displaced by media forms, and a pseudo-culture of indirect relations held to suffer in comparison with the dense moral communities Williams favoured as ideal types during his career as a critic and novelist. In early writing of the same vintage as his Leavisite *Culture and Society* (1958), this idealized community was characterized as the "common culture," an organic bond of meanings once shared by medieval elites and peasants as "tradition," and potentially available again in a socialist future when class and cultural barriers came down. Later, the common culture was reformulated on less idealist terms in the "knowable communities" Williams discussed in *The Country and the City* (1973).

In this book that explored the theme of rural-urban relations in English literature, Williams did not naively seek to construct some pastoral idyll of dense and genuine face-to-face interactions opposed to the anomic city. Although "the problem of the knowable community is...a problem of language" (1973:171), Williams recognized that those to whom we talked, those whom one truly *knew*, were often of the same social class, and that barriers to understanding between classes were chronic. Compared to the tightly choreographed social relations in the country scenes drawn by Jane Austen or Charlotte Bronte, the large numbers of people working the land were "knowable" only in the most general, impersonal, and often panoptic sense of the word.

The class basis to "knowable community" aside, those to whom one talked were also by no means necessarily one's lifelong friends and neighbours. That is, genuine community might be recreated in the urban metropolis if the structure of sensibility found in the country, and captured in images of the rustic life, were recreated there. Williams writes: "It is not so much the old village or the old backstreet that is significant. It is the perception and affirmation of a world in which one is not necessarily a stranger and an agent, but can be a member, a discoverer, in a shared source of life" (1973:298). But Williams's extension of the knowable community to the city is a backhanded compliment: within the structure of his thinking, the metropolis must improbably exist *without* mass media in order to meet his conditions for authentic communication.

In Williams's view, mass media gave form to an urban mode of consciousness saturated with the social relations of capitalism itself. Media produced a state of mind that took its shape not from interpersonal contact, but from arbitrary and non-reciprocal sources of authority: the voices and images of the state, capital, the Other, and consumer desire. To borrow from sociologist David Riesman's famous distinction, knowable community was inner-directed, but urban life was built of external and outer-directed sources in conformity with the vicarious nature of existence under capital. "This paradoxical set of one-way relationships...is then a specific form of consciousness which is inherent in the dominant mode of production in which...our perceptions of the shape of a lifetime, are to a critical extent defined and determined by external formulations of a necessary reality" (Williams 1973:296).

At another level, Williams's opinion that communication is incompatible with mass media can be read through Jentzen's earlier point regarding media criticism as a displaced form of critical anxiety about modernity. Here, media for Williams might be defined as another instance of the classic Arnoldian separation of "culture" and "society," with media and late modernity consigned to "society." However refracted, media represents in Williams's work a form of false community, wherein authentic communications such as those occasioned by the "knowable community" are not possible. The false community of media culture and, arguably, of late modernity, is one most offensively condensed in McLuhan's "global village" concept, but generalized throughout all modern media culture.[8] Williams scorns McLuhan's association of a mass-mediated global village with anything resembling a settled authentic community:

> Much of the content of modern communications is this kind of substitute for directly discoverable and transitive relations to the world....It is a form of shared consciousness rather than merely a set of techniques. And as a form of consciousness it is not to be understood by rhetorical analogies like the "global village." Nothing could be less like the experience of any kind of village or settled active community. For in its main uses it is a form of unevenly shared consciousness of persistently external events. It is what appears to happen, in these powerfully transmitted and mediated ways, in a world with which we have no perceptible connections but which we feel is at once central and marginal to our lives. (1973:295-96)

The irreconcilable nature of mass and interpersonal communication is clearly visible in Williams's refusal to admit that the global village could be anything like the Welsh village of his birth, Llanfihangel Crocorney. The global village is a mental construct synthesized by various external sources in mass media; the Welsh village is the product of individual experiences shared among people living and communicating in proximity. While Williams's localism is not surprising, the recurrence of this theme in the work of Stuart Hall, the cosmopolitan theorist who introduced structuralism to British cultural studies, is.

HALL AND "ENCODING/DECODING"

Hall, given his reputation for high theory, hardly seems a likely champion of a cultural context where "directly discoverable and transitive relations to the world" are the standard by which mass media must be judged and, necessarily, fail. As a Jamaican expatriate, Rhodes Scholar, careful student of French and postmodern thought, and someone who made a much cleaner break with Leavis than Williams did, Hall's sense of place is at the very least more complex. Yet, regarding the model of audience crystallized in the "Encoding/Decoding" article (which represents his theoretical contribution of greatest influence in media studies), a remarkably similar identification of communication with the local and interpersonal—with the frame of reference in which Williams believed culture was appropriately produced—is evident. Although Hall's structuralism forbids him planting his feet in the honest soil of the countryside, as Williams did, his commitment to a bounded locale is just as strong.

The encoding/decoding model represents British cultural studies' formal alternative to the long-dominant "effects" model of mediation. Using elements of Althusser and Gramsci to construct a model of "active audience" that credited television viewers with relative interpretive autonomy, Hall's model offered an alternative to models of raw media manipulation taken from the propaganda theory of the 1920s and the all too easy populist resistance later personified by John Fiske. Hall imagined audiences to take their part in hegemonic negotiation at the moment that the message was decoded at reception, and the linguistically encoded message in the program was subsequently turned into social structure and ideology. Hall insists: "we must recognize that the discursive form of the message has a privileged position in the communicative exchange (from the viewpoint of circulation), and that the moments of 'encoding' and 'decoding,' though only 'relatively' autonomous in relation to the communication process as a whole, are determinate moments" (1980a:129). Hall's encoding/decoding model marked the decisive break with what Roger Silverstone calls "mediation" models of audience which emphasized the power of the medium as a technological, ideological, or textual artifact, and the gradual shift to "reception" models which emphasized audience agency and control over interpretation (Silverstone 1994). That much was revolutionary.

However, these audiences, clustered at the imagined decoding places, their subjectivity opaque and their class, gender, or ethnic characteristics muted, are made coherent through no effort of their own, but rather through the determining power of structure.[9] Their agency is confined to the "knowable community" available in their living rooms, and in which they are to summon up what counterhegemonic energy they can to interpret the ideology present in television discourse. Their relationship to discourse is purely instrumental, and they decode according to their whim. But no matter how radical the interpretation, the meanings have no social afterlife, notably because the audience is defined as stranded in some structural no-man's land outside language, culture, and history. Indeed, though the very encoding/decoding model is committed to the ideological alchemy possible as discourse turns into social structure (i.e., where viewers turn what they watch into action on the world), discourse is not given its due, so its "privilege" extends no further than the time that passes between reception and execution. Decoding may go on, but communication does not happen where it matters most: between the isolated clusters of viewers. It is as if Williams's "mobile privatization" thesis had not been read and absorbed as an object lesson in British media studies.

Discourse, for Hall, is not shared with viewers in other living rooms, and is not sustained much beyond the moment of watching or listening, or the brief sharing of conversation with the others lounging on the sofa. Hall is not clear about where discourse goes once decoding happens; but it is highly uncertain just what form of politics could ensue. The problem with Hall's and similar models of active reception is that the sphere of media consumption is allowed to define the limits of the social, dramatically limiting its scope and emancipatory potential. Jody Berland sees it this way: "As the production of meaning is located in the activities and agencies of audiences, *the topography of consumption is increasingly identified as (and thus expanded to stand in for) the map of the social*" (Berland 1992:42). The "knowable community," as was seen in Williams, is therefore restricted to a context incompatible with the real mobility and dispersal of people in late modern society.

The power to encode is granted exclusively to the production specialists at the source of transmission, and denied to those being interviewed, or more importantly, those whose words and lives contributed to the world encoded in the first place. Their contributions represent a code that was not developed in isolation, but derives from many sources including their own and others' viewing experiences. What "goes around" in television discourse, in other words, "comes around" in a constructive circularity that the encoding/decoding model does not encompass. Hall can't seem to countenance that the moment of "decoding" is also one of "encoding." Indeed, recalling Hall's failure to develop the positive nature of the audience, it is difficult to imagine how active audiences build any kind of solidarity or politics beyond that of the living room. One can hardly blame Hall for the enormous popularity of the "Encoding/Decoding" essay, and its ready assimilation within the more liberal strains of American cultural studies. His work has long grown past the cardboard silhouettes of audiences battling for control of their culture. But it remains a fact that this article, published twenty years ago, inspired a generation of audience research, and has been fixed in many imaginations as the definitive essay in cultural studies.

Although the audience studies inspired by Hall would stretch the limits of the encoding/decoding model by incorporating ethnography and some post-structuralist literature (e.g., Ang uses Foucault in *Desperately Seeking the Audience*), this later research did not accept that audiences might have relatively more power over interpretation than the Leavisian and semiotic models predicted. Many accounts of audience favouring an active audience approach accept the implicit authority of the text by first interpreting its meaning, then asking how and whether the audience matches or varies within that interpretation (Turner 1990:127). Alternately and more pessimistically, the very category of "active audience," given its initial impetus by the encoding/decoding model, is open to criticism. The simple fact that audiences generate multiple responses to a given media text, irrespective of their relationship to its ideological content, does not answer the nagging question of whether this activity is significant. Many television researchers have argued that "all the television-related activity in the world does not necessarily lead to greater liberation, and may indeed...only serve to provide private compensations for public hurt" (Silverstone 1994:154).

Media theory influenced by Birmingham arguably remains trapped by a "line of sight" view of mediation which cannot account for the invisible bodies and virtual communities existing outside the scope of conversation and consumption. This leaves British cultural studies with little room to discuss the relationship of media to society as we know it today. We need to get beyond the descriptions of the reliable push and pull of hegemonic struggle, or the increasingly rare sightings of stable interpretive communities. What the romantic precedent developed in the interwar period demonstrates is that media theory has somewhere to go to find alternative models that allow for genuine communication, even amid media spaces that have become ever more wild, boundless, and surreal. It is false and misleading to believe that our conceptual horizon begins and ends in the tensions between British cultural studies and the media effects tradition. Rather, between the wars, and at a time when publics were terribly frightened at the modernity they had made, there is an alternative—and arguably romantic—view of media and modernity as an uncanny yet humane conjunction.

Chapter 4

The Enemies of Love

MISUSING ROMANTICISM

The only cure for postmodernism is the incurable illness of romanticism.

—Richard Appignanesi and Chris Garratt,
Postmodernism for Beginners, 173

It is in debates over the "information society" (the influential model through which the larger pattern of relationships among digital media, the "new" economy, and other novel features characteristic of post-World War II society has been imagined) that the politics of enchantment are made most visible. Central to these politics is the ownership and use of the romantic legacy as it continues to surface in contemporary culture. The issue of how romanticism is arguably "misused" by theoretical traditions that compete with cultural studies, and how its properties are appropriated for undesirable ends, takes romanticism outside the politics of theory and into the realm of power.

The information society is one where information is the all-purpose economic commodity, social adhesive, and cultural fetish. The concept's great architect is the American sociologist Daniel Bell, whose 1976 book *The Coming of Post-Industrial Society* organized a number of changes that had been separately noted, such as the growth of service industries, the reliance on computers, and the loss of industrial employment, into one highly marketable metaphor. A new model of society was needed, one sensitive to the perception that Western capitalism had put its polluting and fractious industrial phase behind it, and was entering a *post*-industrial phase built on a clean services economy and a classless social harmony.

Notes to chapter 4 are on pp. 178-82.

While the information society concept is normally associated with a line of argument continued by popularizers of Bell's work, such as best-selling futurists like Alvin Toffler, George Gilder, and Nicholas Negroponte, the concept has also become central to more formally academic post-structuralist media criticism by David Lyon, Arthur Kroker, Mark Poster, and Shoshana Zuboff. Post-structuralism, the product of a reappraisal of the basic premises of structuralism in late 1960s France, brings its enormous philosophical sophistication to the problem. The result is a concept far more elastic than even Bell conceived, as the implications for the nature of reality and the self largely buried in his work come to the surface. As sociologist Krishan Kumar (the great critic of the information society) finds, these recent variations on Bell's original thesis are far more sweeping in their claims:

> Those [post-industrial] theories are still with us, but they have been joined by others with a more ambitious scope. In these newer theories we encounter claims that go beyond economics and politics to encompass western, and indeed, world civilization in their entirety. In the information and communication revolution, in the transformation of work and organization in the global economy, and in the crisis of political ideologies and cultural beliefs, these theories see the signs of a turning point in the evolution of modern societies. (1995:vi)

That we are at a "turning point" is not in question. But it may not be a turn from modernity to some brave new epoch, as both these traditions argue, but rather a change in how we read and defend the persistence of the modern in theory, culture, and history. Despite the many real differences between post-industrialism, with its origins in American technocratic utopianism, and post-structuralism with its intensely cerebral French style, there is evidence to suggest that these "enemies of love" share much, including a devoted opposition to modernity and modern thought, and a strategy for making use of romanticism in ways not originally intended by its makers. In reading them together, and treating their separate interpretations of media and culture as a joint problem, a more complete understanding of the real and urgent nature of what is at stake in romanticism is possible.

THE POWERS OF MIND: ANTI-MODERN THEORIES OLD AND NEW

Former Speaker of the United States House of Representatives, *Time* magazine's 1995 "Man of the Year," and tribune of the Republican right in the 1990s, Newt Gingrich argued that ever faster and more powerful digital media demonstrate that "the powers of mind are everywhere ascendant over the brute force of things" (1994:1). While it may seem strange that a major architect of neo-conservatism would champion advanced technologies, the convergence of traditionalism and technology is consistent with the extraordinary history of new media theory. Gingrich meant by the "powers of mind" those technologies that burn intelligence in place of fossil fuels, marvellous machines that anticipated a future no longer defined by physical labour and natural resources. But the phrase can apply equally to a pair of highly abstract theories both organized thematically around the problem of knowledge, and which take as the object of their serious contemplation that historical epoch known as modernity.

Modernity, to recall chapter 2, is that period in cultural history dating roughly from the eighteenth-century Enlightenment, out of which most of the institutions and values that make up the Western world have emerged. Almost since its inception, new media theory has been at odds with modernity, typically because the existence of technological wonders like the personal computer, virtual reality, and the Internet are taken as a sign that an unprecedented new epoch in cultural history has arrived. Whether these theoretical positions are anti-modern and neo-conservative (such as post-industrialism), or postmodern and politically ambiguous (such as post-structuralism), the combination of nostalgia and futurism, reaction and high technology, has made for a strange spectacle. Despite their evident differences, both theories share surprisingly similar opinions on modernity, and the related themes of politics and history.

Both post-industrialism and post-structuralism are critical of modernity—the first on behalf of values attributed to a pre-modern past, the second on behalf of a postmodern future—because each problematizes modernity while locating itself outside of modernist theoretical frameworks.[1] Their anti-modernism and conservative ideological bias are integral to each other, and their opposition to modernity gives their politics a more than usual profundity. That is, when neo-conservatives argue against abortion or gun control, or post-structuralists against the possibility of truth, their particular arguments are rooted in a more fundamental antipathy to the modern cultural and intellectual foundations of what they are addressing.

Post-industrialism's anti-modernism is founded on its distaste for liberal culture. Whether it is Bell's attack on the corruption of capitalism's core values by consumerism, or futurist Alvin Toffler's negative identification of "second wave" industrial society with class struggle, post-industrialism describes a technological revolution so transformative it eclipses the modern. A post-industrial society of abundance ends the scarcity and socio-economic differences that lead to social strife; the state withers away because the redistribution of power to a wired populace makes centralized government obsolete; and a "culture of the individual," as the video version of Toffler's *The Third Wave* breathlessly promises, transcends the joyless homogeneity of mass culture. With these changes, the modern no longer exists.

Post-structuralism's anti-modern affiliation is a convention of its own open affiliation with the postmodern. Modernity insisted on discourses that made claims to referential truth (i.e., an object is out there, and a word or image points to it), such as science and journalism, an assumption that post-structuralism cannot support. But a sea change is alleged to have come over the West in the 1960s, and a shift from modern culture to postmodernity began. Postmodernity answers the emphasis on rationality, universalism, and humanism in the modern with the irrationality of image and spectacle in our media-rich societies, the fragmentation and incoherence of global culture, and a view of the self as without a centre.

Of chief concern to post-structuralism, a theoretical position born of and used to describe life in postmodernity, is the problem of truth. Post-structuralism argues that referentiality in a highly mediated culture is moot, since our social worlds have collapsed upon themselves, and we can no longer with any confidence argue that language addresses reality. Information society critic Frank Webster (1995:188), though agreeing with the post-structuralists that the increase in the number and plasticity of signs in culture makes understanding it more difficult, argues that "complexity is no grounds for asserting that, with interpretation being variable, interpretation itself is lost."

Politically, post-industrial theory is usually identified with neo-conservatism, which is defined conventionally as a position that reconciles socially conservative (e.g., pro-capital punishment, against the welfare state) with economically liberal or "pro-market" opinions. Neo-conservatism developed as a post-World War II alternative to the skepticism conservatives historically felt toward laissez-faire capitalism, since free markets tended to destabilize the social order conservatives so prized.[2] Bell, a member of a small group of Jewish intellectuals who publicly denounced their leftist credentials and became founding members of the "New Right" in the 1950s, is one of neo-conservatism's elder statesmen. The organizational basis of much neo-conservative "info-populism" has been traced to the US Sunbelt states, and the nexus there of southern conservatism, Pentagon contracts, and Republican-affiliated futurist projects such as the Conservative Opportunity Society, a "major political voice of the Information Age" (Roszak 1986:25).

Post-structuralism owes its ideological character to the events defining its origins in the climactic year of 1968. The defeat of the Paris Commune and other radical protests across Europe led to a collective questioning of the

1960s student movement, and rightly called for the kind of anti-foundation-alist critique that the later Roland Barthes, Julia Kristeva, Michel Foucault, and other post-structuralists tendered. But the more severe forms of post-structuralism, which deny the very possibility of meaning and social change, represent "a convenient way of evading such political questions altogether" (Eagleton 1983:143). Post-structuralism "has been able with a good conscience to praise the Iranian mullahs, celebrate the USA as the one remaining oasis of freedom and pluralism in a regimented world, and recommend various forms of portentous mysticism as the solution to human ills" (Eagleton 1983:147).

These urgent criticisms from known partisans aside, simply characterizing post-structuralism as a bastion of reaction is to reduce its complex and often constructive critique to a caricature. It is better to characterize post-structuralism as often apolitical, and in places potentially conservative. But its withdrawal from rational engagement with institutions or causes, its post-modern anti-modernism, and its affinity for information technology suggest certain parallels with post-industrial theory that warrant examination.

There are also certain features in the development and nature of information technologies that appeal to these theories. Post-industrialism draws from a model of communication known as "information theory." As represented in the wartime computer research of Claude Shannon and Warren Weaver, information theory was deeply positivist in nature, and was steeped in the Cold War paranoia and the ideological bias dictated by its origins in Pentagon funding and Bell Telephone's corporate labs. More to the point, information theory was conceived as the basis of the computer logic used in programming and engineering. Post-structuralism, on the other hand, cannot help but be intrigued by the fluid meaning-structures and the floating signification inherent in computer systems. There is furthermore an attractive analogue for both positions in the stateless, ungovernable, and market-friendly nature of the Internet, as well as in the promiscuous play of signs there. Technology journalist Clive Thompson recognizes the neo-conservative potential in the Internet's very structure:

> Cyberspace, it seems, has tilted quite heavily to the right....In a McLuhanesque way, it makes perfect sense. The Net is a classic case of the medium being loaded with a message—it's custom-built for a fiercely free-market outlook. Multinational, anarchically free, and laughably beyond the grasp of any government, cyberspace is an elegant metaphor for the new right's way of doing business. And for the resurgent conservative movement that was searching for a way to outflank squishy-liberal mainstream media, the Net was an answer in search of a question. (1995:14)

Post-industrial and post-structuralist theory also share similar premises about history. Both positions trade strongly on similar claims of an epic "break" with the modern past, vitiating modernity and modern positions alike. In their mutual call for the "end of ideology," a phrase Bell coined in his early major book of the same name, each wins exemption from one of the risks that comes with modern life: having to choose among competing ideologies in order to create the good society. By banishing ideology, each position in a complementary way asserts control of how we understand new media, and more importantly, how we represent the future. Post-industrial theory addresses the political and economic issues relevant to the information society, while post-structuralism takes upon itself questions of language, identity, and culture.

Post-industrialism argues that the informational world of bounty and classlessness means that there is no more rationale for ideology, given that the very best possible society is a mouse click away. Post-structuralism argues that the conditions under which the ideology concept was created (i.e., to match manufactured images of reality with what is known to be true) are over, since reality can no longer be confidently represented. The key post-structuralist concept of "discourse"—that discounts the real in favour of the idea that all reality is ultimately linguistic—replaces ideology. Without alternatives, and spared the second opinions and nagging questions generated by ideology, history is reformulated in simpler terms that welcome self-serving models of cause and effect such as technological determinism.

All this is not to suggest that an intellectual conspiracy is intended here, since two more improbable allies are difficult to imagine. Rather, the new media have drawn out a certain convergence between these two theories as a function of the force field they have created in intellectual culture. Though unintended, this alliance has the effect of developing a discourse around the new media's development that serves both neo-conservative and postmodern ends, and displaces a progressive and modern critical perspective. In summary, then, we might appreciate that these theories share enough to warrant consideration as a joint problem for romantic reflection.

INSTRUMENTAL RATIONALITY AND THE LIMITS OF RATIONALIST CRITICISM

Any attempt to redeem modern thought or culture must confront the problem of instrumental rationality, perhaps the modern period's greatest problem, though it's not immediately identified with new media technologies. The proliferation of digital media has stimulated debate over privacy and surveillance, the Internet's promise for reviving democracy, and the commercialization of cyberspace, among the many others that feature in *Wired, Fast Company,* and other popular sources. But a common theme behind these (and many other issues relating to information technology and culture) is digital media's role in the radical extension of instrumental rationality.

The persistent nature of this particular scourge, like the devil in Christian lore, has earned it many names, each reflecting a different attribute of its personality. Sociologist Max Weber's model of rationalization identified it early on as a contradiction built into modern culture itself, one especially involved with bureaucracy's power to lock up freedom and innovation. Philosopher Jacques Ellul's theory of *la technique* charged technology with being the primary vehicle for its transmission, and credited machinery with a monstrous autonomy. And the Frankfurt School's concept of "instrumental rationality" directly related it to capitalism, ironically comparing this perversion of human intelligence to the now distant ideal of reason on which the Enlightenment had been built.[3]

Whatever we choose to call it, instrumental rationality is a cultural pattern or social force that insinuates itself inexorably, transferring its characteristic values of efficiency, amorality, and control deeply into society. Although it is the unintended consequence of bringing reason to bear on the world, in the form of science, administration, classification, and other similar enterprises, it attacks critical thought and inspires cultural narratives that justify its presence, such as the rhetoric of technological determinism. It is expressed in the means-oriented and self-reproducing logic of state and private bureaucracies; it is magnified and spread by science and technology, as if it were an intrinsic aspect of our gadgets themselves; and it is a fellow traveller of capitalism, enhancing the way in which this near universal socio-economic system commodifies everything.

Instrumental rationality is not limited by any of these forms, nor did it begin with modern culture. But modernity has amplified its power enormously. As David Held claims: "The transformation of what was once liberating reason into a repressive orthodoxy, of the Enlightenment into totalitarianism, can be understood as a result of elements integral to this very form of enlightenment itself" (1980:152). In what the Frankfurt School famously called "the dialectic of Enlightenment," during the course of modern history, critical human intelligence produces its instrumental opposite. The process leads to a false synthesis in which mind and now-oppressive rationalistic structures, such as numbing bureaucratic routines or impersonal market forces, are fused, ironically limiting our ability to think or act freely. This is the stuff of which Monty Python's best punchlines are made.

Technology represents the classic condensation of instrumental rationality.[4] Technology is defined by the Frankfurt School as "not just a collection of new devices but rather something with an inner unity" (Leiss 1990:68). Technology's "unity" extends itself through economic and cultural production and consumption (the latter captured in the Frankfurt School's "culture indus-try" concept), conforming individual behaviour to the system's own impera-tives. "A technological rationale is the rationale of domination itself," explained Horkheimer and Adorno (1972:121). The results of this domination in the cultural arena, for example, can be seen in the willingness of Hollywood to serve as a propaganda tool for American foreign policy; in the way that spe-cial effects in blockbuster films have reduced plot and characterization to after-thoughts; and in the deepening commodification of television and film in the form of product placements, cross-promotion, and merchandising spin-offs.

Instrumental rationality has grave consequences for humanity. We are sub-ject to bureaucracies, technologies, and economic models that are unac-countable and destructive, which result in rampant military spending, massive layoffs, and a citizenry paralyzed by every twitch of the stock market. With the best of intentions, we build rational models for delivering social services, har-nessing nature, or facilitating communication among far-flung populations, and get such irrational outcomes as poverty, pollution, and a public inundated by information.[5] Reification, particularly as the suppression of the human presence in society, is just one of the many effects that follow this terrible social disease. In William Leiss's words, "each successive step in industrializa-tion pushed the natural condition of human labour further into the past; each such step fostered the iron cage of rationalization and reification more securely about humanity" (1990:66).

New media technologies exacerbate the problem of instrumental rational-ity, including reification, with every exponential gain in computing power. Edward Tiryakian believes that the "[information] revolution is a radical extension of the process of rationalization and mastering the world through exact calculations" (1992:80). David Lyon acknowledges that Western cul-ture's "supposed dependence on rational forms of thought...is intensified by reliance upon that acme of logical operations, the computer" (1988:138). And media critic Michael Shallis (1984) writes more apocalyptically of the potential scope of this computer-assisted reification of reality: "The metaphor of the computer, the machine that 'thinks,' redefines the world in terms of 'information.' People are seen as 'information-processing systems,' the uni-verse is interpreted as a vast 'information system'; all human and social inter-actions are analysed or discussed or even just referred to in terms of informa-tion content" (172).

The remedy most commonly offered for instrumental rationality and its attendant problems, such as reification, is to assert the priority of human intelligence and to find ways to ground it so that it resists rationalization. This remedy is evident in John Dewey's project for a rationalist "Great Community," or Jürgen Habermas's hopes for communicative rationality in the public sphere. But relying on reason alone to correct a problem it inadvertently caused in the first place is a kind of intellectual homeopathy that invites more trouble. Instrumental rationality has extended its influence in the culture despite more than a century of criticism from such intellectual icons as Lewis Mumford, Neil Postman, Ursula Franklin, and many others. Despite the best efforts of some of its finest champions, reason by itself can't do much more than rattle the cage.

That's because reason is part of the very problem it seeks to solve. Arguments such as those developed by Dewey's pragmatism, the Frankfurt School, or Habermas to throw a wrench in the works remain rationalist in orientation. This leads to a built-in lack of congruence in understanding media and popular culture, given that these phenomena are far more romantic than rational in nature. That is, simply making rational sense of irrational phenomena like cyberspace or rave culture constantly misses the point. It also means that critical commentary tends to favour solutions, such as Dewey's and Habermas's plans to restore a space in society for rational debate, that are impatient that even in the best of possible worlds, much of human conversation and culture would remain irrational, absurd, and carnivalesque.

Where the solutions have not been rationalist, they have been fatalistic and pessimistic, as evident in the Frankfurt School, the most influential of those positions from the theoretical left that have addressed instrumental rationality. The Frankfurt School, product of the cultural genius of the interwar Weimar period in Germany, "was excellent at tracing the lines of domination within media culture, but was less adept at ferreting out moments of resistance and opposition," given that they credited the co-opting power of the culture industries with extending even to "seemingly radical and subversive impulses" (Kellner 1995:41). The impotence of progressive criticism has been an important factor in allowing post-industrial and post-structuralist positions their current popularity among lay and academic audiences. Visions of a cosmopolitan wired world—a staple of software advertising—are far more attractive than imagining a joyless life in the iron cage.

By releasing romanticism from what, I will argue, is its appropriation within post-industrial and post-structuralist argument and bringing it into the repertoire of the theoretical left, we can expose the limitations of the "rational" conventional criticism of these theories, and carry the analysis further. So the argument now turns to this romantic reading of the post-industrial and post-structuralist theories. Romanticism is appropriated by these positions to stage an "enchantment" of a world otherwise deracinated by instrumental rationality and reification. But it is a bewitching and undesirable enchantment at best, where these plagues are palliated rather than cured.

If cultural studies' task is to bring the power of culture forcefully to bear on instrumental rationality, reification, and similar evils, then establishing a right relationship with the romantic offers a new epistemological platform for this important work and supplements rationalist solutions to the problem. Arguing for such a platform means establishing a negative critique of how romanticism is employed to do very different kinds of work in post-industrial and post-structuralist media theory, particularly with respect to the information society. Daniel Bell, the major post-industrial theorist, and Mark Poster, perhaps the most systematic of the post-structuralist critics of new media, are given particular attention.[6]

Yet while it is valuable to demonstrate how these theories misuse romanticism in order to solve contradictions of their own, a negative critique isn't good enough. What is intended here is a positive critique that demonstrates how valuable those bohemian writers and philosophers are as sources for making sense of buttoned-down technologies. Chapter 5 will constitute that positive critique.

POST-INDUSTRIALISM AND THE INFORMATION SOCIETY

Daniel Bell's post-industrial utopia is classically captured in *The Coming of Post-Industrial Society*. His book is a strange hybrid of sociological functionalism and Golden Age science fiction, where heavily footnoted essays merge with a technophilic idealism that wouldn't be out of place in a space opera. In appraising Bell's argument romantically, initial consideration of the argument from his other major book of the 1960s and '70s, *The Cultural Contradictions of Capitalism*, is warranted: Bell's *Cultural Contradictions* establishes a problem in the present that the *Post-Industrial Society*, a major source for futurism in its own right, solves at an imagined later date.

Cultural Contradictions is not some obscure academic treatise, but a blueprint for the "culture wars" fought by the neo-conservative movement as it emerged in the 1980s. Its argument—that the problems with capitalism were a result of cultural failure—provided a foundation for neo-conservative attacks on the morality of welfare recipients and unions. *Cultural Contradictions* made it intellectually respectable to argue that an aggressively liberal capitalism, with its tragic consequences for job security, social programs, and human desire, was entirely compatible with traditional morality. Where traditional conservatives had, for several centuries, viewed *laissez-faire* market forces as a threat to social order, neo-conservatives found in this "New Right" titan the means to reconcile themselves with post-World War II economic expansion.

The details of Bell's thesis in *Cultural Contradictions* are suggestive. For Bell, early capitalism enjoyed a harmonious balance between social structure (including the economy, the state, education, the family, etc.) and culture. Social structure provided the social, technological, and economic means by which capitalism had become prodigiously productive, and culture the values—namely the Protestant work ethic and Puritan self-denial—by which workers and consumers were disciplined. Culture instilled the moral discipline necessary to ensure labour's productivity, and to curb its appetites sufficiently so that consumption did not impair the accumulation of capital.

Culture to this point in history is deemed inherently rational and ethical, motivated as it is by such heroic parsimony. And for a careful student of Weber such as Bell, instrumental rationality is otherwise strangely thought to be contained within social structure—the genie quite securely in the bottle. Bell (1976a:53) argues that "to assume, as some social critics do, that the technocratic mentality dominates the cultural order is to fly in the face of every bit of evidence at hand." Agger (1992:72), a Marxist critic closely identified with Frankfurt School "critical theory," argues that contrary to Weber's more critical intentions, functionalists like Talcott Parsons, Robert Merton, and Bell reconstructed Weber as a consensus-theorist, making his work an unlikely platform for "an increasingly fashionable neo-conservative critique of Marxism, grounded in the long end-of-ideology tradition that begins with Weber and Mannheim and extends through Daniel Bell." For Bell, Weber is very much at odds with his own *The Protestant Ethic and the Spirit of Capitalism*—that book was written by a "sunny Weber" who articulates all too well Parson's ultra-functionalist "pattern variables" and overlooks the original critique of rationalization. The irony of using a premier theorist of industrial society to account for the emergence of a *post*-industrial one has not gone unnoticed (Webster 1995:39).

This Jeffersonian vision of capitalism—where the machine and the garden, industrialism and a coherent culture, coexist without contradiction—is, however, the victim of its own success in Bell's view. Capitalism so thrives that the surplus of wealth it creates makes it possible for a non-producing class of artists and intellectuals to emerge. These artists take the form of a modernist avant-garde; they promote decadent values of irreverence and easeful consumption that are antithetical to the social structure, leading to a "radical disjuncture" between the two erstwhile integrated spheres. Over time, this avant-garde's contrarian values are assimilated into mainstream society, becoming the basis for the rude and iconoclastic popular culture of the twentieth century. Culture, once the loyal servant to the social order, develops a bad attitude, so alienating itself from the system that it comes to attack society itself. Arguments made by neo-conservative intellectuals such as David Frum who blame the 1960s for high divorce rates, drug use, or a lack of patriotism, begin with Bell and his indefatigable opposition to modernity.

Bell attacked modernism for its championing of culture's independence relative to social structure. But what's especially interesting is that the modernist movements he scorns represent, to many scholars, the epitome of twentieth-century romanticism. Personalities like Baudelaire, Picasso, and Eisenstein are prefigured in the original romantics. In criticizing culture's relative autonomy, Bell is criticizing perhaps the signature feature of romanticism. As Kumar (1995:94) remarks of modernism's romantic nature, and its powerful advocacy of culture's active, critical role: "Modernism can...be seen as late Romanticism. But it goes so much further in its assault on modernity that we are entitled to regard it as something almost qualitatively different. There is a comprehensiveness in its sweeping rejection of all the idols of modernity that marks something new."

In the fine arts, the culture shifts from Gainsborough to Duchamp, from *The Magic Flute* to *The Rites of Spring*. Classical aesthetic values of harmony, mimesis, and the observer's aloof distance from the object are abandoned in favour of spectacular experiments with form, an anti-realist refusal of limits on representation, and the demolition of the "fourth wall" between performer and audience. And in the popular realm, the radical experiments of the early twentieth-century avant-garde are incorporated within the endless novelty of consumer capitalism, as their surrealistic words and pictures become the basis for sensationalist advertising, media sex and violence, and tabloid culture. This irrational culture's new supremacy thus overturns what had been the traditional authority of reason in Western civilization.

Although the rational social order may be betrayed by a blasphemous culture according to *Cultural Contradictions*, rationality is conspicuously innocent of all charges. How can this leading American sociologist, who has inherited the defining problems of his discipline, dismiss instrumental rationality as an illusory issue that flies in the face of "every bit of evidence at hand"? Why is an irrational culture, not a reckless and inhumane rationality, his central concern? The answer is that instrumental rationality is useful to Bell, and key to his larger intellectual strategy. In *Post-Industrial Society*, instrumental rationality is tamed and transformed, returning as technological determinism, the motive power behind his utopian vision. That cultural pattern or social force, so worrisome to a century of critics, is in Bell's program made into a benign if all-pervasive power that drives the information society into the future.

Technological determinism is the doctrine which holds that technology is the most important variable shaping human society. It is not just another manifestation of the hydra-headed phenomenon that is instrumental rationality, but a positive evaluation of this power with enormous ideological and material consequences. Arguments in technological determinism's name are heard regularly in the media, among policy makers, and in the technology sector itself, as we are told that this or that new device—the steam engine, the personal computer, the cell phone—will change the world as we know it. Three main premises characterize the phenomenon: "that technology develops without conscious planning, that it is neutral, and that our thought processes and ideas must be adjusted to close the cultural lag" between the technology's entry into society and our adjustment to it (McCormack 1994:21).

The reifying nature of this or any determinism is apparent when human factors are humbled before a simple, monocausal explanation for historical change that exists outside our control.[7] Technological determinism encourages a fatalistic passivity among populations undergoing rapid change, and allows those elites who are invested in the manufacture and administration of new technologies to identify themselves with what is taken to be the natural and inevitable course of history. A little of both this passivity and the unquestioning authority granted to technological elites was evident in the euphoric public interest in technology stocks in the late 1990s, despite evidence that NASDAQ listings were overvalued and the decimation of Internet start-up companies was likely.

Culture features significantly here, especially as we consider its capacity to criticize and reform social structure. It is important to realize that not just any technology determines the totality in Bell's vision. Rather, it is *information* technology, technology in which culture is deeply implicated, whether culture is defined as "knowledge," "information," "theory" or something similar. Culture's autonomy, which Bell so greatly feared in *Cultural Contradictions,* is broken in *Post-Industrial Society* by turning it into information. Information is not just the particular form of capital on which post-industrial society depends; information is also the means by which the endemic contradictions that otherwise threaten capitalism, including the gap between rich and poor, crises of oversupply and underconsumption, and the destruction of nature, are magically resolved. This is best appreciated in the context of the principal features of the information society concept.

Leiss (1990:129) cites five defining elements of Bell's program, which provide a template for most of the information utopians who would follow him.

These are:

(a) the shift from goods to services production;

(b) the bureaucratic management of society by a technocratic "new class" of engineers, information specialists, and intellectuals, which replaces industrial age classes and their struggles with competition among professional groups for status;

(c) the creation of new technology; and

(d) institutional application and assessment of that technology.

Key to the argument here, however, is the feature Bell himself thought most important:

(e) the central role of knowledge and information technology in extending rational administration to the whole of society.

Bell insists that the "'post-industrial society' emphasizes the centrality of theoretical knowledge as the axis around which new technology, economic growth and the stratification of society will be organized" (Bell 1976b:112). Information, whether in the form of digital technologies, highly trained white-collar specialists, or responsive state and corporate bureaucracies, acts to cybernetically manage and defuse the flaws Marxists thought would rock the system.

Culture's critical potential is diluted both in society at large, and with reference to cultural studies. Culture, once torn from its embedded role in early capitalism and run amok in twentieth-century mass culture, is returned to structure in the post-industrial future, a return made possible by its repackaging as emphatically rational "knowledge" or, as it is more typically characterized, "information." This repackaging of culture as "information" empties it of history and value, leaving culture open to commercial and ideological exploitation. Information is therefore the emasculated form that culture takes once it is identified thoroughly with capitalism, and stripped of its resistant and indeterminate properties. Formerly our chief defence against the seductions of technological determinism, this "informatized" culture now acts to serve instrumental rationality, allowing it to enter irresistibly into our institutions, relationships, and psyches.

Bell's neat bit of intellectual alchemy also has consequences for cultural studies. Culture is a loaded term—Nazi propaganda chief Joseph Goebbels is famously reported to have said that he reached for a gun at the very sound of the word—and full of potential heartache to neo-conservatives because it is critical of ideology and transformative of structure. The more culture is incrementally recast as information, the more cultural studies is denied access to the concept as a basis for intellectual and political action on capitalism. As media theorist Dan Schiller insists, "'information' could be defended...against any full-scale engagement with the radical heterodoxy whose fulcrum was 'culture'" (1996: 169-70). In the theory wars at least (an obscure conflict happening far above pickets at abortion clinics or letters to the editor denouncing *Harry Potter* for encouraging witchcraft), this second-order appropriation matters.

But the tension between culture and information also has romantic consequences. If we might accept that the anti-ideological function of culture—its capacity to challenge the dominant intellectual and experiential frameworks in which our lives are organized—is ultimately romantic in origin, then romanticism is ultimately appropriated too. Bell can't forego the romantic because it offers the only means to check the tendency of structure toward the kind of social entropy any society is vulnerable to. The post-industrial paradise, and the mighty engine of technological determinism on which it depends, uses an informatized culture to do just that. The anti-reifying value of romanticism is crucial to making possible the transformation of a terrifying instrumental rationality into a benign technological determinism.

These permutations may not seem immediately evident from Bell's writings themselves, or even relevant to the general reader. But the matter of post-industrialism's self-serving use of the romantic becomes more clear when the context for this exploitation is drawn. The elements in play are as follows: the origins of functionalism in late German romanticism; the relationship of the post-industrial thesis in the "machine in the garden" tradition in American intellectual history; and the works of the contemporary neo-functionalists who see themselves as continuing Bell's work. Though the evidence is circumstantial, romanticism is the patron saint of loose ends in cultural history, and the relationship between these three themes reveals a clear and visible pattern of exploitation.

A ROMANTIC READING OF POST-INDUSTRIALISM

Late Romanticism and Post-Industrial Utopia

Structural-functionalism is Bell's primary theoretical affiliation. His post-industrialism is a futurist byproduct of this American school of sociological thought which, under Parsons, Bell, Robert Merton, and others, dominated sociology at mid-century. What is less well-known is the fact that key elements of late German romanticism provide a foundation to Bell's sociology. "In fact it is plausible to say that early romantic thought anticipates 20th century existentialism," Saiedi argues, "while the later romanticism agrees with functionalist sociological theory" (1993:65). The compatibility of late romanticism with functionalism is evident after some examination of late romanticism, once the blush was off the rose.

The end of the radical phase in romantic thought and the beginning of the conservative one begins in 1801, after it had become evident to friends of the French Revolution that things had gone tragically wrong. The Terror, Thermidor, and the imperial adventures of a certain Corsican artillery officer would dismay the Republic's allies among romantic German intellectuals and English poets alike, giving rise to nationalistic and traditionalist thinking. The conservative reaction to the disappointment of revolutionary hopes can be read in late romantic thought, especially as it manifests in ideas about language and culture, epistemology and agency.

Language's hermeneutic nature and aesthetic function, as the early German romantics saw it, is lost in late German romanticism. Deeply Catholic in character, the later works of Friedrich Schlegel propose a deterministic view of language. Language is no longer the primary source of culture, but rather passively reflects God-given truths, like those gradually revealed through the universal Christian history thought to underlie experience. Where the early romantics, following Herder, had championed cultural relativism, rejecting "the possibility of a universal definition of progress and evolution across cultures" favoured by the Enlightenment, this late romantic idea of universal history "relates all different cultural forms as successive and related states of a common teleology" (Saiedi 1993:91).

Epistemologically, the early romantic love of irony, chaos, exoticism, and the particular is thrown over for "a dogmatic belief in historical religion, revelation, established traditions and authority, and an individual's submission to the rules and laws of society" (Saiedi 1993:93). Although the irrationalism remains, it is no longer a quixotic challenge to reason on behalf of emotion and the imagination, but rather a mystifying endorsement of authority and the status quo. Romanticism's unique brand of materialism (that acknowledges the relative autonomy of culture to behave as if it were a material force and to shape society) is foregone in favour of an idealism that rejects the world.

Morever, the early romantic belief in difference and the irregular is succeeded by a functionalist holism, where the particular exists only to point to the unfolding Christian revelation. Obsessed with the problem of order in Napoleonic Europe, the Germans developed a view of society as a moral community where authority was ideally based, not on law or abstract principles but rather upon the unconditional love of the people for those who through God's grace had assumed positions of leadership. Predictably, the license granted to the self by the early German romantics is taken away by the late, given their tendency to reduce individuals to the imperatives of the social order.

A simple summary of functionalist premises confirms the parallels between late German romanticism and functionalism. Following neo-functionalist Jeffrey Alexander's own list (Alexander 1985) of premises, functionalism's salient features are as follows: society is viewed as a symbiotic constellation of parts, its energy deriving from the open and pluralistic dynamics of interrelationship, rather than some *a priori* element, such as the economy or culture; the equilibrium between society's parts is taken to be a hypothetical value, though not a practically realizable goal, a position that separates functionalism from "conflict" models of society such as Marxism; personality, culture, and social structure are treated as distinct and separable planes; and social progress follows a pattern of ever-increasing differentiation, with society registering this complexity in the division of labour, social stratification, cultural diversity, etc. In both late romanticism and functionalism, culture's autonomy is reduced to a ghost of itself; order is valued over freedom and change; an arbitrary holism overrules contradiction and dissent; and language and subjectivity exist to reflect and serve the system.

The Organic Metaphor and "Second Nature"

Nature has always been a reliable source of metaphor for thinking by way of analogy about society, and the romantics were especially sophisticated in working with this metaphor. Both early and late romanticisms were committed to an organic model of social reality, a reaction to the mechanistic view of nature upon which the Enlightenment's sociology was predicated. By "organic" here, I mean that society is perceived like nature itself is perceived, as a self-sustaining and synergistic entity, in which each element indispensably contributes to the health of the whole.

The Enlightenment imagined social totality to be a relatively static system of social forces defined as objects—what Saiedi terms their "notion of the natural thinghood of being" (1993:156). To contrast, the romantic model of nature looked beyond the physical fact of the trees in favour of the vital green heart of the forest, defining society in light of an organic metaphor that emphasized life and pattern. Saiedi believes that "this silent transformation of the dominant metaphor in the Romantic perspective was probably the most fundamental revolution in theoretical discourse of the time. In a word, a new pattern of epistemology, theory of action, and political philosophy was built on this new metaphor of nature" (1993:156). Their common interest in organic or naturalistic metaphor apart, early and late German romanticisms model very different values toward nature.

The metaphor of nature was associated with quite progressive ideas in early romantic thought. The early romantics opposed the Enlightenment static conception of nature with a metaphor of a vital organicism denoting life, growth, history, uniqueness, process, activity, freedom, functional interrelations, and totality. Friedrich Schlegel puts words to this plenitude. "Beautiful is what reminds us of nature and thereby stimulates a sense of infinite fulness of life," he declares in *Lucinde and the Fragments*. "Nature is organic, and whatever is most sublimely beautiful is therefore always vegetal, and the same is true of morality and love" (F. Schlegel 1988:198). By contrast, late romanticism replaced this dynamic organicism with an inert one typical of functionalism. Here the same metaphor implies the idea of totality, functional interdependence, priority of the whole to the parts, structural unity, and order. Although neither supports a dialectical conception of social reality, the early romantic organicism allowed an undeniable dynamism and historical character—permission for nature to be nature—that is not present in the later romantic purview.

A remarkable fact about the organic metaphor is that, like dandelions in the spring, it shows up in the most unexpected places. For instance, it enters the debate about the relationship between technology and society, manifesting in our historic ambivalence about machine-ridden modernity. The organic metaphor captures our nostalgia for a past that was presumably more simple and harmonious, and is therefore set in tension with technology, modernity, and most particularly, instrumental rationality. Especially significant here, instrumental rationality, with its tendency toward control, harmonization, and efficiency, is at odds with irrepressible nature. The different forms of organicism make for different adaptive responses to instrumental rationality, notably since that rationality regularly acts to monopolize nature in its various forms—be it human nature or the natural world. Nature, as condensed in the organic metaphor, provides a point of analytical and critical access to this most modern of problems. Technology critic Thelma McCormack describes this dialectic of holism and technique: "We bring to this Information Age a set of attitudes toward technology that reflect our ambivalence toward it, pro and con, attract and repel, and this in turn rests on a deeper conflict inherent in modernity between the world of organic harmony and the world of differentiation and constant change. We may feel more comfortable with one, but never forget the other; we may be more competent in one, but belong emotionally to the other" (McCormack 1994:13).

Leo Marx's classic work of cultural history, *The Machine and the Garden*, argues that the dream of compatibility between nature and technological modern society is "the central theme in the ideology of American industrialism" (Marx 1964:158). The "middle landscape," as he called this imaginary vista of harmonious progress that attracted charismatic builders of planned communities like Robert Owen and George Pullman, salved the conscience of an industrializing nineteenth-century America fearful of making the same mistakes that Old World Europe had made. The "machine and the garden"—the garden signified both external nature and an organic, harmonious society—was an ideological fiction that argued that the destruction of the environment, and what is more, the class warfare and alienation that the Industrial Revolution had brought Europe, could be avoided in the paradisical New World. Nature supposedly served to purify capitalism, and to absorb its contradictions.

Bell inherits the "machine in the garden" tradition, but substitutes a computer for the steam engine. His post-industrial utopia assumes the same compatibility of technology and nature as did his American forebears. But in Bell's technologically advanced world, nature in the verdant, outdoors sense of the word is not at issue, and the emphasis shifts to the organic society. Bell gives sociological legitimacy to what Frankfurt School critic Theodor Adorno called "second nature." Second nature was the term Adorno used to describe the artificial and manufactured technological environment in which humanity had come to operate, cut off from the natural world and subject to seasons, pulses, and rhythms dictated by the machine. Technology is no longer destructive of, or even in an ambivalent relationship with, culture. Rather, technology creates a synthetic "second nature" which Bell (unlike Adorno) defines in positive and utopian terms.

And so Bell closes the circle begun with *Cultural Contradictions*. Drawing upon the conservative model of the organic derived from late romanticism, and that persists in functionalism, Bell goes "back to the future" in the strange manner supported by other conservative futurists of a later vintage, like George Gilder, Newt Gingrich, and Alvin Toffler. Having defined the great problem of modernity as an irrational culture, rather than a perverse instrumental rationality, Bell makes culture into a "simulacrum" (i.e., a sophisticated simulation, a copy for which there is no original) years before post-structuralist Jean Baudrillard coined the phrase.

This is strikingly different than most conservative interventions in the culture wars; rather than return society to the past in the name of traditional values, Bell looks to a future free of the strife and surrealism associated with modern culture. (All the more reason to consider this *neo*-conservatism.) The great scourge of modern life, instrumental rationality, is made over as a benign technological determinism, and culture and capitalist society are returned to their former happy coexistence. But it should be understood that late romanticism ultimately provides Bell with the resources he needs to manage instrumental rationality, employ a conservative organicism, and finally ensure that the future is safely placed beyond modernity.

The very different organicism typical of early romanticism recommends a critical dialogue with technology through the organic metaphor. Theirs is a technological ethics that neither utterly rejects technology nor, as Bell did, accepts technology on its terms. Some evidence of this organicism is present in what Raymond Williams calls the "green language" of the early nineteenth-century English romantic period. Poets like William Wordsworth and the rustic John Clare broke with the eighteenth-century tradition of pastoral poetry that idealized nature as an Arcadia, and instead wrote boldly of the enclosure movement, the ravages of industrialism, and the decline of rural English society. Just as Europe was entering into its industrial capitalist phase, romanticism put forth a trenchant critique of this development, aimed squarely at the mutual alienation of physical and human nature by industry, technology, and capitalist social relations.

The "green language"—the term comes from a poem of Clare's entitled *Pastoral Poesy*–was the new style of nature writing, raw and realistic. Poetry in the green language was based on close observation of nature; it characterized nature as something alive, something with which the poet actively identified as a fellow sufferer. It vividly described the injuries done to the land and to agrarian culture, often through the eyes of a wanderer or dispossessed person who played a lonely witness to the lost idyll. Yet this new poetry of nature was also a poetry of a distinctly modern and worldly human nature, so a knowing relationship was struck between the realism of poems like Wordsworth's *Tintern Abbey* and the psychological realism of the poetry's protagonists. They took no consolation in nostalgia, melancholy, or Luddite rage, but sought instead to reinvent what it meant to be human in a world where nature, internal and external, had been so dramatically betrayed. Williams says of these new men and women that in them "an essential isolation and silence and loneliness have become the only carriers of nature and community against the rigours, the cold abstinence, the selfish ease of ordinary society" (1973:131).

The "green language" spoke for something other than mere reactionary opposition to technology—what Wordsworth called "the fever of the world"— because that led all too readily to the conservatism of the later German and English romantics. The early romantic period, whether in Germany or England, did not sentimentalize the countryside as an escape from civilization or home to a reactionary "primitivism." Rather, the early romantics preferred a sense of contradiction, a feature of the more sophisticated forms of pastoral reflection that could "manage to call into question, or bring irony to bear against the illusion of peace and harmony in a green pasture" (Marx 1964:25). Of course, this complex response does not begin or end with romanticism. Rather, in Leo

Marx's view, it is as old as Virgil's *Eclogues* and as young as Fitzgerald's *The Great Gatsby.*

Romanticism is modernity's particular expression of this complex compatibility of technology with human nature and the physical environment. Romanticism promises a way of making life whole within, rather than despite, the necessary contradictions in modern society. The depth to which this commitment to conceiving reality in non-reified terms is evident in the romantic view of the categorical relationship of humanity to nature. No prior separation of subject from object is assumed, and therefore to this extent "we cannot finally draw a line between nature and consciousness" (Bowie 1995:12). Romanticism is founded on the idea that all beings, animate and inanimate, sentient and not, share a similar nature, and therefore are answerable to the same forces and values. Humanity, the natural world, and the machines created from the interaction of human skills and natural resources, are therefore neither categorically distinct from nor reducible to each other. They must share a planet, and at a great but unavoidable risk, evolve together.

Neo-Functionalism and the Romance of Theory

The latest instance of the functionalist appropriation of romance is neo-functionalism, a recent attempt by sociologists such as Roland Robertson, Jeffrey Alexander, and Edward Tiryakian to revise and update the work of Bell, Parsons, and Merton. Alexander (1985:16) represents neo-functionalism as an intellectual position which, heeding the arguments of functionalism's critics, is an improvement upon its parent tradition. Its several features are evidence of a theory that apparently wants to learn from its mistakes. Within a neo-functionalist framework, culture and personality are defined by less idealist and more materialist terms; a concept of ideology is developed, admitting the relationship between power and representation; and theories of integration share the historical stage with conflict models that accept the reality of social contradiction. In short, "The Parsonian legacy—if not Parson's original theory—has begun to be reconstructed" (Alexander 1985:8). Critics of neo-functionalism have been quick to respond, among them social theorist Ben Agger, who argues that "calling functionalism neo-functionalism advances theory only neologistically" (Agger 1992:69). For Agger, neo-functionalism merely restores the functionalist status quo.

But neo-functionalism is interesting for its references to romanticism. Recent articles by Alexander and Tiryakian represent the beginning of a more programmatic exploitation of romanticism from the neo-conservative side of the theoretical spectrum that bears examining. Alexander argues for a "neo-modernist" theoretical project aimed at understanding modernization, that historical process by which traditional societies are transformed into modern ones with a market economy, liberal democracy, and a free press.

Modernization was a central issue for the social sciences at mid-century, taking the form there of "modernization theory," a prescriptive doctrine developed by Walter Rostow, Wilbur Schramm, Daniel Lerner, and other major modernization theorists. They elaborated a formula for how "Third World" nations might become modern, one that played a major role in Cold War *realpolitik* by offering the West a liberal capitalist alternative to Soviet socialism. Societies didn't simply enter modernity: they followed a precise pattern with the teleological outcome being their emergence as liberal capitalist democracies.

Working from a blueprint developed by Rostow in a book bullishly titled for the times, *The Stages of Economic Growth: A Non-Communist Manifesto*, modernization theorists acted as consultants to a number of US and Western government-brokered development projects, culminating in the 1970s Green Revolution which brought agribusiness to developing nations in order to expand food production.[8] In Alexander's view, modernization was a thematic staple of post-World War II sociology that never lost its relevance, a fact demonstrated by the collapse of the Soviet system and the extension of capitalist globalization, developments which advance the scope of economic and political change on modern terms. For the original modernization theorists and for Alexander a generation later, modernization is a timeless universal process through which all societies pass, regardless of their nature.

Alexander identifies what he considers the "romantic" character of modernization theory. The 1930s and '40s had given voice to what he terms "heroic" progressive projects of social reconstruction, such as the New Deal, while the 1960s would witness a revival of such "heroic" themes in Third World nationalism, as well as the theory and politics of the New Left and the counterculture. The 1950s, despite a Cold War climate of political realism, made for a noticeable romantic tendency in social theory, typical for him of the very spirit of functionalism. Alexander's romanticism is an ethos of benign goodness without any of its radical and anti-reifying qualities. It is a romanticism that regards modernity, as did the modernization theorists Alexander emulates, as an inflexible set of features utterly conforming to liberal capitalism. And it is a romanticism with which he, and other neo-functionalists, ally themselves again:

> Yet, while realism was a significant mood in the postwar period, it was not the dominant narrative frame through which postwar social science intellectuals charted their times. Romanticism was. Relatively deflated in comparison with heroism, romanticism tells a story that is more positive in its

evaluation of the world as it exists today. In the postwar period it allowed intellectuals and their audiences to believe that progress would be more or less continuously achieved, that improvement was likely. This state of grace referred, however, more to individuals than to groups, and to incremental rather than revolutionary change. In the new world that emerged from the ashes of war, it had finally become possible to cultivate one's own garden. (Alexander 1994:173)

A second concern of the neo-functionalists is to rethink modernity itself, and thereby to develop a "more adequate conception" of this epoch on which to then rebuild functionalism (Tiryakian 1991:174). Where Alexander strategically aligns neo-functionalism with the romantic character of post-war functionalist theory, Tiryakian drafts a virtual policy statement on behalf of a neo-functionalist and, implicitly, neo-conservative program. Here again, romanticism returns to play a surprising role in the politics of enchantment.

For Tiryakian, Weber's account of modernization as a relentless process of structural differentiation and rationalization was too pessimistic. Disenchantment is a reality, to be sure; but modernity yields powerful counterprocesses, such as subcultures, nationalism, and fundamentalism, by which instrumental rationality is curbed. Greater than these examples, however, "romanticism is one of the most powerful instances of re-enchantment as a feature of modernity," and indeed, "perhaps the most important Western cultural movement of the modern period" (Tiryakian 1992:84-84). Although some date romanticism's demise to the Dickensian sentimentalism of the mid-nineteenth century, Tiryakian identifies himself with those who take a "bolder stance and propose that romanticism has remained a powerful cultural current since its emergence" (84).

To this point, that of Tiryakian's belief that romanticism lives on today, there is no quarrel. Yet the neo-functionalist version of romanticism depicts it as the saviour, not the critic, of liberal technocratic capitalism, contrary to the original intentions of the German and English romantics. Although the neo-functionalists give less emphasis to technology than Bell does, they are no less committed to the societal status quo. A technologically engineered enchantment, ideologically underwritten by a romanticism functionally incorporated as a counterprocess of rationalization, is the platform for the neo-functionalist politics of enchantment. "Reenchantment and dedifferentiation, in their diverse manifestations, have served to renew and regenerate the Western societal system," claims Tiryakian (1992:92). They have done so through "social movements that challenge existing patterns of structural differentiation or by movements of the imagination that challenge the finitude of material reality and have thereby contributed to its ongoing reconstruction" (92). So although they advocate a revival of modernist social theory, and a romanticized model of modernity, the neo-functionalists would use romanticism to buoy the same Western societal system and the rationalizing modernization process the romantics dedicated their lives to criticizing.

Traceable in the work of Bell and his neo-functionalist successors (Alexander and Tiryakian) is a pattern of appropriation wherein the original romantic critique of capitalism and instrumental rationality is overturned in favour of a romanticism consistent with the deeply conservative later variant. Romanticism here is made fundamental to the maintenance of a highly technocratic and liberal capitalist status quo, a means to sustain an enchanted "second nature" of the type feared by Adorno and antagonistic to the modern. In a culture ever more given over to synthetic miracles produced on-line, in Hollywood, or at the local mall, it is urgently necessary that we appreciate that romanticism is part of our fate among these spectacles and simulacra.

Romanticism never was and never will be one thing, and the issue here is not that post-industrialism and neo-functionalism corrupt some authentic impulse with which I'm conveniently aligning myself. Assuming that romanticism's meaning can be fixed, or its capabilities owned, would be the real betrayal. All that can be done here is to argue for a particular version of it that resembles romanticism at its inception, that is a friend to humanity at a bad time. One thing is clear. Whether Western society becomes a house of mirrors in which we can sometimes recognize ourselves without distortion, or will be a highly polished hell, depends on how romanticism is defined and who is using it.

POST-STRUCTURALISM AND THE MODE OF INFORMATION

Post-structuralism's obvious affinity for media systems that are themselves as language-intensive as computers and computer-mediated communications has attracted several premier post-structuralists to the study of new media; the most comprehensive and schematic of them is arguably Mark Poster. Drawing on classic post-structuralist sources, Poster argues that digital media are emblematic of what he terms a "second" media age, where the modernity of the "first" mass media age of print, radio, and television is irrevocably overturned. "Electronic communications systematically remove the fixed points, the grounds, the foundations that were essential to modern theory" (Poster 1995:60). Modernity and modern theory are therefore no longer able to contain and explain the media or the social relations that result from them. In their place, postmodernity and post-structuralism, a body of theory both born of and most commonly used to explain postmodern culture, are together best suited to explaining a wired world.

In Poster's view, once the second media age is installed, the familiar commonplaces of modern media culture disappear. The humanist subject is destabilized, revealing a self that is endlessly refashioned, that merges with technology to create a "cyborg"; the play of signifiers displaces dialectical social patterns, creating a highly unstable and unpredictable social world; epistemological categories collapse, allowing the convergence of phenomena once thought irreconcilable, such as silicon and consciousness in the form of AI; representation is foregone in favour of a rhetorical and performative model of language that's given up on finding truth in an opaque world; metanarratives like Christianity and socialism fracture into shards of culture like so much colourful broken glass; cultural difference is allowed full expression once it's free of such grand explanatory frameworks; and Marx's mode of production is displaced in favour of Poster's signature concept, the "mode of information." The magnitude of these changes means that the coming world will be unrecognizable, and in Poster's view, the modern preference for models of discursive communities full of chatty rational subjects is no longer viable: "The mode of information betokens a restructuring of language so drastic that the figure of the subject that it will constitute cannot readily be discerned. Relations of mind to body, person to person, humanity to nature are undergoing such profound reconfiguration that images of community are presented if at all only in science fiction books and films" (Poster 1995:52).

By the term "mode of information," Poster offers a means of characterizing historical process by the medium of communication that prevails in a particular period, demarcating cultural history according to successive oral, print, and electronic phases. Obviously, Poster here displaces the Marxist "mode of production" concept, by which Marx condensed the meaning of a whole epoch as something reflected in the economic model (slavery, feudalism, capitalism, etc.) dominant at a given time. In a post-structuralist variation on Bell's post-industrial vista, history *is* information, because every medium throughout time has structured certain kinds of relationships between subject, culture, and the world outside. Poster's signature concept highlights the fact that each phase "may be periodized by variations in the structure...of symbolic exchange," represents "an analytically autonomous realm of experience," and denotes the fetishistic attention granted information in contemporary culture (Poster 1990:6, 8).

What is exceptional about digital media in Poster's view is the fact that language is no longer a medium or even a structure within which other more material entities (i.e., subjects, technologies, and referents) are located. Rather, language is everything. Digital media, by allowing the user to entirely immerse him or herself in a linguistically constructed world, are the best example of this effect Poster calls the "wrapping of language." That is, language is no longer a means to represent the outside world but, according to the self-referential logic of simulation, so saturates the world that the real is no longer mediated. Although this is most evident in virtual reality and the World Wide Web, newer technologies (such as digital text messaging and the coming third generation or "3G" mobile broadband Internet revolution) "wrap" reality up in language far more tightly still. The medium is therefore the message to a degree even McLuhan didn't anticipate. Media theory in this recognizably post-structuralist mode dedicates itself to tracing patterns within the liquid perimeters of discourse alone—in "an unavoidable context of discursive totalization" in which the real has disappeared behind a diaphanous curtain (1990:6). Poster continues: "In the mode of information it becomes increasingly difficult, or even pointless, for the subject to distinguish a 'real' existing 'behind' the flow of signifiers" (1990:15).

As Poster sees it, modern theorists like Adorno and Marcuse were mistaken in their assumption that the subject, living under the sheer weight of instrumental rationality, could no longer be regarded as a free being. Their assumption made for a static, ahistorical, and highly vulnerable self. Poster rejects what he believes to be the Frankfurt School's binary model of the human (i.e., either rational and whole, or abjectly subordinated) for one that allows, under the influence of digital mediation and postmodern conditions, that the subject is still present and accounted for. In dropping the binary subject, the problem of instrumental rationality is also made analytically redundant, since technology and the subject are no longer deemed incompatible.[9]

For too long, Poster argues, modern media theory has been preoccupied with the problem of the "stalled dialectic." This Frankfurt School notion that historical change (tending ideally toward a utopian future) can be halted by instrumental rationality, depends, however, on an artificial separation of technology and culture. In light of the linguistic dissolution of reality into one non-dialectical whole, technology, culture, and other elements in society take up highly mutable relations to each other of a kind not readily captured in the dialectic model. The production metaphor so central to Marxist and neo-Marxist thought must yield to a reality where the philosophical basis for materialism has disappeared. It is a reality Baudrillard describes as "the narcissistic and protean era of connections, contact, contiguity, feedback and generalized interface that goes with the universe of communication" (1983:127).

A society defined by the circulation of information, though no post-industrial utopia, suggests an end to the authoritarian top-down politics of the broadcast model of mass media. It favours instead a decentralized system of multiple producers, distributors, and consumers—a "global village" closer to the disorganized "sprawl" of William Gibson's cyberpunk fiction than to McLuhan's ideal. Domination now exists in a lack of information. Poster defines domination as that condition whereby we are denied knowledge of the terms by which the self is constituted in a world of discourse. Without the means and know-how to make ourselves in a culture of otherwise abundant information and technology, we are not free.

That is, domination is not exercised through the limits placed on a subject's autonomy from external sources, since nothing can be said to be "external" any longer. Rather, it is a function of the subject's failure to recognize the grounds of her or his social constitution as a subject, an ignorance enforced by power. Emancipation is consequently a process whereby "subjects recognize that they are constituted and that they may, with the proper mediations of others, reconstitute themselves and their world so that subject constitution becomes its designated goal and social end" (Poster 1995:11). Social change, albeit defined in these highly individualistic terms, is a matter of better communication.[10]

A ROMANTIC READING OF POST-STRUCTURALISM

The romantic critique of Poster's post-structuralism begins on familiar terms: the straw man of Enlightenment modernity. For Poster, the new media produce a culture so identified with the instability of the signifier, the self, and of fundamental categories that they are outside the "Enlightenment opposition of reason and the irrational" (1995:16). This makes these phenomena all but inscrutable to modern critical theories, given their rationalism, since the fluid nature of contemporary media and culture simply overwhelms any truth-seeking of a conventional kind. Poster addresses cultural studies—its origins in the Western Marxism of Gramsci, Lukács, and the Frankfurt School of which he speaks directly here—and its limitations: "The theoretical tendency of Western Marxism has been to approach the question of a politically stabilized modernity from orientations themselves far too rooted in modernity and its communication technologies. Like modern thinkers since Descartes, they attempt to establish an atemporal or universal foundation for theory which usually takes the form of some definition of the human" (1995:73).

If post-structuralists tend to identify modernity with an overdeveloped rationality typical of the Enlightenment, they ally themselves with the irrational and the romantic. This alliance is aided by the neo-Marxist habit of disavowing anything romantic (with the obvious exceptions of Thompson and Williams here), or indeed, broadly departing from rationalism. Again, Poster confirms the persistence of the romantic stereotype, and the advantage and comfort post-structuralists find in such a characterization.

However, the relationship of post-structuralism to romanticism goes much further back to the very origins of the post-structuralist project in the work of Friedrich Nietzsche. To understand how the romantic is appropriated by post-structuralism, and thereby made available to media theorists in that tradition, it's useful to compare the standard post-structuralist incorporation of Nietzsche, the famous Habermasian criticism of that incorporation, and a third "romantic" interpretation of Nietzsche's intervention.[11]

The standard account is adequately represented in the work of Azade Seyhan. For her, Nietzsche is the source of many of the basic premises of post-structuralism and postmodernism. These include their disregard for foundations and essences, skepticism toward Enlightenment notions of reason and truth, lack of faith in metanarratives, etc. But Nietzsche is far more than the author of these contrarian principles: he is the ultimate broker for early German romanticism as it speaks to the twentieth century. "Nietzsche is an important figure of transition, for he is a reluctant heir to Romantic idealism yet represents in full measure the paradoxical and ironic vision of early Romanticism" (Seyhan 1992:136-37). Nietzsche draws upon a number of defining early romantic themes, including aestheticism, anti-philistinism, the embrace of difference, the search for a new mythology, and the interest in Greek ideas of art and culture, then develops these into "a preamble to post-structuralist criticism" (Seyhan 1992:137).

Chief among Nietzsche's post-structuralist propositions is his belief that there is no metaphysical basis to the terms by which we know and organize the world intellectually, except for the brute assertion of the "will to power." Knowledge, as elaborated later by Michel Foucault, is not really about discovering truth, but is a means of defining human nature and the social world to control them to our advantage. The romantic contribution to the "will to power" thesis is the romantic criticism of metaphysics as fiction. Metaphysics are evidence of the mind trying to cope with the sheer uncertainty of existence by overlaying it with self-deceiving philosophical premises, and building a culture—an Apollonian world of appearances and illusions—on the quicksand of the Dionysian will and appetite. For Nietzsche then, reason, the crown of the Enlightenment, is therefore just a sophisticated form of metaphysical violence.

In this line of thought, all language must be then considered "aesthetic" in nature because, lacking any access to an intellectual foundation, the world's meaning is entirely in play. At best, we can draw ourselves pictures of the world, but these can make no claim to any kind of representational veracity, though we retain our sanity by collectively forgetting that knowledge is metaphorical and the world unknowable. "The understanding that joins

Nietzsche with his Romantic forebears is the realization that there is no mino-
taur of dictatorial truth at the center of the labyrinth, but rather an energetic
and restless inquiry consistent with the desire to face the flux of becoming"
(Seyhan 1992:140).

Habermas's account of Nietzsche's reltionship to romanticism, as discussed
in Habermas's essay "The Entry into Postmodernity: Nietzsche as a Turning
Point" (Habermas 1987), is as insightful as it is problematic for a project concerned to use romanticism as a contemporary critical tool. For Habermas,
Nietzsche represents the first major philosopher to refuse to confront the
dialectic of Enlightenment—the rationalizing disenchantment of the world
effected by bringing reason to bear on it. Beginning with Hegel, then the idealist Schelling and the romantic Friedrich Schlegel, a long line of German
(and other) philosophers, social theorists, and theologians sought to find
some means to put the shattered modern world back together again. With
each attempt, intellectual confidence at restoring wholeness to modernity
ebbs, so that by the romantic period Schlegel tenuously offers the aesthetic
alone as a faculty that might create a new mythology for modern humankind.

Nietzsche, the ultimate naysayer, "renounces a renewed revision of the
concept of reason and *bids farewell* to the program of an intrinsic dialectic of
Enlightenment" (Habermas 1987:86). Like the post-industrialists and post-
structuralists who would follow him, Nietzsche's decision to drop out of the
modern project means that modernity's singular nature must be reduced and
subjected to a "conspicuous levelling," and the epoch made to seem a passing
phase in cultural history. Modernity is thus characterized as the last moment
in "the far-reaching history of a rationalization initiated by the dissolution of
archaic life and the collapse of myth" (Habermas 1987:87).

Nietzsche argues that a new culture can be created only in a future *after*
modernity. Modernity's progressive and linear sense of time forbids a return to
the mythos of pre-rational humanity, and thus we must look to the future after
modernity in order that a new mythology be built. "Only the future constitutes the horizon for the arousal of mythical pasts," writes Habermas of
Nietzsche's vision (1987:87), a future where the will to power is taken as the
only motive force once everyone has awakened from the sleep of reason. The
future thus retrieves a pre-modern past, gloriously alive to the expression of a
primitive human nature and which, unlike the modern world, does not dress
up its savagery in polite debate or scientific rationale.

The romantic conception of language as aesthetic in nature—albeit an aesthetic function with some capacity to connect with the real—is the condition
then of Nietzsche's categorical break with reality. Nietzsche's aesthetic, however, means the negation of the romantic heritage in Habermas's view, an

observation that no doubt contributes to its poor reputation among critical and progressive theorists. Both romanticism and Nietzsche embraced the trope of the Greek man-god Dionysus as the personification of non-rationality. However, argues Habermas, where Dionysus was for the romantics a Christ-like figure whose non-rationality would ultimately rejuvenate Western society, Nietzsche defined him as the avatar of an anti-metaphysics that would guarantee the very impossibility of the "social" in any meaningful form and the utter loss of self. In other words, "this identification of the frenzied wine-god with the Christian saviour-god is only possible because Romantic messianism aimed at a *rejuvenation* of, but not a departure from, the West. The new mythology was supposed to restore a lost solidarity but not reject the emancipation that the separation from the primordial mythical forces also brought about for the individual as individuated in the presence of the One God" (Habermas 1987:92).

With that passage, Habermas identifies early German romanticism as an unwilling accomplice in post-structuralism's emergence. He also implies that romanticism's political credentials are questionable insofar as romanticism isolates the aesthetic sphere from reference to the moral and the rational. This opinion is made more explicit in Habermas's essay, "Modernity: An Incomplete Project" (Habermas 1993), where romanticism's aesthetic project is held to lead to the aesthetic-political movements of the late nineteenth and early twentieth century, e.g., futurism, expressionism, surrealism (a connection this essay endorses), and those movements to the postmodern (a connection it doesn't). Habermas claims that, "in the course of the nineteenth century, there emerged out of this romantic spirit that radicalized consciousness of modernity which freed itself from all specific historical ties" (1993:99). Moreover, and pointedly, reification can be solved, in his view, only if the separate parts of the human sensibility are reunited, a solution he shares with Williams. That is, "a reified everyday praxis can be cured only by creating unconstrained interaction of the cognitive with the moral-practical and the aesthetic-expressive elements. Reification cannot be overcome by forcing just one of those highly stylized cultural spheres to open up and become more accessible" (1993:105).

With all due respect to Habermas's brilliant analysis of communicative rationality and the ideal speech situation in which this reunification of human sensibility is to occur, we would have to wait a long time indeed for this program to solve the crises we face. A different perspective on romanticism yields a glimpse of a project at once more realistic and more attainable than the one Habermas proposes, if not quite so wholesome.

Early romanticism is not intrinsically committed to the Western project, if we take its radicalism and present adaptability as given. True, its founders had faith in the French Revolution, a supreme precedent in the development of Western politics and culture. However, the Western project is currently defined in neo-conservative and neo-liberal terms, and faced with arguments from the likes of anti-globalization activists and queer theorists, it's difficult to believe that such a project, pending its release from neo-conservatives, would be recognizable to Habermas. It is similarly difficult to believe that critical reason can deliver us from the dialectic of Enlightenment, however digitally enhanced, given the permanent fact of uncertainty, difference, and a reality that has perhaps become too large and complex to be interpreted in rationalist terms.

Rather than lump romanticism with Nietzsche's awful fate, Bowie argues that a careful distinction needs to be made between Nietzsche's rejection of metaphysics (substituting power instead), and a romantic epistemology (one hesitates to call it a metaphysic) where, though foundations are logically impossible, the search for these foundations is taken to be progressive and necessary. Bowie claims:

> As is well known, Nietzsche will later, not least via the influence of Romanticism, ask what *value* truth possesses, thereby attempting to undermine the idea that truth *qua* representation of a ready-made world could ever be grounded. Nietzsche's questioning has had a decisive influence on subsequent discussions of the "end of metaphysics" in contemporary literary theory. The Romantic understanding of truth both prefigures Nietzsche's question and implies that any determinate answer to it, for example, in terms of power as the ground of truth, fails to understand the real nature of truth. (Bowie 1997:72)

If the romantic "ground" is always shifting, always refusing the infinite regress of trying to find proof for one's metaphysical origins by reference to those same origins, Nietzsche, for all his philosophical bluster, is no different. He is forced to argue for the validity of his own claims while denying that there is any ground for truth—another performative contradiction in Bowie's view (1997:182). By positing a future where myth is to be made, outside modernity and outside history, Nietzsche allows those grand contemporary myth-making projects—post-industrialism and post-structuralism—just the room they need. No wonder that functionalism and post-structuralism are so attracted to new media, since these media provide the very ideological conditions necessary to follow Nietzsche into the future he defined.

We can accept that truth is difficult to have and to hold, and is not always accessible in mere rational terms. But rather than allow the intransigent nature of truth to persuade us to accept Nietzsche's claim that every act of communication is an exercise of the will to power, we can follow Bowie and the romantics in believing that truth is "at least potentially present in *any* kind of communicative act in relation to another person" (1997:189). To paraphrase the *X-Files*, maybe the truth is not "out there" but we can trust "someone" with whom we can discover it together in the act of communication.

We may live in a world subject to digitally accelerated reification and instrumental rationality, but that fact does not require that we give up on the difficult work of finding mutual accommodation for ourselves and our machines. But the technological pastoral of Bell (and the neo-functionalists) or Poster is a sophisticated "second nature," an unreal world of media-delivered enchantment that leaves us still more vulnerable to the characteristic problem of modernity. They declare modernity over and the victory against instrumental rationality consequently won.

Whether this vision of technological humanity takes the form of ads for cell phones celebrating our new mobility (while ignoring the panoptic consequences of constantly being "in touch" with head office), or for video games promising us ever greater mastery over virtual worlds (while neglecting the lessons of simulacrum), the appropriation of romance by post-industrialism and post-structuralism allows both positions freedom from actually wresting the world from instrumental reason, even as we try to live with its most powerful technological agents. As Leo Marx indicated earlier, "new symbols of possibility" are needed, and the tenets of early German romanticism are a resource that warrants a little of what's left of our attention spans.

So as promised, it is to a positive and romantic criticism of contemporary media and culture, using new media as a case study, that I now turn.

Chapter 5

Information Wants to Be Free

A ROMANTIC APPROACH TO NEW MEDIA

I find certain older structures stubbornly trying to reassert themselves in a technosocial milieu that to them seems to have gone berserk. These are the structures of individual caring, love, and perhaps most poignant, of desire.

—Allucquere Rosanne Stone, *The War of Desire and Technology at the Close of the Mechanical Age*, 36.

CULTURAL STUDIES AND THE NEW MEDIA

Cultural studies, given Raymond Williams's feeling for the Welsh countryside and Birmingham's gritty Midlands locale, has a sustained relationship with place. In the imaginary landscape of early works by Williams, Thompson, and Hall, pastoral imagery abuts on working class rowhouses and the "candy floss" culture of urban modernity. The distance from this moral landscape to the bodiless spaces of contemporary media environments is long; the journey between them is complicated by how rooted many of those concepts and categories dearest to cultural studies are, whatever the national tradition in question. Making cultural studies a more productive source for thinking about media today requires that many of its conventional assumptions about subjectivity, technology, communication, social totality, and the nature of culture be revised to suit a society that moves at the speed of light.

But no matter how ephemeral the environment, romanticism is, to borrow a phrase from a classic Japanese animé, the ghost in the shell. Its themes—

Notes to chapter 5 are on pp. 182-84.

imagination, love, anachronism—resurface within a media system we often think of as cold and indifferent as metal, to establish a human presence even where bodies have disappeared. The persistence of these older structures are more remarkable given the Strangelovian origins of the Internet. The Internet first emerged in 1969 as an exclusive computer network for military scientists working on US Department of Defense projects, and was called ARPANet after its Department institutional sponsor, the Advanced Research Projects Administration. Conceived by a Defense Department-spawned research institute, the RAND Corporation, as a communications system that could survive a nuclear attack (through the network's capacity to reroute data "packets" around damaged or absent nodes in the computer network, if these were obliterated by enemy missiles), the Internet's early culture is steeped in Cold War paranoia and overkill.

Over time, as the various components of the personal computer were built, the technology began to exit the controlled mainframe networks of the military scientists and gradually enter the public sphere. This first entrance took the form of Fidonet and other prototype computer communities roughly analogous to ham radio in the mid-1980s, then to universities and homes in the early 1990s as user-friendly World Wide Web interfaces were developed.[1] In this digital form of Williams's "long revolution," the new media technology followed an old dialectical pattern of state and, particularly, military investment in research and development on the one hand, and popular resistance, appropriation, and innovation on the other.

The argument that these new media should be interpreted in the context of earlier electronic media and within modern cultural history should not detract from the compelling novel features of computers, the Internet, and virtual reality. Among these features are: the exponential growth of processing power and the miniaturization of technology; the cybernetic function, where computers, unique among other technologies, can adapt to their environments through feedback; the radical decentralization of media power possible as computer networks replace the rigidly hierarchical broadcast model, allowing for "many to many" communication; and the Internet's arguably natural resistance to ready absorption within state regulatory and market structures. The Internet recognizes censorship of the political or commercial variety as damage too, and routes around these powers just as it would a cruise missile strike. The cyberpunk credo puts it best: "information wants to be free."

Yet freeing information for theoretical, let alone political and cultural purposes, has proven difficult for media critics in the Birmingham tradition. Compared to the prolific literature favouring post-industrial and post-structuralist positions, a framework for studying new media strongly identified with cultural studies has been absent. To be sure, there have been tentative and speculative pieces by Andrew Ross, Constance Penley, Donna Haraway, Vincent Mosco, Herbert Schiller, David Morley, Frank Webster, Kevin Robins, and others, but none with the sure sense of project and self-consciousness of a Bell or a Poster. This is not to suggest that a cultural studies position on new media should be definitively developed, of course, respecting the caveats about establishing a unified analysis of anything. Rather, it is to argue that society increasingly takes its shape from these "new" media and that, without a more substantial view of digital culture, cultural studies risks becoming as obsolete as a 5^1/4-inch floppy disk.[2]

In this chapter devoted to an assessment of romanticism's value as a resource through which cultural studies might be retooled for a positive critique of media, three issues are selected from the large inventory available. They are: the nature of the on-line subject; ideas about technology and its relationship to culture; and what it means to be authentic in virtual conditions. Even though the subject matter is digital, the implications for media and cultural criticism are more general because older media are being rebuilt in binary terms (e.g., books in PDF format, high-definition television, digital telephones), and the culture itself is being re-encoded. That said, no tradition has realized better than romanticism how the products of the imagination become real, and how enchantment is possible even in systems like the new media, which are rigidly logical in character.

NEW MEDIA AND THE SUBJECT

The post-structuralist subject is purely informational when considered with reference to new media, and its being is unbearably light. Sherry Turkle claims that "when reduced to our most basic elements, we are made up, mind and body, of information" (1995:265). Jean Baudrillard (1983:129) reduces the human form to a fleshy afterthought, left within a television environment where "as soon as behaviour is crystallized on certain screens and operational terminals, what's left appears only as a large useless body, deserted and condemned." Kroker goes further, eliminating the body altogether: "Indeed, why the concern over the body today if not to emphasize the fact that the (natural) body in the postmodern condition has *already* disappeared, and what we experience today as the body is only a fantastic simulacrum of body rhetorics?" (in Probyn 1987:351). The informational nature of the body has inspired a small industry of works like David Lyon's *The Electronic Eye,* Shoshana Zuboff's *In the Age of the Smart Machine,* and Mark Poster's *The Mode of*

Information, which assume that the body is now a matter of data, and use Foucault and other primary sources in post-structuralism to examine how this corporeal information is manipulated. Although these works have their value, they tend to accept without question the dissolution of the body defined as information, a premise that worries feminists like Elspeth Probyn.

In Probyn's view, feminism has only just recently reclaimed the body from centuries of patriarchal exploitation. For post-structuralists to declare the body purely informational, vestigial, or absent in the context of new technologies is to invite the question whether postmodernism, like modernism before it, will again be built on the backs (disembodied or not) of women. In the spirit of a line paraphrased from Lawrence Grossberg—that the postmodern may be too real and too important to be left to postmodernists—Probyn argues that the body is more, not less, central to these admittedly new conditions. "If the postmodern shows us anything, it is that we now have more subjectivities than ever, that our bodies are more acutely articulated, and that a surface is only one way of reading" (Probyn 1987:357). One of the most influential of arguments about the subject and new media is Donna Haraway's "A Cyborg Manifesto: Science, Technology, and Socialist-Feminism in the Late Twentieth Century." It helps put the argument for the future of the body in a highly technological world into perspective.

Donna Haraway's celebrated essay is the most influential work of a progressive cast on technology and the subject, and her cyborg has since become one of the most popular metaphors in cultural theory. In the cyborg, half-human and half-machine, Haraway finds a happy medium between the essentialist self (where our identity as a woman or man, African or Asian, is considered nondiscursive and unchanging) and the fluidly informational body theorized by Turkle, Baudrillard, and Kroker. Cyborgs are everywhere: in the heart patient with an animal organ transplant; in the kid with the Discman listening to an MP3 music file taken from Napster and burned into a CD; and in a popular culture in which *Star Trek*'s Data and *The Matrix*'s Neo are folk heroes. The cyborg breaks down the binaries by which modern subjectivity is fashioned—self and other, white and non-white, culture and nature—and when on its best behaviour, the cyborg liberates us from their dreadful power.

Yet, while Haraway borrows from post-structuralism to fashion her argument, she does not dissolve contradiction into the electric current like Poster does. Rather, the fundamental categories that she believes are ruptured in contemporary culture (those between humans and animals, the organic and inorganic, and the physical and non-physical) maintain an important degree of tension. That is, where Poster eliminates the structure of reality itself by reducing everything to free-floating information, Haraway complicates that structure in terms appropriate to a complex world. The categories on which modernity was founded do not disappear or lose their integrity, but rather reappear in a fused and hybrid form. Haraway's cyborg is well aware of the hazards of that state of being: programming, surveillance, and a Tin Man's clock in the place of a heart. She says of the occupational hazards of the cyborg that, "the home, workplace, market, public, arena, the body itself—all can be dispersed and interfaced in nearly infinite, polymorphous ways, with large consequences for women and others—consequences that themselves are very different for different people, and which make potent oppositional and international movements difficult to imagine and essential for survival" (1991:163).

But the critical potential of Haraway's feminist cyborg, reclaimed from the ultra-masculine cyborg lore of *Robocop* and *Terminator,* does come with problems attached. Haraway's post-structuralism tends to overwhelm her good materialist intentions, leaving that materialism largely gestural. For example, in the anticlimactic conclusion of the essay, Haraway counsels that cyborg politics are best defined as cultural politics, rather than actions with specific reference to liberal democracy and capitalism. The cyborg's revolution is one organized around "the struggle for language and the struggle against perfect communication, against the one code that translates all meaning perfectly, the central dogma of phallogocentrism" (176). Given the tight integration of technology—notably communications technologies—with economic and political globalization, the lack of a more definite politics makes it dangerous to take on an identity this novel and uncertain. We risk asking for R2D2, and getting HAL or *Star Trek*'s Borg instead.

Critics of the cyborg subject have complained of Haraway's tenuous materialism, of her politics that are consequently very short on specifics. Probyn, for example, finds that "the 'historical materialism' which she rightly emphasizes as inherent in a feminist critique is vaporized in her argument" (1987: 355). There are "no strategies of how we get from here to there or there to here" (355), and therefore no tenable basis to Haraway's entire project for techno-emancipation. Dery (1996:246) charges the manifesto with being "maddeningly short on practical politics for working-class cyborgs and disappointingly long on odes to 'partiality, irony, intimacy, and perversity.'" Although Haraway's essay is aimed squarely at those who would reduce the body to pure information, her lack of materialism and political practicality weakens the articulation of body and material world. What is needed is a self neither reducible to information, nor vulnerable to essentialist definition— an action hero committed to saving the world while keeping his or her feet on the ground.

The romantic conception of the self meets these criteria. The romantic self was located in a world, similar to the post-structuralist, where binaries were deemed unworthy of the undivided nature of experience. Wheeler, for example, says of the English romantic poet and critic Percy Bysshe Shelley that "dualisms collapsed as Shelley conceived of mind/world, subject/object, thoughts/things as mere conventions, rather than independent existents passively perceived" (1993:5). Metaphor, the rhetorical trope by which unlike categories are conjoined for cultural and political purposes (as in, war is a gathering storm, love a red rose) was to the German and English romantics the primary vehicle for the active romantic mind. Mind and reality were believed part of a shared continuum, a Shelleyean "poetry of life." The reality thus formed was remarkably ecological, "the result of the primary activity of the power of imaginativeness—within and without—creating metaphors and relations which themselves form the substance of experience" (Wheeler 1993:10). If the original cyborg was Frankenstein's monster, then the romantics might be seen as pioneers in the making of recombinant beings and worlds.

But it is not enough to define the self as a relation or as something that dances at the edge of categories. A cyborg, much less a person, can't live on metaphor alone or be expected to stare into the abyss before the morning's first cup of coffee. Kant's theory of the subject unknowable to itself launched the romantic pursuit of a more tenable model of subjectivity. That is, in answer to the classical Socratic imperative to "know thyself," Kant argued that language necessarily intervenes between self and consciousness, thus limiting what we can know. The early romantic solution was to compensate for this unknowable ego with an action-oriented, ironical, and playful subject who was forever constituting both self and world. It's a solution that owes much to Kant.

That is, the permanent uncertainty that Kant introduced in the very constitution of who we are—that we cannot know ourselves completely, given the limitations of language and consciousness—frees us to play, to experiment, and to take chances. This made the experience of being and acting aesthetic in nature because the endless work of pairing the phenomenal reality inside our heads with the noumenal world outside is not altogether different from what the artist or poet does, gazing out at nature and society and finding words and pictures to match. We cross the Kantian gap by relating the ideal to the material, without having definitive knowledge of either or of how they might connect. Schiller held that "this combination of the formal and material aspects of human existence is precisely what constitutes artistic practice and experience," play and art being "the essence of human nature and the human condition" (Saiedi 1993:117). Life, yet again in that incomparable romantic way, imitates art.

Rejoicing in the contingent nature of the self is a comfortable romantic solution to the Kantian problem. Freed from self-knowledge, we are liberated from narcissism and solipsism to take action and to build a world where those parts of ourselves that we are denied direct knowledge of might be indirectly reflected in art, literature, and more mundane human products. Yet, the vacuum between consciousness and the unknowable self created in the Kantian ego leads to a desperate lack of the predictability and coherence necessary to live a life. As Lacoue-Labarthe and Nancy write, this "crisis inaugurated by the question of the subject will preoccupy Kant's successors....And romanticism, among others, will 'proceed' from it" (1988:32). Denied self-knowledge, the subject must create a system of knowledge in which to organize its experience of the world.

The logical extension of one approach to this problem of how we organize our experience in an uncertain world is the Frankfurt School's "one-dimensional" self, or later, the Althusserian "interpellated" subject or the Foucauldian subject constituted by externally imposed power/knowledge. In other words, we may not know ourselves, but we are defined readily enough by an all-knowing system, invested in secretive bureaucracies and databases, that we have ourselves created. Denied self-knowledge, we are made victims of forms of knowledge that are separated from the love of truth, and that have a scandalous affair with power.

In the romantic alternative, however, the subject is defined as the author of a living system, and the subject's very identity is invested in the organic nature of the system. This notion of the living system is what, for Lacoue-Labarthe and Nancy, separates romanticism from various forms of idealism, especially idealism that might include much of the Frankfurt School, and by definition both structuralism and post-structuralism. They write of this vital model of social totality: "The 'philosophy of Spirit' is indeed the System-subject, but it assumes this status only insofar as it is alive, as it is the *living System*—and as such, in keeping with the entire tradition of metaphysics, it is opposed to the philosophy of the letter alone (to dead philosophy) and to system as a simple 'pigeon-holing' by tables and registers" (Lacoue-Labarthe and Nancy 1988:34).

What is also valuable in being unrepresentable is that a subject who is, at some level, unknowable to her or himself is also unknowable and invisible to the system that's built on utter visibility. In other words, the romantic self is relatively immune to reification aimed at the subject because the indeterminacy granted to the system is also present in her or him. This indeterminacy is not borrowed from some essentialist model of the self arguing for the complexity of human personality. It is, rather, the property of a model of self that appeals to the obstinate fact of the mortal body, the ultimate source of our limitations, and not to some humanist nostrum. What for Descartes was an embarrassment—a lovely rational mind haunted by an unlovely irrational body—is returned as a proudly resistant, because unknowable, entity.

The one writer currently studying new media and the subject from what approximates a romantic perspective is Allucquere Rosanne Stone, a trans-gendered former male with an appropriately acute sense of identity. Stone explicitly identifies her work—most notably her essay "Will the Real Body Please Stand Up?" (Stone 1991) and her book *The War of Desire and Technology at the Close of the Mechanical Age* (1995)—with a cultural stud-ies perspective.[3] For her, the new media don't reduce the body to binary code, nor force a retrenchment in some humanist project. Rather, in terms similar to those Probyn identified, they multiply, magnify, and otherwise proclaim the importance of self and body, even as both are extended into cyberspace.

Moreover, rather than detaching self from body, Stone argues for a subtler relationship between the two given the "technosocial" nature of new media. The discursive self (i.e., born of discourse or language, and the consciousness and culture that follow) and the physical body become complex halves of a new whole, a model of the citizen as someone as much alive in cyberspace as she or he is in real life. The body then acts to "warrant" the self as it moves into cyberspace (whether this cyber-self is in a multi-user dungeon, captured in government or corporate demographic data, or writing e-mail), granting the discursive self a grounded and material nature.

The physical and the discursive self are not symmetrical: the body lan-guishes at the keyboard while the cybernetic self takes wing in the electronic ether. But a relationship built on mutual necessity remains, and the on-line Icarus is steadfastly rooted in physical presence, material need, and political economy. Stone insists that "no matter how virtual the subject may become, there is always a body attached," affirming the value of "keeping the discus-sion grounded in individual bodies" (1991:111-12). Forgetting the body, she writes, is "an old Cartesian trick," and the centrepiece of a project as old as modernity that over time has gradually isolated the body in labour and the mind in intellectual production, textuality, and most recently, electronic media. Recalling the criticisms of Haraway's vague materialism, Stone warns of the hatred of the body or "cyborg envy" that's experienced by those who would create a life of pure discourse or a body of pure information, those who are jealous of the promise of immortality there.

In a very romantic key, Stone argues that the "natural" is to be recovered in the very heart of the technological matrix, nature defined here as "diversity, flexibility, irruption." There are trickster values owed not merely to the play of discourse, but to the persistence of the physical body in this technosocial environment. If romanticism forbids categorical separation of the real from the imagined, the material from the virtual, then Stone's analysis offers a theoretical solution to the absent materialism in Haraway's work. That's because language is nature in the romantic universe: "language...must be seen as another aspect of a nature which can only ever be understood by the recombination of its elements" (Bowie 1997:73). Cyberspace is in this sense a twenty-first century extension of the world of the imagination that the romantics believed was our everyday reality. In recognizing the need to have the on-line self "warranted" by a warm body, and in accepting that a linguistically constituted cyberspace is natural, we technoromantics find ourselves strangely at home in these new environments.

And yet unlike the more nihilistic post-structuralisms, Stone's technosocial thesis declares valid the search for an epistemological foundation. The post-structuralist cyborg lifts its bionic arm and points to a future that is perpetually deconstructed. By comparison, the technosocial self, with a physical self to feed and shelter, and wracked by the constant tension between body and mind, must work for foundation, however vainly. In this work, the ancient structures of desire, memory, and hope assert themselves, as we seek to historicize and humanize technologies of apparent terrifying novelty. Stone's work offers the most reliable and arguably romantic means to making cyberspace, if not the English Midlands, a real place nonetheless.

NEW MEDIA AND TECHNOLOGY

It was ironic that it fell to Raymond Williams to do much of British cultural studies' thinking about technology, particularly in critical response to the effects school's technological determinism.[4] In Williams's work, from his mid-career *Television: Technology and Cultural Form* to his posthumously published essays on technology and culture, technology remains one of the few social facts not numbered in his famously inclusive definition of culture. This academic elder statesman's policy toward technology remained remarkably consistent throughout his career, even as he began to soften and broaden his preference for bounded, place-specific models of culture. Although the issue of technology was important enough for him to devote some of his last essays to, Williams was unwavering.[5]

For Williams, technology was a secondary phenomenon, an instrument by which a technocratic elite might better extend its will over modern society. In Walter Lippmann's famous phrase, elites engineered hegemonic consensus by bringing the ideologically correct "world outside and the pictures in our heads," thereby compensating for the loss of organic culture that modernity's "mobile privatization" had wrought (Lippman 1922). Yet for Williams, technology neither imparted anything to culture nor could itself be considered a cultural form (a categorical distinction implied by the title of his book on television). Rather, technology was cynically inserted into culture where necessary and its articulation was shaped by already existing ideologies and structures; in short, technology added nothing to the culture that was not already present. The following passage from "Culture and Technology" is a representative and late statement of Williams's position, and affirms the stand taken more definitively in *Television: Technology and Cultural Form*:

> Virtually all technical study and experiment are undertaken within already existing social relations and cultural forms, typically for purposes that are already in general foreseen. Moreover, a technical invention as such has comparatively little social significance. It is only when it is selected for investment towards production, and when it is consciously developed for particular social uses—that is, when it moves from being a technical invention to what can be called an available *technology*—that the general significance begins. (1989:120)

The logic of Williams's culturalism regards as potentially deterministic and threatening anything that does not sit comfortably within the non-dialectical pattern of relationships characteristic of his view of culture. There is really no distinguishing something like technology, which has determining properties or a degree of autonomy, from something that monocausally constructs everything in its path. As Hall notes in his essay "Cultural Studies: Two Paradigms," culturalism suffers from a kind of "radical interactionism," which he defines as "the interaction of all practices in and within one another, skirting the problem of determinacy" (1980a:36).

Moreover, Williams's analysis lends itself to an instrumentalism that credits human agency with too much power relative to other factors, such as technology. While Williams's challenge to technological determinism is highly creditable, his view of technology's relationship to culture finds that culture's victory is too complete and, perhaps, suspect. This ready demonization of technology means that media scholarship in the British tradition tends to move facilely "from an intention/needs analysis to an evil intention/artificial needs analysis, in studies of how a class-based society allows media oligarchists to construct ideologies able to lock the masses into hegemonic structures of domination" (Gronbeck 1990:4).

There is organicism of the settled and unadaptive variety such as Williams's, and there is the more vital and inclusive form, defined by his romantic ancestors, that does not reduce difference. In the romantic conception of the organic, there may be modern means to formulate an alternative conception of culture that includes technology within it rather than abandoning it to that which is not culture—a theory of *technoculture*. As the editors of a volume on cultural studies, science, and technology argue, "perhaps the most effective category for problematizing culture—and for the study of it—is technology" (Aronowitz and Menser 1996:21). Though definitions are rare in the several references to technoculture in the cultural studies literature, "media culture is thus a form of technoculture that merges culture and technology in new forms and configurations, producing new types of societies in which media and technology become organizing principles" (Kellner 1995:2).

This is not to imply that technoculture is of Birmingham vintage. But early concepts of "technoculture" tended toward grand and often oppressive edicts on the "culture industry" and the "medium is the message." While the Frankfurt or Toronto schools might be reckoned, against Williams's isolation of technology from culture, as prior variations on the technoculture theme, both posited a relationship between culture and technology that limited scope for technology criticism. In place of these early attempts that stressed the *formal* properties of technology is a welcome if still underdeveloped working out of the meaningful *content* of technoculture.

The contemporary shift from defining technology's relationship to culture as one of form to content is assisted by the fact that the computer codes or software on which new media depend are both forms of language (or cultural in character), and yet as intrinsically technological as the monitor, the chip, or the wiring within. Andrew Ross is one critic who acknowledges how language is a form of technology. In his introduction to the co-edited *Technoculture*, and in his own text *Strange Weather*, Ross breaks with the formal definitions of technoculture. Technologies are more than devices by which culture is filtered and pasteurized, or given a new scale: they are "intentional linguistic processes" (Ross 1991:3). Both *Technoculture* and *Strange Weather* are devoted to investigating alternative techno-subcultures, such as teenage hackers, cyberpunk afficionados, and New Age devotees, in order to recover their dissident means of reading science and technology against the establishment tradition of Big Science. Ross stresses the cultural, content-oriented character of technology: "However remote, impersonal or alienating these processes are, technologies are also fully lived and experienced in our daily actions and practices, and that is why it is important to understand technology not as a mechanical imposition on our lives but as a fully cultural process, soaked through with social meaning that only makes sense in the context of familiar kinds of behaviour" (1991:3).

Aronowitz and Menser's introduction to the edited volume *Technoscience and Cyberculture* provides a more programmatic analysis of cultural studies' responsibilities to technology and culture. For them, a cultural studies of technology has as its number one task the critique of technological determinism. The second task of cultural studies is then to offer a theoretical alternative to determinism; and the authors oblige by outlining just what such an alternative might be, calling it the theory of "complexity." By "complexity," Aronowitz and Menser (acknowledging their debt to Donna Haraway) mean the real permeability of fundamental cultural categories to each other—human/animal, machine/human, culture/nature—which cybernetic technologies underline and explode still further. Computer-mediated communications and other information technologies "employ and engage human beings and nature in such a manner that a continuity among the three arises that prevents any essentialist isolation of one from the other" (Aronowitz and Menser 1996:21).

Using romanticism to build upon their theory of complexity must begin with a little demythologizing. Because romanticism and technology are customarily thought to be opposites, this antagonism is frequently captured in the romantic character of Luddism.[6] Visions of displaced workers breaking machines in industrial England in the name of the apocryphal Ned Ludd, or contemporary activists going "back to the land" and espousing voluntary simplicity, are common features of the progressive response to technology. Such Luddism has been both a conventional form of technological criticism for theorists and activists, as well as one of the few admitted romantic tendencies in neo-Marxist theory and practice. Clive Thompson speaks to this rage against the machine "among conventional lefties," insofar as "the Net revolution has provoked more fear and denial than anything else." Progressives are "used to seeing technology as evil—destroying jobs, alienating women, and generally being a playground for young white boyz" (C. Thompson 1995:14).

Sale (1995:17) makes the connection between romanticism and Luddism clear: "Another expression of a Luddistic kind, also contemporary with the Luddites, was Romanticism, beginning with Blake and Wordsworth and Byron particularly, who like the machine breakers were repulsed by the Satanic mills and the getting-and-spending of the present and like them were mindful of the ruined paradise of the past." But the neo-Luddites of today differ from those stricken weavers of old in that they oppose the entire technological system, not merely isolated instances of it. The threat of technology is its "instrinsic aspect" that "affects what happens regardless of who uses them or with what benign purposes" (Sale 1995:256). The ultimate effect of the "intrinsic aspect" of technology is that it embeds itself deeply into the life of the user, and makes her or him another tragic cog in the works.

The technophobic aspect of the cruder forms of Luddism, and the romantic associations in those crude forms, point to a deeper antinomy thought to exist between romanticism and technology. Romanticism seems to be concerned for nature, the irrational, and the exotic, while technology is identified with the systematic expression of rationality and the domination of nature in the name of mundane control. Bowie confirms the cliched nature of this supposed antagonism, claiming that "romanticism and technology are often regarded as inherently at odds with each other, one supposedly relying upon a desire to get in touch with a nature in us and outside us which the modern 'technologized' world risks losing sight of altogether, the other upon the domination of external nature for human purposes" (Bowie 1995:5). Technology is depicted as singlemindedly rational, while romanticism is indifferent to reason or otherwise irrational in character (Ong 1971:279).

But the antithesis of technology and romanticism is illusory, and the assumption that this opposition exists is a conceit with dire consequences for theory's critical effectiveness. The romantic poetic "was the poetic of the technological age...romanticism and technology can be seen to grow out of the same ground" (Ong 1971:279). The reader may well ask, given the reputation of romanticism for Luddism, how then are romanticism and technology compatible? And is there a middle ground between Williams's dismissal of any "intrinsic aspect" to technology, and Sale's neo-Luddite identification of this intrinsic aspect with much that is intolerable in contemporary society?

Walter Ong argues in his essay "Romantic Difference and the Poetics of Technology" that the conventional opposition in cultural history between the neoclassical era of Pope, Johnson, and Swift, a period exemplary of Enlightenment values, and the succeeding romantic era, is not all that consequential. Much more significant is the opposition between thousands of years of oral culture, deeply invested in what he terms the "commonplace" tradition in rhetoric, and the romantic movement. Ong refers to the necessity, within preliterate oral culture, of developing verbal formulae (e.g., rhyme and metre, fixed epithets, stock phrases) in order to preserve historical experience in the absence of a written literature. "Commonplaces" are these verbal formulae.

Even with the advent of phonetic written languages, oral culture persisted in the self-conscious rhetorical character of Greek, Sanskrit, and most importantly for the West, Latin. Until the advent of mechanical type press technology in the 1450s, the cultural conservatism of oral culture remained at the core of medieval Latinate intellectual society. The result was relatively slow growth in the accumulation of knowledge, and a paralyzing inhibition about learning more of the unknown world. Writers, for example, would refer to Latin "commonplace" indexes and choose conventional phrases endorsed by Greek and Roman stylists, studding their texts with such boilerplate rather than articulating their own experience.

Gutenberg's revolutionary technology, and the mass production of relatively inexpensive reading material in vernacular languages, would revolutionize society (a process, of course, ably chronicled by Elizabeth Eisenstein and Benedict Anderson). But as Ong demonstrates, this revolution was intimately involved with romanticism. Coming some three centuries after the invention of the mechanical press, romanticism was the mature cultural expression of the cumulative effects of Gutenberg's breakthrough. Print technology allowed for an unprecedented capacity to compress, organize, and store data far superior to human memory. Ong writes of the relationship between this quantum leap in processing power and romanticism: "Technology uses the abundance [of new information stored efficiently in mass volume] for practical purposes. Romanticism uses it for assurance and as a springboard to another world" (1971:279). The romantic movement's intellectual courage and appetite for novelty is the sign of the confidence of a European culture newly able to confront the unknown directly. As Gutenberg's press radicalized the means by which knowledge was stored, romanticism offered moral direction to this formerly conservative civilization, gesturing wildly to real and theoretical places never before dreamt of:

> Romanticism and technology...are mirror images of each other, both being products of man's dominance over nature and of the noetic [i.e., of or involving reason] abundance which had been created by chirographic and typographic techniques of storing and retrieving knowledge and which had made this dominance over nature possible. The atrophy of the commonplaces of discourse...is simply one of the more spectacular signs of the attenuation or etiolation of the massive and venerable old oral noetic economy in the face of technological development reflected and furthered by the evolution of communications media. (Ong 1971:264)

Romanticism's anti-foundationalist epistemology provides a basis for a very different definition of technology. Because no final metaphysical ground for truth is allowed in romantic philosophy, technology is not (as with the Frankfurt School) necessarily the agent by which a fixed and determinate world is established. Technology is rather a matter of art, not empirical science. Certain hermeneutically derived ideas about the nature of reality are entertained, and technology—whether a language, a hammer, or a Palm

Pilot—is used to act on reality while guided by these ideas. But the sheer tentativeness and contingency of this action recommends that technology be seen not as the medium for some anti-dialectical power, but rather as the extension of subjects creatively reworking the mental and material contexts of their lives. The problem of instrumental rationality is not foregone, it's just that the conventional rendering of the dialectic of Enlightenment typically ignores romanticism's capacity to interrupt just this kind of narrative. Anti-teleological, anti-dialectical, and critical of the dualistic separation of subject and object that dogs Enlightenment epistemology, the romantic theory of technology is a cause for optimism.

The extent of determinacy permitted by the romantic theory of technology is described by Kant's concept of "schematism." Following on Kant's argument that our knowledge of reality-in-itself is necessarily circumscribed by the cognitive limits inherent in consciousness, the limits of what we can know of reality are captured in "schemata." These basic assumptions about the nature of the noumena, though not objectively valid, are as close to objectivity as Kant's philosophy allows. The schemata are three in number: that even as the appearance of a phenomenon changes, its essence remains; that cause and effect logic applies in reality; and that elements which coexist in space take part in some form of reciprocal relationship. The alternative to "schemata" is a thoroughgoing Humean skepticism, where any attempt to conceptually transcend the bloom and buzz of experience is taken to belie that experience's empirical basis.[7]

Schematism is the aspect of judgement which is spared the infinite regress that romanticism argues must follow on any attempt to construct a metaphysical foundation on which to define truth. Where each attempt to establish an unshakeable basis invites the eternal romantic question—how do you know this foundation to itself be true?—Kant recognizes that the subject can produce more lasting and definitive forms of knowledge by dint of special talent or effort on her or his part. The epistemological condition of any technological extension of ourselves, then, is this creative if exploratory intervention in material reality.[8] The basis for truth is therefore defined not as a matter of rules, but in terms of a "techne," an "art" which depends on the subject's judgement (Bowie 1995:13).

This, of course, places a considerable burden on the subject; but it is the subject's self-reflexive nature—her or his ability to interact with the environment—that defines the romantic view of things. This environmental epistemology has no definitive foundation in either subject or object, however, but is the product of the interaction between them. Mystery then enters into the most ordinary facts of everyday consciousness, and technology's role is to probe the dark places between subject and object, humanizing this space through artful exploration, not empiricism. "It is this aspect of Romantic philosophy which is most relevant to the question of technology, not a vague aversion to the damage done by science to an innocent nature" (Bowie 1995:12). Technology is thus defined as something that falls between technological determinism and Williams's characterization of it as anti-culture. Neither god nor devil, hero nor villain, it assumes a more substantial identity in technoculture.

NEW MEDIA AND "VIRTUAL COMMUNITY"

Virtual communities are "social aggregations that emerge from the Net when enough people carry on those public discussions long enough, with sufficient human feeling, to form webs of personal relationships in cyberspace" (Rheingold 1993:5). A brief history of virtual communities orders them according to four different stages, establishing a historical identity for them that pre-dates slash fiction sites and dating chatrooms by centuries: (1) textual communities from the mid-1600s onwards, organized around books, newspapers, and magazines that define "imagined communities" for their readers; (2) early electronic mass media, dating from the mid-nineteenth-century telegraph to the radio and television viewing communities in the post-World War II period, and roughly corresponding to McLuhan's "global village"; (3) early interactive computer networks from the mid-1970s to the mid-1980s, featuring text-only interfaces in bulletin-board systems (BBS), such as the famous WELL community; and (4) those contemporary virtual communities given graphic identity and easy navigation since the World Wide Web was established in 1991, the future for which is most densely imagined in William Gibson's 1984 novel, *Neuromancer* (Benedikt 1991). But it's a moot question to ask whether the communication that occurs between academics on a cultural theory mailing list, or among gamers playing an on-line version of *Quake*, is sufficiently dense and rich to constitute a genuine community.

Of the texts and arguments most often marshalled to understand the relationship of communication to place, Habermas's "public sphere" concept is probably the most influential. The public sphere, of course, is the social and communicative space which Habermas argued was opened at the origins of modernity in the early eighteenth century, making possible the emergence of liberal public opinion through then new daily newspapers and magazines, lending libraries, and salons. This space formally closed in the 1870s as commercial and state pressure commercialized and regulated it, but it has become an ideal type against which contemporary media discourse and institutions are judged for their capacity to sustain democratic discourse.[9]

Habermas's signature concept (though it dates to early in his career) is commonly invoked as an antidote to Foucault's equation of discourse with power. McGuigan, for example, argues that after Habermas "what is contentious...is the claim that power and discourse are identical, of the very same coin" (1996:177). Discourse for Habermas, under certain conditions, is inherently democratizing, taking advantage of the dialectical nature of oral conversation appreciated by the Greeks, and documented by Jack Goody, Harold Innis, and Walter Ong in their studies of pre-literate communities and orality. The public sphere is primarily characterized by rational discourse, and under media conditions that optimally recreate the "ideal speech situation," the Habermasian concept that upholds interpersonal communication as the highest, most genuine form of interaction. If public discourse is not faked the way it is in talk shows, consumer surveys, and the instant plebiscites that are featured at many web sites (a degenerative process tending to what Habermas called the refeudalization of the public sphere), the public sphere is recoverable. Given the influence of Frankfurt School critical theory on his work, Habermas believes the general problem afflicting public discourse to be instrumental rationality, which acts to "colonize the life world" or that ideologically resistant space of interpersonal "communicative action."

Progressive media and cultural critics have frequently resorted to Habermas's public sphere concept as an analytical tool and moral object lesson. There is obvious, even romantic, appeal for intellectuals in the public sphere argument's advocacy of vigorous rational debate, and its spiritual ancestry in Socratic norms. For example, Stevenson is like many in decrying the privatization of media consumption, and the alienation of the citizen from intersubjectively mediated truth. He writes of the decline in dialogue within the public sphere (1995:50): "Unlike the print culture of the discursive bourgeois salons, much of the new media (television, film and radio) disallows the possibility of talking back and taking part." The public sphere concept, characterized as a largely informal community of discourse that underwrites the media system, education, and government, has proven to be the political horizon for much media scholarship as scholars and policy makers confront the globalization imperative. Morley and Robins confirm this, writing that "the political and social concerns of the public service era—with democracy and public life, with national culture and identity—have come to be regarded as factors inhibiting the development of new media markets" (1995:11). In their opposition to the public sphere, commercial media networks are no longer constrained by, or responsible to, a public, and define their audiences as consumers, not citizens.

The public sphere concept organizes a number of values that underwrite much media scholarship, and therein that scholarship's attitudes towards the new media. The preference for "place" over some flat and featureless media "space," for reason over other content typical of human communication, and for a liberal humanist self as the source of discourse, are values common to arguments in Habermas's name. Given this preference, application of the "public sphere" concept to new media that, among other things, allow on-line subjects to alter their identities, support the blurring of modern genres and rhetorical styles, encourage emotional display and non-rationality as readily as reasonable discourse, and erase fixed notions of local and national place in favour of generic spaces, often leads to a negative judgement of new media's authenticity and value.

This is particularly evident in popular literature on new media, since the public sphere concept is so permeable to official liberal norms for conversation, community, and country, and not least to homely appeals to the natural and the real. One could list many such books, their theses evident from their titles: Clifford Stoll's *Silicon Snakeoil*, Bill McKibben's *The Age of Missing Information*, Theodore Roszak's *The Cult of Information*, and Neil Postman's *Amusing Ourselves to Death* and *Building a Bridge to the Eighteenth Century*, among a dozen others. Although the concern for the quality of public discourse did not begin with Habermas, of course, the public sphere has gone from being an erudite concept in his *The Structural Transformation of the Public Sphere* to a staple of public and policy common sense. But his concept, and the many popularizations sympathetic to its spirit, favour a normative model of communication as something ideally transacted on direct and immediate terms.

But Habermas's public sphere may be no more than a better theorized version of Williams's knowable community, and just as vexatious. Even if, in the best of all possible worlds, electronic mass media were to be returned to majority public ownership, and the rapid privatization of cyberspace somehow stopped, it is unlikely that mass or new media could ever satisfy Habermas's criteria—if indeed they ever did. What is necessary is a more realistic view of media experience that sees hope in the much-lamented spatialization of cultural geography in late capitalism, a trend set significantly by new media. This contrary reading of the virtual community borrows from recent writing by new media critics sensitive in different ways to romantic concepts, as well as directly from the romantic literature.

The privilege granted to direct and immediate communication over more highly mediated forms, such as mass or new media, has its origins in classical Greek thought. Plato's Socrates "privileges a private and esoteric mode of communication, in which the audience is carefully selected by the speaker" (Peters 1994:124). This Socratic model can be contrasted to the broadcast model which Jesus advocates in the New Testament, where Christ "sows seeds" of meaning to whomever is available in a "radically public and exoteric mode" and the audience "sorts itself out by its responses" (124). Authentic communication in Greek thought is restricted to a few, whereas Jesus is portrayed offering a kind of love that embraces all humanity. These ancient antecedents aside, the priority of direct over mass or distributed forms of communication has distorted communication studies since, and has misled many traditions of media research organized around the problems of "mass society," "mass culture," or "civilization."[10]

We ordinarily think of the distance between sender and receiver as a "gap" that must be bridged in order for successful communication to occur. But the gap—philosophically sketched in Kant's distinction between noumena and phenomena, and iterated much later in Jacques Derrida's concept of différance—in fact allows both direct and mass (or distributed) forms of communication to be understood as similar, since both have the gap in common. No matter how intimate or alienated an act of communication, be it a lover's whisper or a World Cup telecast, the gap intrudes, making every message fraught with risk and intrigue. The gap's normality is the normality of misunderstanding, distance, and the awkward search for the right word or gesture. "The gaps at the heart of communication are not its ruin, but its distinctive feature" (Peters 1994:130).

The communicative gap therefore establishes a problem that the romantics seek not so much to solve as to live with. The powers of imagination are to be marshalled to challenge the epistemological distance between self and world without, of course, assuming that distance may be definitively breached. What is necessary, however, is that the gap be seen to operate in the context of new media. The new media intensify a pattern already established within modernity, characterized by the greater frequency of indirect social relationships, the disarticulation of voice and body, and the asynchronous and dispersed nature of time and space. Like Peters, Calhoun (1992:206) disagrees with the priority given to immediacy in communication, claiming that "such [indirect] relational structures have been neglected compared to other aspects of integration" and that communication has been "conceptualized in ways that focus on face-to-face interaction and obscure the fact that mediated relationships are still social relationships."

The introduction of new media technologies therefore does not much alter the tendency toward indirect relationships, nor represent a break with the modern. Rather, they expand and intensify these relationships, a continuity crystallized in a gap that has endured as long as human communication. Calhoun emphasizes how human patterns have endured despite technological changes, arguing that "new technologies have extended the most basic trends in social integration more often than they have countered them, and this pattern will probably continue unless substantial social effort is invested to the contrary" (1992:218). For good or ill, new media extend the pattern of indirect social relationships which classical social theory saw intrinsic to modernity's *gesellschaft* nature, and confirm that new media might be readily located in a modern episteme. Modernity, as captured in "alienation" and "anomie," is synonymous with indirect social relationships, and information technologies have greatly added to the number and presence of these formations in terms that may not be as destructive or unnatural as Habermas's public sphere metaphor suggests (Calhoun 1992:211).

Once the notion of a gap in signification is accepted as a convention of discourse, and the indirect social relationships that gap represents are seen as typical of media old and new, then the familiar correlation of communication and place is open to question. Physical proximity alone, or models like the public sphere that evaluate media cultures in terms of how close to immediacy and knowable community they come, are no longer guarantees of authenticity. The tendency to devalue "space" in favour of deeply historicized and temporally accented "places" is therefore constructively challenged. Interdisciplinary interest in space is relatively recent, as the contemporary popularity of the work of Edward Soja in theoretical geography, McKenzie Wark and Manuel Castells in media studies, and Arjun Appadurai in cultural anthropology reveals. Jody Berland describes this spatial trend:

> Both positivist and Marxist historians and sociologists...have tended to privilege historical determinations in the interpretation of society and culture, and to render spatial determinants as both static and secondary. This historicism of the theoretical imagination has permeated accounts of every type of social and cultural phenomenon in the Anglo-American and European mainstreams of academic thought. For a number of reasons, which are both historical and geographic in scope, this "bias" is now being challenged in social theory and contemporary theoretical geography. (Berland 1992:39)

Despite the neglect, cultural studies has not significantly incorporated space into its theoretical repertoire. Space's bad reputation, as evident in Harold Innis's influential description of the so-called "space bias" of print and electronic media as synonymous with the logic of capitalism, rapid cultural change, and the loss of collective memory, has made it a less than desirable concept to work with. Contemporary capitalism has given us further cause to disdain space as a helpful theme, since globalization is distinguished by the border-busting nature of capital, the elimination of time through instant communication, and the dilution of historically minded local cultures. Yet, despite the very good reasons not to want to work with space, we might see in digital media something that defines the spatial metaphor in a constructive way. In other words, the point is not merely to recover "space" as an analytical category, but to redeem it as a potentially progressive tendency in the convergent geographies of global capitalism and digital media.

Romanticism, in its love of anachronism and hatred of teleology, is already spatially disposed. To be sure, pre-romantics like Herder are responsible for the place-specific definitions of culture that underwrote the development of cultural anthropology. And post-structuralists, committed to a depthless image-world of screens and floating signifiers, have earned space a poor reputation. But in the short analytic distance between the enduring nature of the common disruptions or misfirings in communication, and the indirect, highly mediated, and unfamiliar social dimension of space, there is potential for seeing spatialization not only as necessary to a society built upon mass and new media technologies, but as a good and valuable thing. That is, community might endure in a social world where the spatial axis is dominant, though it might not be the bounded, knowable, and time-biased community of Innis, Williams, and Habermas. The negative identification of space is but one side of the story. The other, as may be seen, is available to us on romantic terms.

Poster, an exemplary post-structuralist new media critic discussed in chapter 4, defines the problem of the discursive break to offer a counterpoint to a romantic appreciation of self, gap, and space. For him, the gap as imagined in modern terms is a shaky pretext on which a rational self is constructed. From this vantage point, at a critical distance from the text or object, the self is made into the very type of the Enlightenment ego—detached and rational. The gap ensures the integrity of the self's boundaries, and is the source and guarantee of its rational nature. The "ideological force of modern Enlightenment communication theory derives in good part from this move," Poster argues (1995:60). Yet the gap, so vital to propping up the rational modern self, is also a chasm into which modern theory falls in Poster's view. Novelists like Virginia Woolf used stream of consciousness techniques to allow the reader immediate access to the writer's creative process; while the situationists, the anarchist heroes of the 1968 Paris commune, attacked the routines of everyday life through surprising acts of détournément (or the "turning around") in which they confronted society with its own disenchanted state. With these and other incursions, the gap grew unstable, and modernity was for Poster quick to follow.

The problem here is that Poster, like so many other postmodern theorists, identifies the modern with Enlightenment rationality exclusively, and does so to postmodernism's advantage. Calhoun argues that in the writing of many postmodern theorists, of which Poster is an especially talented example, "the Enlightenment is evoked as though it were the archetype of a unidimensional and uncontested modernity" (Calhoun 1993:75). Calhoun then makes room for the argument that other models of the self, and the gaps that constitute the self, are possible in terms both romantic and modern:

> The postmodernist critique...tends to equate modernity with the rationalist Enlightenment. But the Romantics were as modern and as new as the ratio-nalists....There may be an important battle between rationalist universalism and attention to the irrational, between the value of the particular and the repressive, disempowering and deceptive side of individualism. But to equate that with a battle between modernity and its putative successor is to fail to recognize how deeply a part of modernity that whole battle, that whole frame of reference is. (1993:79-80)

Calhoun invites us to see that the uncertainty which postmodern theory claims for itself is an attribute of the romantic side of modern culture. In acknowledging the modernity of chaos and complexity, Calhoun's point authorizes a romantic appreciation of the gap, itself a key source for this cultural instability.

How does a romantic view the gap and its relationship to the self? The romantic solution to the gap is to argue that the modern critical subject is not defined by her or his distance from the text. This argument makes the modern subject a straw man that Poster can easily collapse, given how conceptual categories have come to break down under the pressures of accelerated culture and hypercapitalism. Rather, the modern *romantic* subject is not so much defined by the sharp distance between subject and world, but rather as a subject that lives *inside* the gap. The gap is not a vacuum that seals the subject hermetically from text, only to collapse explosively under postmodern conditions. Rather, the gap is itself a meaning-*full* space. While the gap is categorically unbreach-able, given that definitive truth is impossible, it can expand and contract, can itself be represented in the critical imagination, and has a history and human character granted it by the innumerable crossings made by subjects. The gap is large enough to contain all our failings and misunderstandings. In fact, the gap is potentially nearly infinite in size, since it is the navigational point from which we explore social space itself. Space is the epistemological gap between mind and reality made social. This is something we often experience on-line. The gap between one person and another, manifested in their typed exchanges, is at the same time the dimensions of cyberspace itself. We are as close or as far from another person in cyberspace as is manifested in the distance between utterance and understanding. Space, as the social extension of the gap, is also then deeply human for all its strangeness, terror, and unbounded refusal to behave as "place."

Romanticism's investment in the spatial is evident from the transcendental disposition of romantic conceptions of language and reality (or better, language as reality), typically captured in the idea of "poesis." Meaning exceeds its particular location in a sign, as "every fact...is a sign whose meaning transcends the signifier" (Saiedi 1993:120), and signification proceeds through daisy chains of metaphors in terms familiar to deconstruction. Language's intertextual ambition is such that, as Friedrich Schlegel wrote in the *Athenaum Fragments* (F. Schlegel 1988:193), "it embraces everything that is purely poetic, from the greatest systems of art...to the sigh, the kiss that the poetizing child breathes forth in artless song." Poetry can moreover "hover at the midpoint...on the wings of poetic reflection, and can raise that reflection again and again to a higher power, can multiply it in an endless succession of mirrors" (Simpson 1988:193). The wilfully excessive nature of meaning in the context of romantic philosophy, like Derrida's theory of intertextuality, allows for the disembedding of meaning from the local without denying the possibility of meaning altogether. Nihilism, of course, always threatens. But the romantic solution is to keep meaning moving through space, to write as if one's very life depended on it—as it does.

The fullness of "space" is evident from Derrida's concept of "spacing." Spacing "designates the divisive, traditionally obscured gaps between things, such as the writing within speech which makes writing not a supplement to speech, but the possibility of it as articulation" (Wheeler 1993:215). Space is translated as an active phenomenon and the very pretext for différance (i.e., the constant slippage between signifier and signified, the form of the sign and its meaning). Derrida presses his case by insisting that spacing exists even within entities thought whole and complete (e.g., not between words in a sentence, but within the various elements in words themselves.) Spacing for him is the means of undoing the metaphysics of presence and intention and, as stated, space is the social elaboration of the epistemological uncertainty confirmed by the gap. "This gap, this otherness is Derrida's 'spacing' or articulation; it is the 'writing' inscribed in all speech, writing being a non-concept, the tracing, differance, iteration" (Wheeler 1993:230).

The road from "gap" to "space" spans the distance from the moment one recognizes the necessity of indeterminacy, to the next where one finds the courage to make a home there. Meaning doesn't end with the triumph of space over time, a future defined by "accentuating spatiality" (Soja in Morley and Robins 1995:28) or "the formation of a new historical relationship between space and society" (Castells in Morley and Robins 1995:29) that favours capitalism. Rather, it begins with space. Without the redemption of space—on romantic terms or otherwise—there will be little for progressive critics to say to new media which are as spatial as the capital flows they parallel, serve, and occasionally interrupt.

Morley and Robins are perhaps the most advanced new media critics, working within a cultural studies project, to rethink new media and space in positive terms. As they ask in *Spaces of Identity* (1995:38): "Can we reposition ourself in local space without falling into nostalgic sentiments of community and *Gemeinschaft?*" While short on solutions, Morley and Robins cite the neo-pragmatist Richard Rorty in arguing that we need to move from Enlightenment "objectivity" to (what can only be described as a romantic) "solidarity" in developing some working model of articulation between local and global spaces. Objectivity demanded of the Enlightenment self that s/he create distance from other people and attach her or himself to something that can be described without reference to particular human beings. In sheer rational terms, it is difficult to imagine our relationship with others living far away, and refracted through the images presented in the evening news.

However, a romantic, critical imagination built upon a solidarity that projects outward from deep, textured, and extensive relationships with real people, not distance and category, may be the only means by which the articulation of local and global might effectively be imagined. Solidarity is "referential and contextualised," yet not place-bound. The community to which one relates one's being can be "distant in time or place." The process of bonding "can occur in the context of attachment to bounded territorial locations," but "solidarity and collectivity should also have aspirations directed beyond the locality" (Morley and Robins 1995:40). It is difficult not to see here traces of the romantic call to a radical empathy, and at the very least, the possibility of taking back the very idea of territory from that jaded old rentier, capitalism.

Chapter 6

The Market in the Fallen World

CULTURAL STUDIES AND POLITICAL ECONOMY

> If the doctrine of the Fall entangles humans in each other's
> errors, the doctrine of the Market disentangles each fumbled
> attempt toward a finally concatenated good. Modern capitalism
> lives by a counter-myth to the Fall of Man—one where benign
> nature makes everything go, miraculously, right...Eden was lost
> by free choice in the Fall of Man. It rises again, unbidden, by the
> automatic engineerings of the Market.
>
> —Gary Wills, *Reagan's America: Innocents At Home*, 455

Cultural studies has often been charged with being a glittery gadfly, ambitious in pursuit of trendy exotica as various as dance club etiquette and
Japanese comic books, but unable to engage the larger ideological and structural realities of the contemporary world. To borrow from the vocabulary of
cultural studies' self-reflection, the field finds itself living dangerously
between two daunting poles. First, there is what is called "New Times": the
recognition that neo-conservatism, post-Fordism, digital media, postmodernism, the end of the Cold War, and other features of the 1980s and 1990s
mean that a new era is upon us, with dire implications for society and theory.
Second, there is "cultural populism": the habit in cultural studies of stressing
the critical potential of popular and everyday culture, such as a punk's
provocative fashions or a nightshift worker's stolen hour of sleep, at the
expense of harder questions about inequality, war, and human suffering.
Between these poles, critics have argued that cultural studies has grown too
narrowly focused on rock-and-roll radicalism while the forces of neo-liberal

---

Notes to chapter 6 are on pp. 184-85.

globalization have bought up all the record shops and, more to the point, seized control of world political economy.[1]

Borrowed from the original discipline invented in the early nineteenth century by David Ricardo, the economist who systematized Adam Smith's insights, "political economy" is a concept that recognizes that, contrary to habit, we cannot isolate something called the "economy" from issues of politics, power, and governance. Political economy began as a form of statecraft under Ricardo, who recognized that the emergent capitalist economies he observed could be directly managed by the powerful, albeit with the wise counsel of strategists like himself and Harriet Martineau. Since Marx, the term has increasingly been favoured by progressive critics who, contrary to post-Keynesian economics, refuse to treat the market as a machine innocent of human interest, ideology, or domination. It is both an academic field, as in the "political economy of communications" (which will be discussed soon), and a description of the way the world works. Kellner offers a useful definition: "The reference to the terms 'political' and 'economy' call attention to the fact that the production and distribution of culture takes place within a specific economic system, constituted by relations between the state, the economy, social institutions and practices, culture, and organizations like the media. Political economy thus encompasses economics and politics and the relations between them and the other central dimensions of society and culture" (Kellner 1997:104).

The critics say that, having separated itself from the excessive emphasis given to political economy among its Marxist and neo-Marxist predecessors, cultural studies has gone too far, and abandoned the serious study of issues like free trade and anti-terrorist laws to apologists for reckless capitalism. As the editors of a collection of essays evaluating cultural studies argue in their introduction, "the substantive issue was, and is, cultural studies' failure to deal empirically with the deep structural changes in national and global political, economic and media systems through its eschewing of economics, social or policy analysis" (Ferguson and Golding 1997:xiii).

The most credible critics of cultural studies' lack of attention to politics and economics are those scholars identified with the political economy of communications, a position invested in a more traditional Marxism. The long-standing debate between these two schools of thought over theoretical priorities and critical practices is a good place to begin reflection on romanticism's value for ending what has become an impasse more crippling than any cultural populism. Their movement was born soon after the initial publication of Smith's 1776 *The Wealth of Nations*, so the romantics were the first systematic critics of capitalism, and were sensitive to the relative autonomy of culture long before it was forgotten by true believers in the base/superstructure model. That is, romanticism is uniquely sensitive to the nature of political economy in a time when culture and capitalism converge in ways that even Marx, writing about the cannibalistic nature of commodification more than a century ago, could not have predicted.

"IS ANYBODY ELSE BORED WITH THIS DEBATE?"

The criticisms of cultural studies' difficulty with the dismal science come from inside and outside the field. Among those identifying with cultural studies: Gruneau (qtd. in Harp 1991:210) warns that "there is a significant danger that critical studies designed to seek out and analyze the wide variety of apparently popular cultural forms of resistance to hegemony will be drawn into a theoretical position that loses sight of the importance of political economy and capitalism's powerful forces of containment." Davies (1995:121) explains that both British and American cultural studies' difficulty with political economy results from their overreaction to the crude nature of the base/superstructure model, which conditioned cultural studies to neglect economics generally. Kellner (1995:53) blames the influence of postmodernism on cultural studies for the inattention to the world behind the simulacra, as well as economic illiteracy among cultural theorists. And McGuigan suggests that eliminating the economic enfeebles criticism, insofar as the material grounds for challenging power are abandoned, leaving cultural studies prone to a narcissism that grants excessive importance to trivial cultural phenomena (1992:244-45).

The charges from the rival political economy of communication position are understandably even less sympathetic. Garnham, for example, argues that cultural studies' conception of power and determination is too local and diffuse to be analytically productive, an indiscipline possible because neither concept as used is accountable to the raw facts of *realpolitik*. Cultural products also serve to justify the terms by which a society's economic wealth and inequality are reproduced, something not readily reflected by the utopian potential too carelessly credited to popular culture. Garnham also asserts the necessity of epistemological realism against cultural studies' structuralism, insisting that "discourse is capable of expressing a truth about a world external to that discourse, and further, that discourse has a determinate relation to the actions of human agents, actions about which it is possible to make normative judgements" (1990:5). In a later article (1995), Garnham complains about cultural studies' relative indifference to the priority of production. He argues that much cultural activity is not about resistance so much as everyday coping with the harsh facts of life, and cites how control over the supply and marketing of cultural commodities allows producers great influence over the terms of audience reception or the meanings attributed to texts.

Golding and Murdock (1991) argue that cultural studies doesn't understand cultural industries *as* industries, and thus it fails to adequately balance the considerable autonomy typically granted to audiences against the institutional forces aligned against them. In the most balanced review of cultural studies by a scholar of the political economy of communication, Mosco credits cultural studies with usefully criticizing positivism and persuading political economy to consider gender, culture, and race. However, in this view, cultural studies defines power too generically, failing to identify it with agents, institutions, and structures (Mosco 1996:258). And lastly, Fred Inglis, an iconoclast not easily aligned with any position, writes off the entire enterprise, complaining that "Cultural Studies, indeed, have made great play with their highly politicized and goofily partisan version of political economy, without ever showing any notable address at the subject" (1993:123-24).

Cultural studies, of course, has its own able defenders. Hall's essay, "Cultural Studies: Two Paradigms," represents perhaps the sharpest polemic against the political economy of communication. He argues that political economy makes a theoretical fetish of the cultural commodity, and reduces it to a generic object that ignores the different properties and practices that surround its use. The specificity of culture and ideology is abandoned to economic reductionism. Moreover, cultural production and consumption are analyzed at so high a level of generalization that the presence of real people engaging in particular cultural activities is lost (Hall 1986:47). Grossberg argues that the discipline's emphasis on production is insensitive to how consumers of popular texts make meaning, and how those meanings are employed to expand the scope of their freedom under capitalism. Moreover, cultural studies doesn't neglect political economy as such, according to Grossberg. It simply defines political economy differently, accenting those aspects of economy that escape the rigid Marxist terminology of profit, surplus value, exchange relationships, commodity, and exploitation (1997:9).

Others cite a greater role for political economy found in early cultural studies literature. Normally an unremitting critic of anything from Birmingham, Garnham (1995:63) maintains that cultural studies in its culturalist guise maintained fidelity with a comprehensive analysis of capitalism, an analysis taking the form of "an oppositional, broadly socialist political movement which saw the cultural struggle as part of a wider political struggle to change capitalist social relations in favour of this working class." And Kellner, singling out Hall's "Encoding/Decoding" as an exemplary case, states that "some earlier programmatic presentations of British Cultural Studies stressed the importance of a transdisciplinary approach to the study of culture that analysed its political economy, process of production and distribution, textual products, and reception by the audience" (Kellner 1997:103).

But rearguard defences and nostalgic yearning apart, the project of developing what might be called a "cultural studies of political economy" seems as far away as a tax on international capital flow. By the "cultural studies of political economy," I mean a position within cultural studies that, correcting for what has arguably been a lack of engagement with the problem, addresses capitalism at its current epic scale while still remaining "cultural." Dialogue between champions of the respective sides—among the political economists of communication principally Graham Murdock, Peter Golding, Janet Wasko, Nicholas Garnham, and Vincent Mosco, and among cultural studies critics Stuart Hall, Lawrence Grossberg, Douglas Kellner, and James Carey— has been sufficiently unproductive to lead Grossberg to title his contribution to a colloquy on the issue, "Cultural Studies vs. Political Economy: Is Anyone Else Bored with This Debate?" Over the several decades of polemic, the positions have become only entrenched and hostile, with the political economy of communication scholarship insisting on its variations on base/superstructure and Frankfurt School culture industry models, while cultural studies holds to theories filtered through other western Marxisms, structuralisms and post-structuralisms, feminism, and generally less orthodox positions.[2]

Unique in this deadlocked literature, however, are two articles devoted to reconciling culture and political economy, Harp's "Political Economy/Cultural Studies: Exploring Points of Convergence" (1991) and Kellner's "Overcoming the Divide: Cultural Studies and Political Economy" (1997). Although neither is definitive, Harp and Kellner raise questions that need to be answered; questions about how to make cultural studies relevant to a world where the market has truly become a massive metaphor and cultural system in its own right.

THE DEBATE GETS INTERESTING AGAIN

Harp's largely unheralded work offers a Canadian perspective on the debate, invoking a national tradition of political economy that is precociously aware of culture. Citing fellow Canadian Harold Innis's work as a precedent, Harp argues that political economy and cultural studies can converge to mutual benefit in the study of community. In light of Innis's "staples thesis," which argued that a culture could be interpreted in light of the staple its economy depended on (e.g., fish, fur, timber), Harp suggests that "the encounter between the local and the particular experiences of actors/individuals/subjects and the universalizing institutional structures of society is mediated by community" (1991:216).

Community, in other words, provides a conceptual common ground in which cultural studies can contribute its sensitivity to experience, and political economy its regard for the bigger picture. Against the tendency of political economy to reduce experience to an effect of class, Harp argues that cultural studies brings to the study of community its feel for the grain of subjectivity and place. But however peace-making and precedent-setting, Harp's analysis is not easily generalized above the level of community to the national or global level where economic discourse is abundantly generated. Nor does it outline the terms by which the political economy of communication and cultural studies might be negotiated intellectually, preferring to allow their potential contribution to community studies to speak for the value of convergence.

More intellectually pure and programmatic is Kellner's article. Echoing the argument in his 1995 book *Media Culture*, Kellner calls for a "multiperspectival" approach to cultural analysis. Kellner (1997:117) writes: "To avoid the one-sidedness of reception studies, I am proposing therefore that cultural studies itself be multiperspectival, getting at culture from the perspectives of political economy, text analysis and audience reception." The dichotomy of political economy of communication and cultural studies is a false one in Kellner's view, reflecting a lasting tension between social-science-driven models like "media effects" involved in institutional analysis, and textualist forms of media and cultural criticism. His preferred means of organizing a multiperspectival analysis, and reconciling institutional and interpretive forms of critique in one transdisciplinary framework, is to use Hall's "articulation" concept.

Familiar from chapter 2, where it was criticized for neglecting the properties of discourse at the expense of ideology, "articulation" is a concept more evocative than explanatory. For Hall, it offered a way of imagining how historical patterns unfold without having to resort to the language of dialectic and determination. Phenomena, such as globalization and a generation of baby boom "echo" youth, could converge and create the anti-capitalist social movement that came to life in Seattle. Where a heavy-handed dialectical analysis might seek to define how such a movement was inevitable given certain conditions, the concept of articulation is finely tuned to a reality far more contingent than imagined by Marx. Articulation thus offers a model for historical causation that does not resort to underlying laws or structures, but still is optimistic that the reasons why something happens can be explained. For Kellner, "perhaps the key concept of *articulation* could be deployed to indicate how economics and culture can be combined in doing concrete analyses"

(1997:112). In his view, media production is to be "articulated" with audience reception and textual analysis. That is, the terms whereby a given media text is interpreted are better understood when related to the structures within which they're produced (e.g., the network or studio), with both linked by how the text is consumed and by whom (e.g., a family at home, a couple at a drive-in). Once dissimilar phenomena are related conceptually through articulation, the new ensemble invites the joint "multiperspectival" effort of the several disciplines.

Although it's a timely departure from determinism, articulation remains a vague notion. Downing (1997:191), examining the concept's history and usage in the work of Grossberg and Jameson, argues that no statement regarding articulation is provided "which is not immediately thrown back into a set of unpredictably whirling conceptual dervishes, seemingly to ensure that no reader may assume the analytical game is over." Citing Grossberg's (1992:56) maddeningly generic definition of articulation as "a more active version of the concept of determination" wherein "not only does the cause have effects, but the effects themselves affect the cause, and both are themselves determined by a host of other relations," Downing (1997:191) believes that the concept needs further elaboration (and a greater degree of attention to the material, it might be added) to save it from the mad dance.

Kellner's use of articulation to bind the several perspectives into one multiple form, albeit something of a theoretical stop-gap, does lead inquiry into the relationship between culture and economy in a promising direction. While inviting many questions, articulation and multiperspectival analysis raise *very* good questions that are not yet satisfactorily addressed in this debate. Is there room for negotiation between the harder Marxist materialism favoured by political economy scholarship, and the more qualified cultural materialisms adopted in different forms by cultural studies? Is there some way to bridge the culture industry orientation of political economy and the devotion to agency, praxis, and consumption in cultural studies, or for that matter, the epistemological gap between structure and text? And finally, do post-Fordism, globalization, and the interpenetration of culture and economy in information-based capitalism call for a rationale for the "articulation" of phenomena and perspectives more definitive than Harp's "community" or Kellner's "multiperspectivism"?

Romanticism will be later seen to offer a conceptual vocabulary suitable to the convergence not only of the political economy of communication and cultural studies, but of a political economy and a culture in which information has become the ultimate commodity. First, however, it is important to understand just how the critical potential of romanticism has been diverted by the political economy of communication. For here too, as with the far more unfriendly neo-functionalists, the romantic legacy emerges in surprising and unwelcome ways.

THE POLITICAL ECONOMY OF ROMANCE

What is ironic about the debate between political economists of communication and cultural studies critics is that the former often accuse the latter of being "romantic" in nature. It's ironic because after the culturalist epics of *William Morris* and *Culture and Society*, romanticism is scarcely mentioned in cultural studies literature. McGuigan (1992:65), in a catalogue of definitions of popular culture, identifies the romantic with the "popular culture perspective from below, of which radical populism against mass culture is an instance." The nature of these references by political economists is twofold.

First, the heroic capacity of people to use culture to tilt at structure and ideology—the neo-Gramscian "active audience" with which cultural studies is so often identified—is described as "romantic." This is a mild profanity among political economists because it's used to draw attention to a model of the public that flatters its agency and is heedless of constraint. This is the standard critique of cultural populism up to a point: the symbolic solutions that cultural consumers achieve to their material problems, in their acts of bricolage and détournement, are escapist and inadequate. That is, there is a lot of distance between a karaoke performer singing out the Beatles' "You say you want a revolution" and the real thing. Garnham (1990:1) disapprovingly cites the "bacillus of romanticism" for impelling cultural studies to pursue pop culture ephemera in a guiltless escape from the grim world of structure and alienation. The link between cultural production and the wider system of material production is neglected, a neglect which stems from "that romantic tradition of analysis" that persists in cultural studies and isolates cultural practice in the secondary sphere of leisure and the private (Garnham 1990:13).

In a later essay, McGuigan (1997) argues that the radicalization of cultural consumption is the result of the repression of economics in cultural studies. Abandoning base/superstructure, cultural studies reconstituted the economy as entirely symbolic in nature. This cultural economy, though having no evident relationship to the material economy, and eschewing determination of any kind, in fact borrows from neo-conservative ideology's celebration of consumer sovereignty. That is, the ecstatic consumer with a wealth of market choices, and the wannabe radical posting subvertisements which parody national ad campaigns, have much in common. They are free to shape signs as they please, just so long as no lasting harm is done to the real structure of power. McGuigan juxtaposes the cultural to the material economy, stressing that "we have the idea of a 'cultural' or 'symbolic' economy which consists of exchange relationships and significatory flows but with little discernible relationship to something like a 'real' economy" (1997:140).

But the romanticism under scrutiny is not merely a synonym for escapist subjectivism, but the two-hundred-year-old tradition of theory. Combined with the charges against the "romantic" nature of audience activity is a resolute defence of an Enlightenment heritage by political economy of communication scholars; they are critics who believe in the legacy that was intellectually besieged by Nietzschean postmodernists and politically attacked by neo-conservatives (Garnham 1990:2). That cultural studies is included in the Nietzschean geneaology is confirmed later when Garnham (1990:19) stresses that the Enlightenment project cannot be salvaged unless the "idealizing tendency of most cultural analysis" is stopped, and economics is given its rightful place at the centre of cultural criticism. McGuigan, an internal critic of cultural studies, makes a similar negative association between cultural studies and romanticism, allowing that "in terms of aesthetics, the discovery of popular culture is related to the Romantic reaction to Classicism" (McGuigan 1992:10).[3]

However, the conjunction of cultural studies and romanticism through the mediation of a "romantic" cultural populism represents a misreading of romanticism. Romanticism *is* a primary source for cultural studies; but romanticism is not oblivious to production, structure, and social responsibility. In identifying cultural studies with a caricature of romanticism, the political economy of communications passes over a tradition that is, in its own way, very materialist. Cultural populism does not represent romanticism any more than it summarizes the cultural studies project. Thus, to charge that cultural studies is haplessly romantic, and to suggest in this that the field is blithely heedless of economics, is to misrepresent the romantic tradition and its potential in cultural studies today. Cultural studies has not successfully addressed economics, but far from being the problem, romanticism may in fact offer a partial solution to the impasse.

The second charge against romanticism reveals more of the rationale for identifying cultural consumption with the romantic. Sociologist Colin Campbell (1987; see also Lury 1996:72-77) argues that romanticism was to the creation of consumer culture what the Protestant work ethic was to labour and production as capitalism emerged in its mature form in the eighteenth century. Romanticism acted to provide the experiential basis for the modern consumer society by giving consumption, once a bare necessity for the majority of pre-modern peoples, new meaning and value. It put the "culture" in consumer culture by detaching the experience of pleasure from the simple consumption of food, shelter, and other necessities, and turning it into a form of hedonism—pleasure for pleasure's sake. Pleasure was thus free to be re-attached where it would do the new socio-economic system and culture the most good.

Separated from physical need in an economy of relative abundance, pleasure was increasingly projected onto imaginary experiences, images, and dreams, which in themselves could not be adequate to this appetite. This hedonism thus became chronic and pathological, and was organized as a kind of consumer ethic in the context of an endless cycle of consumption within modern consumer culture. In legitimizing pleasure as a good in itself, stimulating production by valuing and demanding novelty, and liberating the subject from traditional constraints on desire and self-fashioning, "romanticism has served to provide ethical support for that restless and continuous pattern of consumption which so distinguishes the behaviour of modern man [sic]" (Campbell 1987:201).

Although crediting the romantics with good political intentions, Campbell argues that their revolution was a limited aesthetic, one devoted to ideas of art and beauty, and in his opinion, therefore compatible with romantic contributions to a consumer culture in need of a pleasing image. Campbell's romanticism is in the end no more than an ideology that, combined with the Puritan ethos, helps to constitute a modernity indispensable to capitalism. Campbell's analysis might be read as providing the articulate rationale for the more casual relationship between romanticism and consumption drawn by the political economists, though his argument is not normally cited by them. Both link romanticism to consumption: the political economists to the consumption of symbols, and Campbell to the consumption of goods. But the result is the same. Romanticism is pacified, and its capacity for resistance is outmatched by its assimilation by capitalism.

This argument would not be the oddly one-sided contest it is if there were cultural studies scholars actively defending the romantic legacy and its critical potential. But there aren't, and thus the fighting words are evidence of contradictions resident in the political economy of communications more than they are of a covertly capitalist content to cultural studies' arguments.

The political economy of Smith, Malthus, Ricardo, and (later) John Stuart Mill, borrowing heavily from Enlightenment liberalism, was long opposed by English romanticism. What seems apparent in the frequent references to the romantic nature of cultural populism or of consumer culture is that these political economists and sociologists, many of them indebted to Marx, are as much contradicted by romanticism as their Ricardian ancestors were long ago. This is painfully ironic, since romanticism was a ferocious critic of Ricardian political economy when it consolidated in the early nineteenth century and drew on Enlightenment rationalism to create positivist laws. It is for this reason that William Blake wrote with such angry eloquence in his poem "Milton" of "these dark Satanic Mills."

Moreover, the romantics were aware of how the Enlightenment tradition and its rich rationalism were absorbed into political economy; they foresaw the beginning of reason's "instrumental" corruption. Romanticism's self-reflexive nature, long before it became vogue in postmodernism, was its saving grace. Levinson says of this quality: "Romanticism, was, after all, the first critique *of* critique as a practice implicated in the political economy it attacked: the first discourse to try to step outside its own shadow, all the while protesting through its textuality the hopelessness of the endeavour" (1994:271). While the popular conception of romanticism is of a movement unconcerned with the world, preferring painted scenery to the real thing, the romantic use of imagination, emotion, and nature has no less a radical edge than the angry slogans of the Jacobins. Williams argues that romanticism kept alive the memory of the whole being after utilitarianism had stripped humanity of its moral complexity, capitalism the life-affirming nature of labour, and political economy the free will of the citizen and consumer:

> The emphasis on a general common humanity was evidently necessary in a period in which a new kind of society was coming to think of man as merely a specialized instrument of production. The emphasis on love and relationship was necessary not only within the immediate suffering but against the aggressive individualism and the primarily economic relationships which the new society embodied. Emphasis on the creative imagination, similarly, may be seen as an alternative construction of human motive and energy, in contrast with the assumptions of the prevailing political economy. (1958:59)

If we can accept the legitimate nature of romanticism's criticism of political economy in the nineteenth century, what then is its contemporary relevance? There are obvious parallels: the revival of laissez-faire doctrine under contemporary neo-liberalism suggests Ricardo, even as the erosion of the post-World War II welfare state reminds us daily of Malthus's harsh prescriptions. Harriet Martineau, the designated "national instructor" and propagandist who dedicated herself to conveying Ricardian tenets in popular narratives, all the better (in the words of a factory owner character in her novel *The*

Rioters) to "preach patience to starving people," has her counterpart in Francis Fukuyama and the "end of history" thesis. But the ultimate analogy may be a cultural one. The market society, then as now, is where the imagination has suffered a massive failure: we abdicate the creation of relationships among people, with nature, and between categories of experience to the Invisible Hand, mutual fund ads, and structural adjustment policies.

Imagination was the special expertise of the romantics then, and potentially still is now. At a time when, in the absence or failure of other universalizing projects, the market has become the dominant means by which totality and utopia are represented, romanticism's sensitivity to the subtler shadings of the dialectic is compelling. Citing romanticism's value for a time of capitalist triumphalism, Christensen (1994:456) claims that "if we want to discover what possibilities for change remain open now, we might inquire into the untimely back at the beginning of the nineteenth century, when history first ended." To accept the reduction of romanticism to a byword for consumption of several kinds in capitalist culture is to give away the keys to the kingdom. Several romantic concepts can offer cultural studies not only a way out of its "boring" debate with the political economy of communication, but more importantly, the means to recover the field's relevance. In the romantic understanding of the sublime, social totality, and materialism is an outline of a cultural studies of political economy. The critique of our colonization by the market metaphor is the singlemost important task ahead for cultural studies; it is one in which the romantics excelled. As the situationists once proclaimed, "all power to the imagination."

TOWARD A CULTURAL STUDIES OF POLITICAL ECONOMY

The Corporate and the Romantic Sublime

Cultural theory is confronted by the sheer complexity of life in the new millennium, and the difficulty of finding appropriate images to encompass that complexity. Cyberpunk novelist William Gibson captures it as well as anyone in the famous opening to his genre-bending *Neuromancer*: "Cyberspace. A consensual hallucination experienced daily by billions of legitimate operators, in every nation, by children being taught mathematical concepts....A graphic representation of data abstracted from the banks of every computer in the human system. Unthinkable complexity. Lines of light ranged in the nonspace of the mind, clusters and constellations of data. Like city lights, receding" (1984:51).

Twentieth-century theory often drew from eighteenth- and nineteenth-century sources of inspiration, namely in the natural sciences, philosophy, and aesthetics; it stressed order, epistemological realism, and intelligibility in keeping with its Enlightenment influences. In cultural studies, the importance of imagery was acknowledged as early as Williams's chapter "Images of Society" in his 1961 book *The Long Revolution*. The success of the "long revolution" by which democracy was gradually extended to politics, economics, and culture during the modern era depended on bringing forward fresh images of society, the better then to bring a startling new social order into focus. Williams describes the social imagination crucial to political and economic change, an enduring theme in his work. "Such changes, difficult enough in themselves, derive meaning and direction, finally, from new conceptions of man and society which many have worked to describe and interpret" (Williams 1961:141).

The problem visited on theory today is not Williams's task of fitting the image to society, but acknowledging that, more and more, the image *is* the society. This doesn't mean that Baudrillard's simulacrum is upon us or, to paraphrase Robert Venturi's classic book, that we will have to learn to like living in Las Vegas. The material world is no less with us today than it was in the Industrial Revolution or the Middle Ages. However, there is nothing unreal or ahistorical about the images we live inside, and no margin in granting unquestioned priority or privilege to "reality." These images are as familiar, comforting, and deceptive as Norman Rockwell paintings: a worn, weary, but still functional liberal democratic system; a global market that can be relied upon to outlast the business cycle; a natural world that despite evidence of ecological catastrophe exists to serve our appetites; or the clash of civilizations, this time invoked in response to September 11, 2001. The images are credible and meaningful to many; they are of our time, deny it as we might; and they have huge consequences for how we share the world's bounty. But the hyperreal conditions of contemporary capitalist society suggest the need for a new approach to representation in the absence of some intellectual Esperanto. Citing theory's inability to translate contemporary society using the existing stock of images and discourses, Grossberg writes: "Cultural Studies must confront the globalization of culture not merely in terms of the proliferation and mobility of texts and audiences, but also in terms of the movement of culture outside the spaces of any (specific) language" (1997:17).

The sheer plenitude and exoticism of cultural forms, as well as the threat of cultural imperialism, are often designated as the global culture's emergent features. We wonder at the appeal of Japan's Pokémon among Western schoolchildren or the invented tradition of Kwanzaa among African-Americans; we worry about the consequences of a McDonald's in Beijing or cool hunting on the insurgent nature of youth culture. But the convergence of image and reality is perhaps the source of global society's true complexity,

at least where representation is concerned. Image and reality were, as romantically understood, always already inseparable. But media's presence has
amplified this interpenetration of ideal and real today to an unprecedented
degree; the meaning of its consequences is still being revealed. McRobbie
confirms our beguiled state, arguing that "for populations transfixed on images
which are themselves a reality, there is no return to a mode of representation
which politicizes in a kind of straightforward 'worthwhile' way" (1994:22-23).

In the modern era, one of the most common ways of speaking about the
ineffable has been the romantic concept of the "sublime," which came to the
romantics via Immanuel Kant's pre-romantic writings. The "sublime" is the
label we give to what lies outside our powers of representation—the dark matter in our social universe. Yet ironically, for something that cannot be articulated, the sublime has a surprisingly long and verbose history in theory. In his
essay "The Sublime and the Avant-Garde" (Lyotard 1993), Lyotard dates the
first modern reference to the sublime to a translation of the classical author
Longinus, whose thought the French philosopher Boileu introduced in 1674
within his *Art Poetique* and his *Du Sublime*.

Lyotard's genealogy continues with Edmund Burke, the English philosopher
and enemy of the French Revolution, who defined the "sublime" as the awe-
some power of nature, a force constantly challenging the limits of representation. As discussed in Burke's 1759 *A Philosophical Enquiry into the Origin of
Our Ideas of the Sublime and Beautiful*, the sublime was so powerful it threat-
ened to stop representation altogether—and thereby, to paralyze culture and
end history. Lyotard makes the sublime's romantic provenance clear and its
importance to the modern project compelling. He writes that it is in the name
of the sublime "that aesthetics asserted its critical rights over art, and that
romanticism—in other words, modernity—triumphed" (1993:246).

Burke's negative judgement of the sublime, and Lyotard's identification of
the concept with the fate of the romantic, is perpetuated in contemporary
theory. Control of this romantic concept is of strategic importance to postmodern and post-structuralist positions (represented in previous chapters as a
worthy nemesis and usurper of a potential romantic revival). The neutralization of the sublime's critical potential is evident again in Lyotard's essay,
where he argues that the meaning of the romantic sublime has shifted register in light of twentieth-century art and aesthetics. Formerly, the romantic
sublime signalled the possibility of another and better world beyond the ideological frame of reference in a given society. Outside the bloom and buzz of
experience lay a utopia for which words did not yet exist.

In contrast, the sublime invoked in twentieth-century theory and culture
gestures to an inexpressible "now" devoid of social or utopian content.

Twentieth-century avant-gardes think of the sublime as a vacuum or noth-ingness, where the ineffable is not a Kantian dare to frame our words and images better, as will be seen, but an iron burden on action of any kind. Samuel Beckett, the abstract expressionists, and Dada represent brilliant vari-ations on this fatalistic theme. Lyotard follows Kant in bringing the sublime inside the social, but unlike Kant uses it to underscore the impossibility of see-ing and acting upon patterns in human behaviour. He writes: "The inexpress-ible does not reside in an over there, in another world, or another time, but in this: in that (something) happens" (Lyotard 1993:246).

In his disdain for totality and representation, Lyotard offers us the sublime without the possibility of growth. We are left to wonder if action of any kind is possible in the absence of metanarratives that would otherwise explain pat-tern and purpose. Lyotard's appropriation of the sublime gives comfort to a capitalist world that would identify the sublime with its own commercial des-tiny. Here the "automatic engineerings" of the market have replaced Edenic nature as the source of value, and yet the market mysteriously stands outside representation inspiring love and loathing with every stock cycle.

Each time we consume something without lasting satisfaction, spend our savings on something no one really wants or needs, or watch corporations like Nike ("Just Do It") and Coca-Cola ("Always") behave as if they have a spiri-tual role in our lives, that emptiness we feel is a little of the void Lyotard described. As Naomi Klein writes in *No Logo: Taking Aim at the Brand Bullies*, a successful company now looks to "transcend its products and become a free-standing meaning," while its advertising agencies do the work of "identifying, articulating, and protecting the corporate soul" (Klein 2000:23). Taken together, these several features add up to the "corporate" sub-lime, a phenomenon that will only grow in power as capitalism devotes itself to the manufacture of meaning.

The lack of regard for the sublime's critical potential is shared by theorists of a more sympathetic nature. For Dienst, the sublime is an obstacle to the-ory, something to overcome lest we lapse into silence and awe. He writes that "to 'figure out' the contemporary situation without resorting either to the tropes of sublimity or to the schematic shorthand of economics, theoretical work will have to cultivate its own powers of imagination and transmission" (1996:68). Jameson, to contrast, concedes the sublime to Lyotard and post-modern theory. He claims that the "hysterical sublime" is evidence that post-modern theory has guiltlessly given up on the hard work of understanding the world in order to delight itself with pretty pictures. The "hysterical sublime" is a depthless void born "of the limits of figuration and the incapacity of the human mind to give representation to such enormous forces" (Jameson

1984:77). For Dienst and for Jameson, the sublime is synonymous with paralysis and postmodernity, and the very opposite of honest intellectual labour.

Kant's 1790 *The Critique of Judgement* takes a more constructive perspective on the sublime from which cultural studies can learn. Where the beautiful (i.e., that which *can* be represented by the imagination) calls on our understanding to provide a "mimetic" (or realistically accurate) match between image or word and the beautiful object, the sublime presents a superior challenge. Where Burke characterized the sublime as a threatening force of nature, Lyotard treats it as the impossibility of meaningful action in the void; Dienst and Jameson identify it as theory's doom, and Kant believed the sublime an intrinsic feature of the human mind and a positive phenomenon compatible with reason.

Rather than leaving us bewildered, the sublime provokes our rational powers to higher levels of function. Kant (1988:109) writes of the pleasure and possibility of the sublime in *The Critique of Judgement*, stating that "though the imagination, no doubt, finds nothing beyond the sensible world to which it can lay hold, still this thrusting aside of the sensible barriers gives it a feeling of being unbounded; and that removal is thus a presentation of the infinite." At the point where the imagination, meeting with an object too imponderable for representation, fails to supply us with images, the mind grows from this "outrage on the imagination," as Kant termed it, by having to work still harder. The sublime strengthens reason and the imagination, and underscores the mutual dependence between these two faculties. The sublime "can never be anything more than a negative presentation," but the gain in the enlargement of our faculties means that "still it expands the soul" (Kant 1988:109-10). What doesn't kill us, in other words, makes us smarter.

In his "The Impossible Object: Towards a Sociology of the Sublime," subculture theorist Dick Hebdige takes up the Kantian sublime in order to demonstrate its value to cultural studies. In Hebdige's view, post-structuralists have represented the sublime in Burkean terms, insofar as it represents the ultimate constraint on reason and imagination. Theirs is the "asocial sublime," a cynical celebration of the impotence of theory relative to its object and without regard to theory's social mission. The post-structuralist sublime is a source of terror, a depthless mass that exists behind the cool and impersonal network of flickering signifiers. Post-structuralism—to which Dienst and Jameson seem too keen to yield the sublime—defines the limits of representation as the limits also of an emancipatory project of any kind. So as a counterpoint, Hebdige offers an extended metaphor of the "social sublime" in the form of a neighbour of his, a Mr. H., who gives endless lavish care to a classic Ford Thunderbird that, although mute, offers up value sufficient to situate this man in the world.

Marjorie Levinson underlines the romantic content of such an optimistic conception of the sublime. For her the sublime is not necessarily some implacable post-structuralist horror, but the presence of the transcendent in ordinary objects and everyday phenomena in our lives. Levinson believes the romantic sublime to have subversive potential in the here and now. For her, romanticism's "counter-epistemology" depends on a pair of metaphysical premises, nature and mind, and the way they are mutually implicated in the sublime. In the sublime, mind and matter are immeasurably mixed, refusing the imposition of value, resisting circulation, and generally not playing the game. The sublime is a trope or figure for phenomena too refractory for mere rational comprehension—but a symbol that is "also real, also an action in the world" (Levinson 1994: 273). In this, the romantic sublime seems the desired basis for a new aesthetic which is social, which refuses to step back from the abyss between subject and object, and which is committed to thoughtful action in a culture where meaning either comes too cheaply or not at all.

The romantic sublime recommends that we be patient with uncertainty, since in a world where media and reality mingle, reality is always implicated in every act and instance of representation. Given the circumstances, some part of the real is permanently outside our ability to represent. Perhaps romanticism's relevance to contemporary cultural criticism is better demonstrated by looking at the point where the recovery of the sublime meets society. That point is the market-centred nature of social totality today.

Totality and the Market

Lukács did the important work of defining "totality" in his *History and Class Consciousness*. The concept refers to a view of society as a relational whole, where no single element has ultimate determining power. It provided a pretext for Western Marxism to stop looking for the philosopher's stone of the last instance, for some magical formula where the lead of endless dialectic would be turned into the gold of determination. Totality also gave license to the Frankfurt School, Gramsci, Bakhtin, and other revisionists to investigate how other variables, such as culture, civil society, and the body figured in giving shape to experience. Gary Lunn suggests just how important a corrective the concept was, given the habit among orthodox Marxist and liberal economists alike of separating out phenomena from a web of interrelationship. He gives credit where it is due: "In reacting against the deterioration of Marxist theory into a kind of economic determinism, Lukács and still more the Frankfurt School were to stress the Hegelian view of the social whole as a seamless, constantly interacting totality in which production, politics, etc. were all a part" (Lunn 1982:24).

Hall, among others, is on record regarding the pursuit of a theory of totality as the core problem of cultural studies. But Hall's enthusiasm for the project has not spared cultural studies criticism from largely neglecting totality after Williams. Mosco, for example, has argued that "cultural studies is considerably less certain about the value of pursuing the social totality, because it doubts the empirical reality and theoretical usefulness of the concept" (1996:267). He cites its preference for the particular rather than the systemic, a "romanticism of difference" that makes cultural studies averse to drawing relationships between the scattered moments of difference and identity for fear of creating a system by default.

Through the intervention of corporate PR, neo-liberal think tanks, and international economic institutions like the World Bank, the market today impresses itself on global society as the very image of totality. This in itself compels from cultural studies a serious second look at the concept. All the various factors that Lukács and the Frankfurt School might have included in their recipes for totality—the state, media, religion, family, etc.—are increasingly subsumed and privatized by the market. Jameson demonstrates how the market has come to frame the defining image of totality as we know it. "The force, then, of the concept of the market lies in its 'totalizing' structure, as they say nowadays; that is, in its capacity to afford a model of a social totality" (Jameson 1991:272).

Yet the sublime reminds us of the radical significance of admitting our ignorance now and then, and in this we are given a wonderful tool to use against the market. Information-based capitalism, represented in the business pages as the "new" economy of high technology, post-Fordist production, and services, murders sublime uncertainty in declaring everything knowable, a mere matter of accumulating the data and running the spreadsheets. In light of what Foucault's "power/knowledge" theorem has taught us about how knowledge is often not about discovering truth but gaining power, the information society is by definition easily controlled. The sublime tips the balance in favour of culture versus information by declaring some things unknowable, adding culture's rich combination of fact and fiction to the experiential mix, and thus vastly contributing to the world's enchantment again. Once the strategic value of the Kantian sublime, with its romantic pedigree and social nature, is admitted into the analysis, a different model of social totality is invited.

This is a model of a romantic totality as radically open as the prevailing market model is closed, where the sublime represents the impossibility of its closure. This romantic model of social totality is "expressive" or, alternately, a "genetic" totality. Martin Jay, the great contemporary chronicler of the totality concept, dates this aesthetic version of totality to Jean-Jacques Rousseau's work. For the pre-romantic Rousseau, totality was not a given, a kind of organic unity already present in nature. Rather, the social whole was a constant creative work in progress. Social coherence had to be constantly sought by individuals and institutions, and was thus a matter for culture—not capital.

The romantic Holderlin's model of totality is representative of this genetic alternative. For Holderlin, author of the "System Program" cited in chapter 1, the unrepresentability of the sublime forced a different appreciation of the conceptual horizons that defined modernity. Once defined as a project possessed by the dream of representation, modernity's ambitions toward capturing the real meet with the stubborn fact of a world that will not finally yield its meaning. Nor did totality tend to a synthetic homogeneity, as imagined in Hegel's classic model of historical development. The romantic totality was as heterogeneous as these devotees of difference could imagine; it was dynamic without being dialectical; and it unfolded in history without tending to some convenient teleological closure.

The sublime is therefore, as demanded by a metaphysics of tragedy, no longer located in divinity or fate, but brought inside the secular world—a fact requiring what Surin terms Holderlin's "cartography of the sublime." This demonstrates the continuity of the romantic sublime with Kant, who also brought it inside human society. The appropriate theoretical response to this new uncertain space was for Holderlin a "poetic ontology," whereby the material nature of language was recognized and, contrary to a tragic Faustian view of the modern, the power to shape self and society recognized. Surin (1995:163) compares Holderlin's poetic ontology to Williams's "long revolution," allowing that they resemble each other in imagining culture to have the capacity for determination on par with more conventionally economic sources of production.

Cultural Materialism Then and Now

By cultural materialism, Williams argued that we should regard the means of cultural production (e.g., media, conversation, art) as forces comparable in their determinative power to the more conventional forms of economic production.[4] He meant that culture has a material force analogous to the ways we exploit nature for gain, or share wealth among the classes. That is, we should understand that signifying practices are not dissimilar from factories, resource extraction, or technology in their power to set totality in motion or give it shape. This fact requires that we think about culture's material nature, in a systematic way that seeks to understand how culture impresses itself on the objective world—in other words, a cultural materialism. In essays like "Base and Superstructure in Marxist Cultural Theory" and "Means of Communication as Means of Production" (1980), Williams made room for culture's more subtle causal power by softening the orthodox model of economic determinism into a "determination" that set limits on social form.

Cultural materialism separates Williams's work from the harder versions of determination favoured by the British Communist Party to which he once belonged, and from the idealism of F.R. Leavis that had been the major influence on his culturalism. Early versions of the concept cleaved uncomfortably close to Leavis's mystical brand of humanism. But by the time Williams's book *Culture* was published in 1981, his cultural materialism showed a sensitivity to the less than holistic nature of reality. Dropping its insistence on a prior organicism violated by capitalism, and the tendency to overlook difference in the name of a binding "structure of feeling," this much-improved cultural materialism was left unfinished at the time of Williams's death in 1988.[5]

The romantic connection to Williams's cultural materialism is again Holderlin's. Surin (1995:158) credits Holderlin with a sophisticated materialism in which the imagination is the essential component, "since it is the imagination that enables materialism to retain its constructive power in the very moment that materialism has lost its hope." What is important to the narrative here is that recent scholarship has discovered that the continuity between romanticism and Williams (discussed in previous chapters) includes cultural materialism as a key feature. For example, Milner argues that "the whole tradition of Romantic and post-Romantic anti-utilitarianism which we have designated as culturalism," manifestly present in Williams's overtly Leavisian "structure of feeling" concept, "remains much more actively present in the later cultural materialism than is often supposed" (1994a:63).

Recognizing its lasting value, contemporary criticism has sought to finish what Williams began, building on a cultural materialism that in itself was originally a romantic problem. Kellner (1995:43), for example, recommends that cultural materialism grow beyond Williams's emphasis on means, and appreciate that discourse itself has material effects. Others, such as communication theorist Dan Schiller, take cultural materialism much further, building on Williams's later formulation of the "structure of feeling" as a "metaphor of solution" (Williams 1977). That is, rather than arguing that culture was merely parallel with the economic in determining the shape of society, Williams argued that culture was dissolved into economic practices (and vice versa) in an economy so invested in information and service. This was an economy, in other words, that produced culture as much as it produced raw resources and manufactured widgets.

The slippery nature of contemporary information capitalism was something Williams tried to capture with his "solution" metaphor. He wrote that "[structures of feeling] can be defined as social experiences *in solution*, as distinct from other social semantic formations which have been *precipitated* and are more evidently and more immediately available" (1977:133-34). Culture is thus held to be deeply if diffusely present in economic and other practices, an opinion strikingly similar to Holderlin's that imagination is implicated in the material itself. Dan Schiller (1996:193) argues that this more liquid formulation of cultural materialism means that culture "exists not as a separate and autonomous practice, nor even as half of a composite construct which also encompasses activity; it is, rather, again an organic dimension of an ontologically prior category of social labour." Defining culture (including communication) as a material practice with material effects, cultural materialism has the romantic benefit of undoing what Dan Schiller believes to have been the endless reification of communication within the history of communications research. Where it has historically been treated as an easily essentialized and cerebral property—mere words passing between people or via massive technological media—in Schiller's view cultural materialism helps us to restore communication to a more sanguine identity as a sensuous and material form of labour. Communication, as a form of culture, does work too.

This later and more soluble form of "cultural materialism" allows cultural studies to more productively address the problem of political economy in an information-based capitalist society. The opportunity for cultural studies to make itself as current as the communications technologies it needs to analyze is present in the fact that, in the information society, the base is becoming a part of the superstructure. That is, more and more of what we have considered to be the economy in the past is now "culture," an aspect of which is captured above in the "corporate sublime." Reality has caught up with Williams's thesis, meaning that cultural studies scholars now have a means to address economy without having to do calculus. As Stuart Hall himself has said in partial recognition of this shift, "it's possible to get a long way by talking about what is sometimes called the 'economic' as operating discursively" (1996b:145).

In the place where dialectical tensions used to reveal themselves, therefore, a new and arguably non-dialectical kind of space has emerged where base and superstructure used to be. Romanticism offers a non-dialectical model of totality appropriate to "a situation where ideology duplicates or simulates rather than inverts the real, and where production turns around and mirrors ideology" (Levinson 1994:280). Becoming digital means that culture and economy "are identified in such a way as to allow the libidinal energies of the one to suffuse the others without, however (as in older models of our cultural and intellectual history), producing a synthesis, a new combination, a new combined language, or whatever" (Jameson 1991:275). If indeed the dialectical pattern of historical process (which assumed that history proceeded by means of a series of massive implosions, as the contradictions of a given social system gave birth to new and unimagined models of society) is no longer viable, romanticism gives us a way to keep progressive ideas and practices alive in a dark time of capitalist supremacy. The hybrid space of information capitalism is part ideology and part discourse, part technology and part culture, an odd world in which eccentric romanticism is both at ease with and yet anathema to its enemies. Robins and Webster describe this new space at the heart of totality:

> There is an important social space that is invisible to any simple base/superstructure conception of society, a space hardly ever explored in British media theory. This is a space in which capital seeks to influence, not ideas or profits, but the very rhythms, patterns, pace, texture and disciplines of everyday life....And crucially important here is a consideration of how technologies invest and inform the patterns of culture, of the whole way of life. (Robins and Webster 1988:46-47)

As nature is overtaken by technology, our sense of the real is saturated with simulation, and the market commodifies everything that moves, it is more important than ever not to give up on the real—as post-structuralism would have us do. But a new language is needed to account for the remarkable and unprecedented reality that is emerging, where fact and fantasy, the ideal and the real, merge in ways that we can no longer prejudge like we used to. Such a language is no worse for taking as part of its lexicon these three romantic concepts: the sublime, totality, and cultural materialism.

Conclusion

WRESTLING WITH THE ANGELS

I want to suggest a different metaphor for theoretical work: the metaphor of struggle, of wrestling with the angels. The only theory worth having is that which you have to fight off, not that which you speak with profound fluency.

—Stuart Hall, "Cultural Studies and Its Theoretical Legacies," 280

The angels of romanticism, assuming these creatures really are from heaven, hardly fight fair. Just when you believe you understand a point, they break into pentameter or begin speaking in tongues. Take what, on its own terms, is difficult German philosophy, read it in the poetic idioms in which it was expressed (and in English translation where necessary), transport it from its original context to the present day, argue for its contemporary relevance in light of technologies that even the romantics didn't dream of, and there is a risk of clipping a few wings.

It's surprising that, given the challenge I've experienced in adapting their complex and often mystical aphorisms to contemporary culture, the original romantics were not humbler. But where language, media, culture, and political economy are concerned, as well as a good number of other issues besides, there is clearly a need to witness what makes cultural studies special, and remember why the project seemed so timely when the Birmingham Centre was founded in 1964. Beyond the modest limits of this book, a pair of retrospective essays by Williams and Hall prepare the reader for further consideration of romanticism's value as a contemporary archive for and stimulus to modern cultural criticism.

Williams, in his essay entitled "The Future of Cultural Studies," earnestly appeals to us to remember that cultural studies was initially an intervention as political as it was intellectual, built on the militant genius of Leavis and Marx, and on the small victories won on behalf of the long revolution in adult education classes in Britain. Its recent institutionalization worried him, and suggested that cultural studies was increasingly isolated from the social formation that had inspired it originally. In this late essay by Williams, given as a lecture several years before his death, there are strong echoes of the culturalism of his early career. The romantic Williams is eminently intelligible in his caution that "you cannot understand an intellectual or artistic project without also understanding that the relation between a project and a formation is always decisive; and that the emphasis of Cultural Studies is precisely that it engages with *both*, rather than specializing itself to one or the other" (1989:151). If cultural studies has been about "taking the best we can in intellectual work and going with it in this very open way to confront people for whom it is not a way of life," then cultural studies' future is secure (162). But despite its bold and prophetic theme, the essay is anxious, concerned that cultural studies is becoming an arcane version of *Trivial Pursuit*. It may not be imposing on this text to read here a subtle invocation of romanticism's anti-reifying powers, summoning the poets of Jena and the English countryside from the dead in order to appeal to the social responsibility and spiritual vocation of the imagination.

Hall, in "Cultural Studies and Its Theoretical Legacies," repeats some of Williams's own concerns, a surprising gesture for the person responsible for the "idealist" structuralism Williams believed had made cultural studies all too predictably academic. Like Williams, Hall warns of the importance of worldliness, of articulating text to context relentlessly, and of keeping the critical intellect true to experience. In Hall's view, theory has gotten too comfortable in the academy. Cultural studies has theorized power so long it has forgotten what raw force feels like to its victims; it has been overtheorized and overprofessionalized; and its interdisciplinarity threatens to lapse into mere pluralism. But even Hall sounds romantic in the last several pages of the essay, as he recalls the maddeningly elusive nature of culture, and the fact that the best that theory can hope for is a beautiful failure: "Unless and until one respects the necessary displacements of culture, and yet is always irritated by its failure to reconcile with other questions that matter, with other questions that cannot and can never be fully covered by critical textuality in its elaborations, cultural studies as a project, an intervention, remains incomplete....I think that, overall, is what defines cultural studies as a project" (Hall 1992:284).

Romanticism is the one theoretical tradition that cultural studies, unique among the other metanarratives on which it draws, can claim as its own. This present argument is at best merely a prologue for another and more comprehensive application of romantic ideas to contemporary culture, in the spirit of the radical empathy and anachronism which the romantics practised. There are many topics that might be explored: the gothic and romantic criticism; romanticism and gender (given that popular romantic ideology of the kind that fills soap operas and pulp fiction still informs some of our most important life decisions relating to sex, love, and mating); the return of the romantic in subcultures, such as rave and riotgrrls, or in the anti-globalization movement with its situationist style. Many of the topics that postmodern and post-structuralist thought now claims—issues as trivial as music videos, or as epic as subjectivity, textuality, and epistemology—can and should also be rendered in modern and romantic terms. In a time of spectacles and shadows, where modern thought is the condition for making existence tolerable, cultural studies' privileged relationship with romanticism suggests that reviving and adapting key romantic concepts for cultural criticism might make a small difference toward restoring to the world a little of its lost, ancient magic.

Notes

Introduction

1 Christopher Norris's entry on the German philosopher of language, Frege, is helpful in discussing post-structuralism. While Norris is a staunch critic of post-modern and post-structuralist theories, he makes appropriate reference here to how the status of the referent distinguishes structuralism from post-structuralism. See Payne, ed., *A Dictionary of Cultural and Critical Theory*, 7.

2 Given that German romanticism is the original and most philosophically comprehensive of the romanticisms, German sources in translation are used primarily in this argument. Although English romantic sources are used, the measure of English romanticism is taken primarily in the tradition of English culturalism in its several manifestations, notably as these appear in the work of Matthew Arnold, William Morris, F.R. Leavis, and Raymond Williams. The English sources, being primarily poetic, lack the explicit theoretical attention given to concepts and themes in the German writings. Moreover, the early German romantic period is the ultimate source of much of the theoretical infrastructure within cultural studies, despite the intervention of English texts, and also represents the densest and purest expression of the very romanticism cultural studies may be accountable to.

3 I am indebted to Christensen's work for the idea of "using" romanticism in the first place, as well as to a student whose name I've long forgotten who first and inexplicably passed the essay onto me. Christensen writes to inspire: "romanticism is not an object of study—neither the glorious expression nor the deplorable symptom of a distant epoch and peculiar mentality—but a problem in identification and practice" (Christensen 1994:453).

Chapter 1

1 Surveys of the British tradition in cultural analysis differ in their definition of when and what was "culturalism." Some define it as a persistent argument about the nature of culture beginning in the eighteenth-century public sphere (Milner); others (Turner) localize it in the work of Williams, Thompson, and Hoggart which immediately preceded the founding of the Centre at Birmingham, and would thus make it synonymous with left-Leavisism (and far less awkward a phrase). The latter reckoning distinguishes it from the "culture and civilization" or "culture and society" positions assumed by much of the English intelligentsia, and as chronicled in Williams's book *Culture and Society*.

   Given my interest in reaffirming an already acknowledged continuity between romanticism and cultural studies at Birmingham, and more importantly, refurbishing romanticism to argue for and make it adaptable to contemporary critical purposes, I borrow here from Andrew Milner's 1994 book *Contemporary Cultural Theory: An Introduction*, in which the long view is taken. That is, something recognizable as culturalism—asserting the organic character of culture, and its oppositional value vis-à-vis utilitarian, industrial capitalism—begins in the eighteenth century, and despite philosophical adjustments and the change of political stripe in passing from the reactionary "culture and civilization" tradition to left-culturalism, remains recognizable today.

   I also follow Milner's usage as far as the meaning of "British cultural studies" is concerned. British cultural studies here refers specifically to cultural analysis centred in Britain after the founding of the Centre. Thus "British cultural studies" and the work of the Birmingham centre are largely synonymous in my account, except where other British cultural criticism of recent vintage not affiliated with the Centre for Contemporary Cultural Studies is concerned. Such a distinction is necessary because other usage (Turner, among others) allows British cultural studies to stand in for the several centuries of cultural analysis in Britain. But projecting the contemporary cultural studies movement back to Arnold, or even to the public sphere, credits cultural criticism with intellectual and methodological features that it doesn't merit.

2 Its severest critic is one of its own illustrious descendants. See Hall, "Cultural Studies: Two Paradigms."

3 Saiedi does identify several sources in sociology and social thought that have addressed romanticism in some way. But to acknowledge its contributions to social theory is not the same as appreciating its contemporary relevance, and this contemporary aspect is conspicuously rare in the literature.

   Among the sources that refer to romanticism and the social sciences (but not its contemporary relevance), Saiedi cites the following sources: Robert Nisbet, *The Sociological Tradition* (New York: Basic Books, 1966); Steven Seidman, *Liberalism and the Origins of European Social Theory* (Berkeley: University of California, 1983), and Irving Zeitlin, *Ideology and the Development of Sociological Theory* (Englewood Cliffs: Prentice Hall, 1968).

From personal observation, the following also qualify as having some reference to romanticism in social thought: Jacques Barzun, author of *Classic, Romantic, and Modern* (Garden City: Anchor Books, 1961) and *Romanticism and the Modern Ego* (Boston: Little, Brown, 1943); Karl Mannheim's writing, particularly his *Essays on Sociology and Social Psychology*; Marshall Berman's *All That's Solid Melts into Air: The Experience of Modernity* (New York: Simon and Schuster, 1982); and of course, Alvin Gouldner himself, in the essay, "Romanticism and Classicism: Deep Structures in Social Science."

4 I follow the periodization offered by Norman Hampson's *The Enlightenment: An Evaluation of Its Assumptions, Attitudes and Values* (London: Penguin, 1968). He divides the period into two parts: the first phase or "early" Enlightenment dating from 1715 to 1740, a period when the Enlightenment was at its most optimistic about the human prospect; and a second or mature phase, dating from 1740 to the revolutionary year of 1789, a period when most of the canonical works of the Enlightenment were published, e.g., Rousseau's *Social Contract*, Voltaire's *Candide*, Montesquieu's *The Spirit of Laws*, Diderot's *Encyclopedia*, etc. Hampson acknowledges a pattern of cultural pessimism emerging in Europe in the 1760s, as the political and economic stasis of the early Enlightenment gave way to political wars and protocapitalism. So-called pre-romanticism finds its basis in this disquiet. Conor Cruise O'Brien rather tendentiously distinguishes the early from the later Enlightenment in terms of the earlier period's greater respect and compatibility with religion and tradition, and the latter's cynicism. (Note that all foreign language titles are provided in their conventional English translations.)

5 The dichotomy of early and late romanticism reflects primarily on its development in Germany, since radical and conservative strains of romantic thought were jointly present throughout the history of English romanticism. In other words, the German periodization does not apply when cultural radicals like Blake (respecting that he was a generation older than the others), Shelley, and Byron, and conservatives like Coleridge (whose knowledge of German romantic literature was superior to that of the other English romantics), exerted influence over English romanticism at roughly the same time. Keats, the precocious nightingale, did not exhibit the same degree of political intention in his work, but could be classified among the more liberal of his peers.

6 They appear here unchanged from the authoritative translation taken from Surin, though the order of their appearance in the list has been rearranged to better suit exposition. Original text of the System Program is set as a subhead for ease of reference.

7 Their "humanist pantheism" is discussed in Blechman, *Revolutionary Romanticism*, 27.

8 Blechman writes: "While the most generous contemporary readings of the romantic new mythology view it as a charming utopianism, one need only consider the emergence of liberation theology in Latin American in the 1970s, or the recent synthesis of Mayan tradition with democratic humanism by the

Zapatistas, to see that the romantics were grappling with ideas that can be emancipatory" (1999:29).

9   Jay argues that most partisans of the romantic, "genetic" model of totality in England have been right wing where totality was favoured at all. England, spiritual home to utilitarianism and other forms of individualist and liberal thought, didn't suffer holisms gladly. This makes Williams all the more unusual—as a socialist and a holist—although his being Welsh probably had something to do with it. Jay writes of Williams's unusual stance: "Even in England, which, for most continental thinkers and Marxists in particular, was the bastion of individualism in thought and politics, a counter-trend can be observed....The tradition of seeking solace for the disintegrative effects of individualism in the realm of culture, which Raymond Williams trenchantly followed in *Culture and Society*, was often the repository of more holistic hopes" (1984:68).

10 Although Hunter takes a Foucauldian direction that I can't ultimately follow, his definition of aesthetics as a technology of ethics—as a model for better living through beauty—is attractive.

Chapter 2

1   As discussed at length in McGuigan's famous critique of cultural studies, *Cultural Populism*.

2   Stuart Hall's relationship to the modern is discussed later in this chapter in the context of his structuralism.

3   By the "long revolution" Williams meant the slow but gradual democratization of the West, a process precipitated by the growing presence of working class culture in public life through the modern period. This was intended as an alternative to the quick fix promised by the orthodox view of proletarian political revolution, and as a means of bringing democratic scruple and culture into socialist debates on historical change that often neglected these issues. See Williams's volume, *The Long Revolution*.

4   French romanticism, as represented in the writing of Chateaubriand and Lamennais, lacked the political and temporal unity of romanticism in Germany and England, and is not accounted for in this analysis.

5   Prendergast explains: "In this context, the emphasis on wholeness, continuous connected practice, and so forth reveals...the continuing and probably unexpungeable traces in Williams's own thought of the tradition explored in *Culture and Society*, in particular the paradoxical Arnoldian-Leavisite view of culture as distinct (from 'society') but whose distinctness consists in making whole what has been divided and atomized" (15).

6   In this view, Williams is regrettably consistent with the position taken by the neo-conservative critic Daniel Bell in his essay, "The Cultural Contradictions of Capitalism," with the difference that Bell identifies the loss of a traditional culture supportive of capitalism, rather than Williams's socialism. Bell's thesis in this founding document of the post-war New Right is that once upon a time,

before the advent of avant-gardism, capitalism and culture enjoyed a harmonious, mutually beneficial relationship. Capitalism generated wealth, and culture generated the values necessary to ensuring that people kept to the Puritan work ethic and the Pilgrim pledge of self-denial. Twentieth-century avant-gardes, however, counselled ease, consumption, and a breakdown of cultural authority, and their modernist values poisonously entered the mainstream culture where they today allegedly support a liberal bias in the media, and contrarian and consumerist values born of the 1960s. "The commonplace observation," Bell opined, "that today there is no longer a significant avant-garde—that there is no longer a radical tension between new art which shocks and a society that is shocked—merely signifies that the avant-garde has won its victory....In effect, 'culture' has been given a blank check, and its primacy in generating social change has been firmly acknowledged" (1976:35).

Ideological enemies though they may be, Williams and Bell shared organicism and a categorical separation of culture and society (Bell famously addresses the "disjuncture" between the two) as a central value in their work. Bell has been duly criticized for using his functionalism to separate the market society from culture, and argue that the American Dream could be renewed through a restoration of the lost moral order—as if somehow the market itself did not have a part in everything from consumerism to institutional decay, and culture separately determined economy. Bell's thesis has long given aid and comfort to neoconservatives who would reconcile economic liberalism and social conservatism, largely by denying the economy-culture connection, at least insofar as the economy affects culture.

7 As a shorthand for Williams's feelings about modernity, mobile privatization underlines his discomfort with several of modern culture's key features: relentless change, and the challenge to the integrity of community.

8 Definitions of ideology and discourse abound, and any choice is bound to offend. I prefer the following definitions as benchmarks, making reference to variations in Marxist-semiotic and Foucauldian texts where appropriate. From Mike Cormack, *Ideology:*

> Ideology...is a process which links socio-economic reality to individual consciousness. It establishes a conceptual framework, which results in specific uses of mental concepts, and gives rise to our ideas of ourselves. In other words, the structure of our thinking about the social world, about ourselves, and about our role within that world, is related by ideology ultimately to socio-economic conditions. (1992:13)

From John Fiske's essay, "British Cultural Studies and Television":

> A discourse is a socially produced way of talking or thinking about a topic. It is defined by reference to the area of social experience that it makes sense of, to the social location from which that sense

> is made, and to the linguistic or signifying system by which that sense is both made and circulated....A discourse is then a socially located way of making sense of an important area of social experience. (1987:168)

9 These works are Eagleton's chapter on "Ideology and Discourse" in his book, *Ideology*, which is a primary source in this chapter; Hall's essay "The Rediscovery of 'Ideology': Return of the Repressed in Media Studies"; and Williams's chapter, entitled simply "Language," in *Marxism and Literature*.

10 Average North American television consumption is approximately 22 hours a week, 1,144 hours a year, and 91,520 hours over an 80-year lifespan. That's good for 3,813 24-hour days, or about 10.5 years. Allow for sleep and 16 waking hours in a given day, and the total is closer to 15 years of television watching over a lifetime.

11 Media effects, a blend of information theory, behaviourism, and sociological functionalism, was the dominant tradition of media analysis in the 1940s and 1950s, and particularly identified with American media scholars such as Paul Lazarsfeld, Wilbur Schramm, Elihu Katz, and others. Still a force to be reckoned with, it has since come under heavy criticism for, among other things, its complicity with the media industries' own conception of audience, information, and technology, etc.

Chapter 3

1 John Fiske's *Understanding Popular Culture* (and its companion volume of case studies, *Reading the Popular*) is an important exception to the lack of attention to media among primers in cultural studies. However, what is notable about Fiske's extensive reading of various media—from tabloids to TV wrestling—is that his analysis tends to be sufficiently post-structuralist in its theoretical origins, and so emphatically committed to the "active audience" at the expense of structure, that he has effectively been expelled from the ranks of Birmingham-affiliated authors. Whether Fiske is fairly shunned is outside this argument's mandate. But it is worth noting that again it is post-structuralism which is conspicuously invoked when the subject is mass media, and not other theoretical traditions.

2 Although Peters never uses the "R" word in the several articles of his used in this section, he has confirmed in personal e-mail correspondence the romantic character of media theory in the interwar period: "I am persuaded of the importance of romanticism and I like the deep tracing of it" (personal e-mail, 24 January 1998).

3 By American cultural studies, I refer here to the work of James Carey, Lawrence Grossberg, and others to create an American equivalent of the Birmingham project. Although there are as many differences in American cultural studies as there are in the British—Carey is very much a Williams-like romantic, seeking a revival of pragmatism, while Grossberg is as intensely theoretical as Hall—

this American cultural studies is worlds apart from earlier work in its sophistication and critique.

4 Lest this dichotomy be overstated, it should be said that the Centre for Mass Communication Research at the University of Leicester undertook research in media effects during the period of Birmingham's growth and maturity. Moreover, in the USA, scholars like George Gerbner and David Riesman, though part of the functionalist empire, sought to make room for culture quite early in the form of Gerbner's "Cultural Indicators" project and "cultivation" model of mediation, and Riesman's "lonely crowd" metaphor.

5 This idealization of culture within a model of communication is demonstrated at its most sincere in the work of James Carey, notably his essays in *Communication as Culture*, and at its most worrisome in the work of anthropologist Clifford Geertz.

6 Williams's *Television: Technology and Cultural Form* rates a single paragraph in *Politics and Letters*, a series of interviews with Williams by the editors of *New Left Review* which represents one of the best secondary sources on Williams's work. Alan O'Connor's book, *Raymond Williams: Writing, Culture, Politics*, for years the major systematic review of Williams by a single author, doesn't offer much more on Williams's media analysis than *Politics and Letters*. So conspicuous was the absence of the television book that an interview was conducted by Stephen Heath and Gillian Skirrow, and later published in Tania Modleski's edited *Studies in Entertainment: Critical Approaches to Mass Culture*, to rectify the minimal coverage in *Politics and Letters*. The result is disappointing.

7 Williams writes in the *Television* study: "In the young radical underground and even more in the young cultural underground, there is a familiarity with media, and an eager sense of experiment and practice, which is as much an effect as the more widely publicized and predicted passivity" (1974:133). Williams throws a crumb to the resistant possibilities in media reception, but it is a meagre one. The mass audience at large is consigned to that same passivity, captive to the television "flow," and there is no discussion of how these notes from underground might circulate back to the mobilized and privatized mainstream.

8 Williams's deep ambivalence toward modernity in the more contradictory form it takes after the late nineteenth century, a period convergent with the emergence of electronic media, has already been cited as evidence of this persistent dislike of refractory social phenomena.

Yet, the thesis identifying the lingering effects of the "culture and civilization" tradition is not without its critics. For example, O'Connor (1989b) reproves Grossberg for failing to appreciate that Williams transcended the culturalism of his early career enough that the opposition of culture and structure was relaxed. Citing Grossberg's reference to "structure of feeling" particularly, O'Connor asserts that Grossberg's "partial and reductionistic" reading of Williams overlooks that this concept had only a residual role in Williams's work after the mid-1970s.

O'Connor's review article in *Critical Studies in Mass Communication* is conspicuous in arguing that Williams had dropped the particular formulation of the "culture and society" tradition, i.e., the "structure of feeling" concept, by the mid-point of his career. O'Connor (1989b:408), however, does not actually disprove Grossberg's claim that Williams remains loyal to "culture and society," only that Williams's use of "structure of feeling" "is actually a contradictory and ad hoc formulation and has only a residual role in Williams's work after the mid-1970s."

Fair enough. But it's unclear why O'Connor cannot bring himself to say that Williams actually drops the "culture and society" tradition altogether, unless as commentators like Prendergast (1995) and Grossberg (1997) indicate, Williams never did. Arguing that Williams dropped this particular usage, "structure of feeling," rather than directly addressing Williams's allegiance to the tradition, is not persuasive.

Out of fairness to Williams, there is evidence of a certain relaxation of his definition of common culture later in his work. Morley and Robins (40) cite Williams in *The Year 2000* for encouraging the reimagining of community to "explore new forms of variable societies and variable identities."

But given that his "When Was Modernism?" and "Culture and Technology" essays were published very late, essays that indicated an impatience with contradiction and phenomena like technology that did not reduce easily to his model of social totality, I have reservations about how new and variable these societies and identities were to be. What is apparent from Williams's essays published at the end of his career, in *The Year 2000* and *The Politics of Modernism*, is that the priority of culture over society is not a residue but a recurrent and enduring theme in his work. The point here is not to genuflect to Williams, but to pay the honour due to him by being respectfully critical. I believe he would understand.

9 In fairness to Hall, the encoding/decoding model was intended as a generic theoretical model to be given flesh later by audience researchers like David Morley, Ien Ang, and Charlotte Brunsdon using ethnographic techniques (e.g., interviews, surveys, observation).

Chapter 4

1 Post-structuralism's postmodern pedigree is obvious enough. However, suggesting a relationship between Bell and postmodern positions may come as a surprise, particularly given the inclusion of postmodernism among his many targets in the essay, "The Cultural Contradictions of Capitalism." Postmodernism, Bell believes, is the mature and exaggerated form of late modernism, and likewise "tears down the boundaries and insists that *acting out*, rather than making distinctions, is the way to gain knowledge" (1976a:52; see also 1976b:53).

Yet, following Kumar (1995), Calhoun (1993), and Alexander (1994), we can mark a transition from high modernist to someone wanting to put modernity behind him (a transition echoing his famous passage from Trotskyist to neo-conservative). The technocratic high modernism of *The Coming of Post-Industrial Society*, a work reissued with a new foreword in 1976, is directly contradicted by the argument in the "Cultural Contradictions" essay (published in *The Cultural Contradictions of Capitalism* in the same year) whereby high modernism is held to have betrayed capitalism by domesticating avant-garde values in the form of consumer culture. Bell's appeal to nostalgia as a means to knit the disjunction of culture and society is a keynote of postmodernism. As Alexander has found:

> What is so striking about this phase of Bell's career, however, is how rapidly the modernist notion of post-industrial society gave way to postmodernism, in content if not in explicit form. For Bell, of course, it was not disappointed radicalism that produced this shift but his disappointments with what he came to call late modernism. When Bell turned away from this degenerate modernism in *The Cultural Contradictions of Capitalism*, his story had changed. Post-industrial society, once the epitome of modernism, now produced, not reason and progress, but emotionalism and irrationalism, categories alarmingly embodied in sixties youth culture. (1994:181-82)

But Bell's protestations to the contrary, Calhoun confirms the inclusion of post-industrial theory within the canon of postmodern works, underlining how both post-industrial and more patently postmodern arguments, such as post-structuralist media theory, agree to there being a definitive "break" with the modern past, to the postmodern centrality of media or knowledge in lieu of a modern emphasis on production, and again, to the obsolescence of modernity itself. As Calhoun sees it,

> postmodernism includes sociological and political economic claims to identity as a basic transition from "modernity" to a new stage of (or beyond) history. These variously emphasize "post-industrial," information or knowledge society as the new societal formation. A new centrality is posited for media, information technology and the production of signification (for example, cultural industry) as an end in itself. Key figures in this line of argument (notably Bell and Touraine, and popularizers like Toffler and Naisbitt) are not directly a part of the postmodernist movement, but their arguments have influenced it substantially. (1995:78)

However, defining Bell as a "postmodernist" may confuse the issue more than is useful, and crudely include him among post-structuralists with whom he may share a certain resemblance in some ways, but with whom he is clearly not a blood relative. It may be sufficient to say that in his resolute opposition to modern culture (but not, of course, to technology or capitalism, which in his analysis are separable from modern values), and in his ambition to propel society beyond modernity, Bell's analysis bears comparison with expressly postmodern arguments. While he is no postmodernist, neither is he a merely reactive traditionalist, and it is his identification with the "break" with modernity and technological determinism that suggests the analogy with Poster and certain aspects of post-structuralist new media theory.

2 "Neo-conservative" is a term originally used to refer to those left-liberal Jewish and American intellectuals, including Bell, Horowitz, Kristol, novelist Saul Bellow, and others, who made a spectacular turn to the political right in light of revelations of Stalin's atrocities, as well as tension between the Jewish and African-American communities. They and their children (Adam Bellow at the Free Press, publisher of *The Bell Curve;* and William Kristol, chief advisor to former US Vice-President Dan Quayle) subsequently took up leadership roles in the post-war Right, and provided the ideological brain trust for Nixon and, most importantly, Reagan. However, the term is more generally used today to refer to the movement they fostered, again, reconciling social conservative and liberal economic positions—as evidenced so instructively in Bell's *Cultural Contradictions.*

Neo-liberalism is a related though different ideology. While sharing a similar faith in market freedom and an aversion to state regulation, neo-liberalism is not conspicuously conservative where social policy is concerned. It is a liberalism freed of that ideology's post-World War II adherence to a Keynesian welfare state, but equally unencumbered by pro-life, pro-gun, anti-crime, or anti-homosexual politics. Neo-conservatism, at its acme of influence in the 1980s, arguably made possible the separation of liberalism from its affiliation with statism, and thus the "New Democrat" and "New Labour" politics in the 1990s US Clinton and UK Blair governments.

Note that post-industrial theory does have adherents who articulate a decidedly radical position; these are often identified as post-Fordist in nature, and generally don't anticipate a paradise that follows on the end of industrial society.

3 It's identified here as "instrumental rationality" because its instrumental, process-oriented values are central to the logic of digital technology, and because of the Frankfurt School's lineage within Marxist criticism, a position with which cultural studies would be sympathetic. But the choice of this name, among the several possibilities available, should not suggest that I favour a Frankfurt School style analysis.

4 It is important to keep in mind Jacques Ellul's concept of "technique," meaning "the totality of methods rationally arrived at and having absolute efficiency in every field of human activity" (Ellul 1964:xxv).

5 This effect is often referred to as the "law of unintended consequences" or, in a more Weberian key, the irrationality of rationality.

6 Some explanation of why Poster, and not Jean Baudrillard, is singled out for attention here is warranted. Baudrillard is unquestionably the most cited and influential post-structuralist theorist of new media. However, though his many books and articles refer to new media, his work rarely addresses the specific

character of these technologies, but rather works within a broad outline of a world in which such media are a central fixture. That is, rather than attend to the post-structuralist implications of binary code or databases, Baudrillard writes on the cultural consequences of simulation at large.

Poster is much more attentive to the technologies themselves, and moreover, his work is a systematic and explicit synthesis not only of Baudrillard, but of the ideas of Foucault, Derrida, and Lyotard as they relate to new media. While Baudrillard is more important as intellectual *provocateur*, Poster is more comprehensive, having the advantage of hindsight and a formal and schematic academic approach to the post-structuralist literature. Baudrillard is anything but formal, schematic, or academic.

7 To be fair to Bell, a considerable thinker in his own right, he does formally disavow technological determinism, i.e., the idea that technology is the principal engine of history, in the foreward to the 1976 edition. In explaining his having attributed to technology a great deal of importance within the argument in *The Coming of Post-Industrial Society*, he hedges: "such emphasis does not mean that technology is the primary determinant of all other societal changes. No conceptual scheme ever exhausts a social reality. Each conceptual scheme is a prism which selects *some* features, rather than others, in order to highlight historical change or, more specifically, to answer certain questions" (1976b:x). This disclaimer aside, Bell's analysis still reads as a case study in technological determinism. To be sure, every conceptual scheme must select some features. But every conceptual scheme must also account for its ideological and structural consequences (whether imagined or real), and Bell does not satisfactorily explain the implications of his having highlighted technology as he has.

8 It should be noted that contemporary "structural adjustment" policies, whereby nations are compelled by international lenders such as the World Bank to privatize their social programs, open their markets to international trade, and generally reduce the state's presence in the national economy, are very much in the spirit of post-war modernization.

9 In a noteworthy digression, Poster here editorializes on the possibility of cooperation between cultural studies and post-structuralism once the modern subject is abandoned:

> If one works outside the binary autonomy/heteronomy, bypassing technological determinism, an alternative is still open of an analytic of technologies of power: this brings into relief the discourse/practices which etch contours of identity versus an analytic of modes of appropriation/resistance which highlight the agency of reception. The former is characteristic of post-structuralist strategies, the latter of the Birmingham school of cultural studies. I regard the two as complementary. (1995:22)

Among many other problems that might beset wholesale cooperation between cultural studies and post-structuralism (though American cultural studies is

THE POLITICS OF ENCHANTMENT [181]

conducting an ongoing experiment in this vein), is the future of the "culture" concept. Although Poster believes that the relative optimism about the subject shared by both cultural studies and post-structuralism offers common ground, he decidedly prefers "information" to "culture."

10 To his credit, Poster is sensitive to post-structuralism's faults, particularly that of linguistic reductionism, i.e., viewing reality exclusively as a matter of language. "While the practice of some post-structuralists may lend itself to this accusation," he writes, "my effort, in theorizing the mode of information, has been to counteract the textualist tendency by linking post-structuralist theory with social change, by connecting it with electronic communications technology, by 'applying' its methods to the arena of everyday life, by insisting on communication as a historical context which justifies the move to an emphasis on language" (Poster 1995:75).

11 To remain focused on new media theory, and not digress into post-structuralism at impossible length, I have not considered the deconstructionist wing of post-structuralism, though reference is made to deconstructionist concepts in later chapters. Poster is not a deconstructionist, nor is much of that media theory inspired by post-structuralism—but Derrida does appear in places. Moreover, deconstruction does not always share with other strains of post-structuralism their disregard for some metaphysical or epistemological bottom line. Thus deconstruction may in this sense be regarded as more romantic and less Nietzschean in character.

Chapter 5

1 Understanding the Internet is a matter of finding metaphors to describe and analyze a system with an internal complexity that exceeds the technical knowledge of many media critics, including this one. Chapter 4 ("Visionaries and Convergences: An Accidental History of the Net") of Howard Rheingold's book, *The Virtual Community,* provides an excellent abridged history of the Net's development.

2 On a similar note, it is worth reflecting whether the "linguistic turn" would have been possible without the coincidence of the early electronic media. In what sense did these media make possible a theory, albeit intensely and technically linguistic in nature, that pointed to the relative fluidity of meaning, language's part in social construction, and the contingency of the relation between signifier and referent?

3 Stone (1995:21) says of her relationship to cultural studies: "My chosen method of representation for this attempt—a kind of adventure narrative interspersed with forays into theory—developed out of earlier work....I feel that it is only through the process of trying out various forms of representation, some experimental and some not, that I can properly grapple with the formidable challenge of finding viable pathways into academic discourse in the time of cultural studies."

4 "Technology" might be defined as the system(s) which supports the achievement of practical tasks or "techniques" (Williams 1983b:315), and in this symbolizes that which most crystallizes the human relationship with the non-human, because technologies enable us to modify our environments (however defined). Media technology symbolizes a still purer case, since it is the means by which we formally make coherent and meaningful that relationship between self and world, being and non-being, whether we are cyborgs or not.

Irreducible to discourse and yet a channel for it in its media form, an inorganic entity and yet at times eerily almost human, technology confirms that something alien has indeed landed on the planet. It forces on media analysis the issue of media's relationship to the material world, because the book or the television box are metonyms both of the "hard" political-economic structure that made them, and of the ineffable materiality of the referent behind the sign. I cite Williams's preferred definition of technology here because it is not incompatible with my objectives; it is his articulation of technology with society that remains a problem.

5 With the qualified exception of elements of his 1962 book, *Communications*, which featured some pragmatist content.

6 The reader is advised to refer to the discussion of Luddism as an ultimately unhelpful response to new technology—even when this Luddism is made philosophically sophisticated.

7 Details on Kant's concept of "schemata" are drawn from the entry for "Kant, Immanuel" in *The Cambridge Dictionary of Philosophy*, ed. Robert Audi (Cambridge: Cambridge University Press, 1995).

8 The similarity of this point to McLuhan's argument in *Understanding Media* about technology being an extension of our bodies and their senses, and the value of seeing the use of technology as something best guided by artists sensitive to the shifting "ground" of perception, is unintended but by no means regretted.

9 Habermas succinctly defines the public sphere:

> The bourgeois public sphere may be conceived above all as the sphere of private people come together as a public; they soon claimed the public sphere regulated from above against the public authorities themselves, to engage them in a debate over the general rules governing relations in the basically privatized but publicly relevant sphere of commodity exchange and social labor. The medium of this political confrontation was peculiar and without historical precedent: people's public use of their reason. (1989a:27)

This is extended more significantly to the mass media in a later encyclopedia entry written by Habermas, and reprinted in Douglas Kellner and Stephen Bronner's edited volume, *Critical Theory and Society: A Reader:*

> By "the public sphere" we mean first of all a realm of our social life in which something approaching public opinion can be formed. Access is guaranteed to all citizens....Citizens behave as a public body when they confer in an unrestricted fashion...about matters of

> general interest. In a large public body, this kind of communication requires specific means for transmitting information and influencing those who receive it. Today, newspapers and magazines, radio and television are the media of the public sphere. (Habermas 1989b:136)

10 Peters himself examines mass media forms only. The Internet is a "distributed" medium because messages don't emanate from a single source (e.g., radio or television station transmitter) to a mass audience, but from an infinitely variable number of senders to an infinitely variable number of receivers. As such, the medium is "distributed" because information is transmitted from any number of points in the Internet, and the Internet itself as a physical artifact is radically decentred among many web sites, institutional servers, Internet providers, and various nodes on backbones, etc. The Internet, in contrast to the "mass" model of mediation characteristic of broadcast, is often regarded as a "many to many" model of mediation.

Chapter 6

1 Globalization may be defined as "the growth and acceleration of economic and cultural networks which operate on a worldwide scale and basis" (O'Sullivan et al. 1994:130). It is synonymous with the tilt toward transnational corporations, worldwide media networks, a "casino capitalist" turn away from manufacturing and toward finance capital, and "postmodern" culture.

2 I attended a day of panels and papers hosted by the International Communication Association at Carleton University, 29 May 1998. The ICA, largely composed of scholars identified with a political economy of communication position—Hamid Mowlana, Janet Wasko, Graham Murdock, Jeremy Tunstall, and Vincent Mosco being in attendance at this particular conference—seemed more receptive to cultural theory than the passionate arguments of a Nicholas Garnham would suggest. Mowlana gave the keynote address on the topic of how Islamic culture is largely unintelligible to Western cultural analysts, and there were occasional remarks from the floor about the importance of understanding culture on other than reflectionist terms. This suggests that there may be counterparts to Harp and Kellner emerging from political economy's side of the polemical divide, although this is not yet reflected in much of the published literature.

3 The full quote indicates the degree of McGuigan's correlation of romanticism and cultural studies:

> In terms of aesthetics, the discovery of popular culture is related to the Romantic reaction to Classicism, the attempt to break with excessively formalistic, dry and unemotional art. To recover something of the vital impulses of ordinary people, their apparent spontaneity and disregard for propriety, their "naturalness," are amongst the themes which cut both ways: back to a myth of an "organic" past in contrast to a "mechanical" present, or forward to a Utopian

future of popular emancipation. It is no accident that the great Welsh cultural theorist Raymond Williams should most famously have opened his account of "culture" with a book on English Romanticism and its conservative and radical strands: *Culture and Society*, published in 1958. (McGuigan 1992:10)

4 Williams defined cultural materialism in "Notes on Marxism in Britain since 1945," *New Left Review* 100 (November 1976-January 1977): 88, and quoted in Schiller (1996:187): "What I would now claim to have reached...is a theory of culture as a (social and material) productive process and of specific practices, of 'arts', as social uses of material means of production (from language as material 'practical consciousness' to the specific technologies of writing and forms of writing, through to mechanical and electronic communicative systems)."

5 Prendergast documents the growing sophistication of cultural materialism, by way of Gramsci's influence on Williams, Williams's exposure to 1960s social movements that celebrated difference rather than a class consensus, and the complexity of an information-based transnational capitalism:

At the level of general theory, one possibility might be to retain the indispensable emphasis on connection while detaching it from the more holistic and value-laden notion of wholeness, thus permitting a way of thinking the social that is more compatible with a sense of the fluid, heterogeneous, and fragmentary character of social formations. The later work, notably the book *Culture*...moves toward just this view; by consistently approaching "totality" ("the whole social order") from the notion of "complex real processes," the argument both demands and engenders as crucial to the actual analytical programme of a "sociology of culture" a strongly maintained attention, alongside the continuing stress on the connected, to the concrete and differential specificity of cultural practices. (1995:16)

Bibliography

Agger, B. 1992. *The Discourse of Domination: From the Frankfurt School to Postmodernism*. Evanston: Northwestern University Press.

Alexander, J. 1985. "Introduction." In *Neo-functionalism*, edited by J. Alexander and J. Turner, 7-18. Berkeley: Sage.

——. 1994. "Modern, Anti, Post and Neo: How Social Theories Have Tried to Understand the 'New World' of 'Our Time.'" *Zeitschrift fur Soziologie* 23, 3: 165-97.

Ang, I. 1991. *Desperately Seeking the Audience*. London: Routledge.

Appignanesi, R., and C. Garratt. 1995. *Postmodernism for Beginners*. Cambridge: Icon.

Arnold, M. 1986. *Culture and Anarchy*. 1869. Reprint, Cambridge: Cambridge University Press.

Aronowitz, S., and M. Menser. 1996. "On Cultural Studies, Science and Technology." In *Technoscience and Cyberculture*, edited by S. Aronowitz, B. Martinsons, and M. Menser, 7-30. New York: Routledge.

Baudrillard, J. 1983. "The Ecstasy of Communication." In *The Anti-Aesthetic: Essays on Postmodern Culture*, edited by H. Foster, 126-34. Seattle: Bay Press.

Bell, D. 1976a. *The Cultural Contradictions of Capitalism*. New York: Basic.

——. 1976b. *The Coming of Post-Industrial Society: A Venture in Social Forecasting*. New York: Harper Collins.

Berland, J. 1992. "Angels Dancing: Cultural Technologies and the Production of Space." In *Cultural Studies*, edited by L. Grossberg, C. Nelson, and P. Treichler, 38-55. New York: Routledge.

Berman, M. 1982. *All That Is Solid Melts into Air: The Experience of Modernity*. New York: Simon and Schuster.

Billig, M., and H.W. Simons. 1994. "Introduction." In *After Postmodernism: Reconstructing Ideology Critique*, edited by M. Billig and H.W. Simons, 1-11. London: Sage.

Blake, W. "Marriage of Heaven and Hell." In *The Complete Poetry and Prose of William Blake*. Edited by D. Erdman. Garden City: Anchor.

Blechman, M. 1999. *Revolutionary Romanticism: A Drunken Boat Anthology*. San Francisco: City Lights.

Bowie, A. 1991. Review of *The Ideology of the Aesthetic* by Terry Eagleton. *Radical Philosophy* 57 (Spring): 36-37.

———. 1995. "Romanticism and Technology." *Radical Philosophy* 72 (July/August): 5-16.

———. 1997. *From Romanticism to Critical Theory: The Philosophy of German Literary Theory*. London: Routledge.

Brantlinger, P. 1990. *Crusoe's Footprints: Cultural Studies in Britain and America*. New York: Routledge.

Calhoun, C. 1992. "The Infrastructure of Modernity: Indirect Social Relationships, Information Technology, and Social Integration." In *Social Change and Modernity*, edited by H. Haferkamp and N.J. Smelser, 205-36. Berkeley: University of California.

———. 1993. "Postmodernism as Pseudohistory." *Theory, Culture and Society* 10, 1: 75-96.

Campbell, C. 1987. *The Romantic Ethic and the Spirit of Modern Consumerism*. Oxford: Basil Blackwell.

Carey, J. 1988. *Communication as Culture: Essays on Media and Society*. Boston: Unwin Hyman.

Christensen, J. 1994. The Romantic Movement at the End of History. *Critical Inquiry* 20, 3: 452-76.

———. 1997. "Thomas De Quincey, Bill Gates, Johns Hopkins and the Romantic Ethic of Digital Media." Department of English, Johns Hopkins University. Manuscript.

Connor, S. 1997. *Postmodernist Culture: An Introduction to Theories of the Contemporary*. 2nd ed. Oxford: Blackwell.

Cormack, M. 1992. *Ideology*. Ann Arbor: University of Michigan Press.

Crisell, A. 1986. *Understanding Radio*. London: Methuen.

Davies, I. 1991. "British Cultural Marxism." *International Journal of Politics, Culture and Society* 4, 3: 323-44.

———. 1995. *Cultural Studies and Beyond: Fragments of Empire*. New York: Routledge.

Dery, M. 1996. *Escape Velocity: Cyberculture at the End of the Century*. New York: Grove Press.

Dienst, R. 1996. "The Futures Market: Global Economics and Cultural Studies." In *Reading the Shape of the World: Toward an International Cultural Studies*, edited by H. Schwartz and R. Dienst, 67-92. Boulder: Westview.

Docker, J. 1994. *Postmodernism and Popular Culture: A Cultural History*. Cambridge: Cambridge University Press.

Douglas, S.J. 1999. *Listening In: Radio and the American Imagination*. New York: Random House.

Downing, J. 1997. "Cultural Studies, Communication and Change: Eastern Europe to the Urals." In *Cultural Studies in Question*, edited by M. Ferguson and P. Golding, 187-204. London: Sage.

Dworkin, D. 1997. *Cultural Marxism in Postwar Britain: History, the New Left, and the Origins of Cultural Studies*. Durham: Duke University Press.

Eagleton, T. 1983. *Literary Theory: An Introduction*. Oxford: Basil Blackwell.

———. 1990. *The Ideology of the Aesthetic*. Oxford: Basil Blackwell.

———. 1991a. *Ideology: An Introduction*. London: Verso.

———. 1991b. Review of *Aesthetics and Subjectivity: From Kant to Nietzsche* by Andrew Bowie. *Radical Philosophy* 57 (Spring): 37-38.

Easthope, A. 1993. *Wordsworth Now and Then: Romanticism and Contemporary Culture*. Buckingham: Open University Press.

Eksteins, M. 1989. *Rites of Spring: The Great War and the Birth of the Modern Age*. Toronto: Lester and Orpen Dennys.

Elam, D. 1992. *Romancing the Postmodern*. London: Routledge.

Ellul, J. 1964. *The Technological Society*. New York: Vintage.

Featherstone, M., ed. 1990. *Global Culture: Nationalism, Globalization and Modernity*. London: Sage.

Ferguson, M., and P. Golding, eds. 1997. *Cultural Studies in Quesion*. London: Sage.

Fiske, J. 1987. "British Cultural Studies and Television." In *Channels of Discourse: Television and Contemporary Criticism*, edited by R. Allen, 254-90. Chapel Hill: University of North Carolina.

———. 1989. *Understanding Popular Culture*. London: Unwin Hyman.

Foucault, M. 1979. *Discipline and Punish: The Birth of the Prison*. Translated by Alan Sheridan. New York: Vintage.

Frank, T. 1996."When Class Disappears." *The Baffler* 9: 3-12.

Garnham, N. 1983. "Towards a Theory of Cultural Materialism." *Journal of Communication* 33, 3: 314-29.

———. 1990. *Capitalism and Communication: Global Culture and the Economics of Information*. London: Sage, 1990.

———. 1995. "Political Economy and Cultural Studies: Reconciliation or Divorce?" *Critical Studies in Mass Communication* 12, 1: 62-71.

Gibson, W. 1984. *Neuromancer*. New York: Ace.

Gingrich, N. 1994. "Cyberspace and the American Dream: A Magna Carta for the Knowledge Age." Release 1.2, 22 August 1994. Progress and Freedom Foundation. www.hartford-hwp.com/archives/45/062.html

Golding, P., and G. Murdock. 1991. "Culture, Communications and Political Economy." In *Mass Media and Society*, edited by J. Curran and M. Gurevitch, 15-32. London: Edwin Arnold.

Gouldner, A. 1973. *For Sociology: Renewal and Critique in Sociology Today*. New York: Basic.

———. 1976. *The Dialectic of Ideology and Technology: The Origins, Grammar and Future of Ideology*. New York: Oxford University Press.

Gronbeck, B.E. 1990. "Communication Technology, Consciousness and Culture: Supplementing FM-2030's View of Transhumanity." In *Communication and the Culture of Technology,* edited by M.J. Medhurst, A. Gonzalez, and T.R. Peterson, 3-18. Pullman: Washington State University Press.

Grossberg, L. 1992. *We Gotta Get out of this Place: Popular Conservatism and Post-modern Culture.* New York: Routledge.

——. 1995. "Cultural Studies versus Political Economy: Is Anybody Else Bored with this Debate?" *Critical Studies in Mass Communication* 12, 1: 72-81.

——. 1996a "History, Politics and Postmodernism: Stuart Hall and Cultural Studies." In *Stuart Hall: Critical Dialogues in Cultural Studies,* edited by D. Morley and K.H. Chen, 151-73. New York: Routledge.

——. 1996b. "On Postmodernism and Articulation: An Interview with Stuart Hall." In *Stuart Hall: Critical Dialogues In Cultural Studies,* edited by D. Morley and K.H. Chen. 131-50. New York: Routledge.

——. 1997. *Bringing It All Back Home: Essays on Cultural Studies.* Durham: Duke University Press.

Habermas, J. 1987. *The Philosophical Discourse of Modernity.* Cambridge: MIT Press.

——. 1989a. *The Structural Transformation of the Public Sphere: An Inquiry into a Category of Bourgeois Society.* Cambridge: MIT Press.

——. 1989b. "The Public Sphere." In *Critical Theory: A Reader,* edited by D. Kellner and S. Bronner, 136-42. New York: Routledge.

——. 1993. "Modernity: An Unfinished Project." In *Postmodernism: A Reader,* edited by T. Docherty, 98-109. New York: Columbia University Press.

Hall, S. 1980a. "Encoding and Decoding." In *Culture, Media, Language: Working Papers in Cultural Studies, 1972-79,* edited by S. Hall. D. Hobson, A. Lowe, and P. Willis, 128-38. London: Hutchinson.

——. 1980b. "Cultural Studies and the Centre: Some Problematics and Problems." In *Culture, Media, Language: Working Papers in Cultural Studies, 1972-79,* edited by S. Hall. D. Hobson, A. Lowe, P. Willis, 15-47. London: Hutchinson.

——. 1980c. "Introduction to Media Studies at the Centre" In *Culture, Media, Language: Working Papers in Cultural Studies, 1972-79,* edited by S. Hall, D. Hobson, A. Lowe, and P. Willis, 117-21. London: Hutchinson.

——. 1982. "The Rediscovery of 'Ideology': Return of the Repressed in Media Studies." In *Culture, Society and the Media,* edited by M. Gurevitch, T. Bennett, J. Curran, and J. Woollacott, 56-90. London: Methuen.

——. 1986. "Cultural Studies: Two Paradigms." In *Media, Culture and Society: A Critical Reader,* edited by R. Collins, 57-72. London: Sage.

——. 1992. "Cultural Studies and Its Theoretical Legacies." In *Cultural Studies,* edited by L. Grossberg, C. Nelson, and P. Treichler, 277-94. New York: Routledge.

Hampson, H. 1968. *The Enlightenment: An Evaluation of Its Assumptions, Attitudes and Values.* London: Penguin.

Haraway, D. 1991. *Simians, Cyborgs and Women: The Reinvention of Nature.* New York: Routledge.

Hardt, H. 1992. *Critical Communication Studies: Communication, History and Theory in America*. New York: Routledge.

Harp, J. 1991. "Political Economy/Cultural Studies: Exploring Points of Convergence." *Canadian Review of Sociology and Anthropology* 28, 2: 206-24.

Harris, David. 1992. *From Class Struggle to the Politics of Pleasure: The Effects of Gramscianism on Cultural Studies*. London and New York: Routledge.

Harvey, D. 1989. *The Condition of Postmodernity: An Enquiry into the Origins of Cultural Change*. Oxford: Basil Blackwell.

Hebdige, D. 1996. "The Impossible Object: Towards a Sociology of the Sublime." In *Cultural Studies and Communications*, edited by J. Curran, V. Walkerdine, and D. Morley, 66-92. New York: Arnold.

Held, D. 1980. *Introduction to Critical Theory: Horkheimer to Habermas*. Berkeley: University of California Press.

Hewitt, R. 1997. *The Possibilities of Society: Wordsworth, Coleridge, and the Sociological Viewpoint of Romanticism*. Albany: State University of New York.

Horkheimer, M., and T. Adorno. 1972. *Dialectic of Enlightenment*. 1944. Reprint, New York: Herder and Herder.

Illouz, E. 1997. *Consuming the Romantic Utopia: Love and the Cultural Contradictions of Capitalism*. Berkeley: University of California Press.

Inglis, F. 1993. *Cultural Studies*. Oxford: Blackwell.

Jameson, F. 1984. "Postmodernism, or the Cultural Logic of Late Capitalism." *New Left Review* 146 (July/August): 53-93.

———. 1991. *Postmodernism, or the Cultural Logic of Late Capitalism*. Durham, NC: Duke University Press.

Jay, M. 1984. *Marxism and Totality: The Adventures of a Concept from Lukács to Habermas*. Berkeley: University of California.

Jentzen, J. 1990. *Redeeming Modernity: Contradictions in Media Criticism*. Newbury Park: Sage.

Kant, I. 1988. "Excerpts from The Critique of Judgement." In *The Origins of Modern Critical Thought: German Aesthetic and Literary Criticism from Lessing to Hegel*, edited by D. Simpson, 89-123. Cambridge: Cambridge University Press.

"Kant, Immanuel." 1995. *The Cambridge Dictionary of Philosophy*. Edited by Robert Audi. Cambridge: Cambridge University Press.

Kellner, D. 1995. *Media Culture: Cultural Studies, Identity and Politics between the Modern and the Postmodern*. New York: Routledge.

———. 1997. "Overcoming the Divide: Cultural Studies and Political Economy." In *Cultural Studies in Question*, edited by M. Ferguson and P. Golding, 102-19. London: Sage.

Kern, S. 1983. *The Culture of Time and Space, 1880-1918*. Cambridge: Harvard University Press.

Klein, Naomi. 2000. *No Logo: Taking Aim at the Brand Bullies*. Toronto: Knopf.

Kroker, A. 1987. "Body Digest: Theses on the Disappearing Body in the Hypermodern Condition." *Canadian Journal of Political and Social Theory* 11, 1-2: i-xvi.

Kumar, K. 1978. *Prophecy and Progress: The Sociology of Industrial and Post-Industrial Society.* London: Allen Lane.

——. 1995. *From Post-Industrial to Postmodern Society: New Theories of the Contemporary World.* Oxford: Blackwell.

Lacoue-Labarthe, P., and J.L. Nancy. 1988. *The Literary Absolute: The Theory of Literature in German Romanticism.* Translated by Philip Barnard and Cheryl Lester. Albany: SUNY Press.

Leavis, F.R. 1930. *Mass Civilization and Minority Culture.* Cambridge: Minority Press.

Leiss, W. 1990. *Under Technology's Thumb.* Montreal and Kingston: McGill-Queen's University Press.

Levinson, M. 1994. "Romantic Criticism: The State of the Art." In *At the Limits of Romanticism: Essays in Cultural, Feminist, and Materialist Criticism,* edited by M.A. Favret and N.J. Watson, 1-19. Bloomington: Indiana.

Lippman, W. 1922. *Public Opinion.* New York: Harcourt Brace.

Livingston, I. 1997. *Arrow of Chaos: Romanticism and Postmodernity.* Minneapolis: University of Minnesota.

Lowery, S., and M. DeFleur. 1983. *Milestones in Mass Communications Research: Media Effects.* New York: Longman.

Lukács, G. 1971. *History and Class Consciousness: Studies in Marxist Dialectics.* Translated by Rodney Livingstone. Cambridge: MIT Press.

Lunn, E. 1982. *Marxism and Modernism: An Historical Study of Lukács, Brecht, Benjamin, and Adorno.* Berkeley: University of California Press.

Lury, C. 1996. *Consumer Culture.* New Brunswick, NJ: Rutgers University Press.

Lyon, D. 1988. *The Information Society: Issues and Illusions.* Cambridge, UK: Polity Press, 1988.

——. 1994. *The Electronic Eye: The Rise of Surveillance Society.* Minneapolis: University of Minnesota Press.

Lyotard, J. 1993. "The Sublime and the Avant-Garde." In *Postmodernism: A Reader,* edited by T. Docherty, 244-56. New York: Columbia University Press.

Mannheim, K. 1953. *Essays on Sociology and Social Psychology.* London: Routledge and Kegan Paul.

Marcuse, H. 1964. *One-Dimensional Man.* Boston: Beacon Press.

Marx, L. 1964. *The Machine in the Garden: Technology and the Pastoral Ideal in America.* New York: Oxford University Press.

McCormack, T. 1994. "Must We Buy into Technological Determinism?" Paper presented at Symposium on Free Speech and Privacy in the Information Age. University of Waterloo, Waterloo, ON. 26 November.

McGuigan, J. 1992. *Cultural Populism.* New York: Routledge.

——. 1996. *Culture and the Public Sphere.* New York: Routledge.

——. 1997. "Cultural Populism Revisited." In *Cultural Studies in Question,* edited by M. Ferguson and P. Golding, 138-54. London: Sage.

McKibben, B. 1993. *The Age of Missing Information.* New York: Plume.

McRobbie, A. 1994. *Postmodernism and Popular Culture.* London: Routledge.

Milner, A. 1994a. "Cultural Materialism, Culturalism and Post-Culturalism: The Legacy of Raymond Williams." *Theory, Culture and Society* 11, 1: 43-73.

———. 1994b. *Contemporary Cultural Theory: An Introduction*. London: University College of London Press.

Modleski, T. 1986. *Studies in Entertainment: Critical Approaches to Mass Culture*. Bloomington: Indiana University Press.

Montgomery, M. 1995. *Language and Society: An Introduction*. 2nd ed. London: Routledge.

Morley, D., and K. Robins. 1995. *Spaces of Identity: Global Media, Electronic Landscapes and Cultural Boundaries*. London: Routledge.

Mosco, V. 1996. *The Political Economy of Communication: Rethinking and Renewal*. Thousand Oaks, CA: Sage.

Norris, C. 1992. *Uncritical Theory: Postmodernism, Intellectuals and the Gulf War*. Amherst: University of Massachusetts Press.

Novalis (F. von Hardenberg). 1988. "Monologue." In *The Origins of Modern Critical Thought: German Aesthetic and Literary Criticism from Lessing to Hegel*, edited by D. Simpson, 273-76. Cambridge: Cambridge University Press.

O'Brien, C.C. 1994. *On The Eve of the Millennium*. Toronto: Anansi.

O'Connor, A. 1989a. *Raymond Williams: Writing, Culture, Politics*. Oxford: Basil Blackwell.

———. 1989b. "The Problem of American Cultural Studies." *Critical Studies in Mass Communication* 6, 4: 405-13.

Ong, W.J. 1971. *Rhetoric, Romance and Technology: Studies in the Interaction of Expression and Culture*. Ithaca: Cornell University Press.

O'Sullivan, T., J. Hartley, D. Saunders, M. Montgomery, and J. Fiske. 1994. *Key Concepts in Communication and Cultural Studies*. 2nd ed. New York: Routledge.

Payne, M., ed. 1997. *A Dictionary of Cultural and Critical Theory*. Oxford: Blackwell.

Peters, J.D. 1994. "The Gaps of which Communication is Made." *Critical Studies in Mass Communication* 11, 2: 117-40.

———. 1996. "The Uncanniness of Mass Communications in Interwar Social Thought." *Journal of Communication* 46, 3: 108-23.

———. 1999. *Speaking into the Air: A History of the Idea of Communication*. Chicago: University of Chicago Press.

Pietila, V. 1994. "Perspectives on Our Past: Charting the Histories of Mass Communication Studies." *Critical Studies in Mass Communication* 11, 4: 346-61.

Pinkney, T. 1989. "Raymond Williams and the 'Two Faces of Modernism.'" In *Raymond Williams: Critical Perspectives*, edited by T. Eagleton, 12-34. Boston: Northeastern University Press.

Porter, D., and D. Prince. 1998. *England from $60 a Day*. New York: Macmillan.

Poster, M. 1990. *The Mode of Information: Poststructuralism and Social Context*. Chicago: University of Chicago.

———. 1995. *The Second Media Age*. Cambridge: Polity Press.

Postman, N. 1987. *Amusing Ourselves to Death: Public Discourse in the Age of Show Business*. New York: Penguin.

——. 1999. *Building a Bridge to the Nineteenth Century: How the Past Can Improve Our Future*. New York: Random House.

Prendergast, C. 1995. "Introduction: Groundings and Emergings." *Cultural Materialism: On Raymond Williams*, 1-28. Minneapolis: University of Minnesota Press.

Probyn, E. 1987. "Bodies and Anti-Bodies: Feminism and the Postmodern." *Cultural Studies* 1, 3: 349-60.

Pyle, F. 1985. *The Ideology of Imagination: Subject and Society in the Discourse of Romanticism*. Stanford: Stanford University Press.

Radway, J. 1984. *Reading the Romance: Women, Patriarchy and Popular Culture*. Chapel Hill: University of North Carolina Press.

Rheingold, H. 1993. *The Virtual Community: Homesteading on the Electronic Frontier*. New York: Harper Perennial.

Robertson, R. 1992. *Globalization: Social Theory and Global Culture*. New York: Sage.

Robins, K., and F. Webster. 1987. "The Communications Revolution: New Media, Old Problems." *Communication* 10, 1: 71-89.

——. 1988. "Cybernetic Capitalism: Information Technology, Everyday Life." In *The Political Economy of Information,* edited by V. Mosco and J. Wasko, 44-75. Madison: University of Wisconsin Press.

——. 1999. *Times of the Technoculture: From the Information Society to the Virtual Life*. New York: Routledge.

Ross, A. 1991. *Strange Weather: Culture, Science and Technology in the Age of Limits*. New York: Verso.

Ross, A., and C. Penley. 1991. *Technoculture*. Minneapolis: University of Minnesota.

Roszak, T. 1986. *The Cult of Information: The Folklore of Computers and the True Art of Thinking*. New York: Pantheon.

Saiedi, N. 1993. *The Birth of Social Theory: Social Thought in the Enlightenment and Romanticism*. New York: University Press of America.

Sale, K. 1995. *Rebels against the Future: The Luddites and Their War on the Industrial Revolution: Lessons for the Computer Age*. Reading, MA: Addison-Wesley.

Schiller, D. 1996. *Theorizing Communication: A History*. New York: Oxford University Press.

Schlegel, A. 1988. "Lectures on Dramatic Art and Literature." In *The Origins of Modern Critical Thought: German Aesthetic and Literary Criticism from Lessing to Hegel,* edited by D. Simpson, 251-72. Cambridge: Cambridge University Press.

Schlegel, F. 1988. Selections. *The Origins of Modern Critical Thought: German Aesthetic and Literary Criticism from Lessing to Hegel,* edited by D. Simpson, 177-208. Cambridge: Cambridge University Press.

Seyhan, A. 1992. *Representation and Its Discontents: The Critical Legacy of German Romanticism*. Berkeley: University of California Press.

Shallis, M. 1984. *The Silicon Idol: The Micro Revolution and Its Implications*. Oxford: Oxford University Press.

Sholle, D. 1988. "Critical Studies: From the Theory of Ideology to Power/Knowledge." *Critical Studies in Mass Communication* 5 (March): 16-41.

Silverstone, R. 1994. *Television and Everyday Life.* New York: Routledge.

Simpson, D. 1993. *Romanticism, Nationalism and the Revolt against Theory.* Chicago: University of Chicago Press.

Skirrow, G., and S. Heath. 1986. "An Interview with Raymond Williams." In *Studies in Entertainment: Critical Approaches to Mass Culture,* edited by T. Modleski, 3-17. Bloomington: Indiana University Press.

Stevenson, N. 1995. *Understanding Media Cultures: Social Theory and Mass Communication.* London: Sage.

Stoll, C. 1996. *Silicon Snake Oil: Second Thoughts on the Information Highway.* New York: Anchor.

Stone, A.R. 1991. "Will the Real Body Please Stand Up? Boundary Stories about Virtual Cultures." In *Cyberspace: First Steps,* edited by M. Benedikt, 81-118. Cambridge: MIT Press.

———. 1995. *The War of Desire and Technology at the Close of the Mechanical Age.* Cambridge: MIT Press.

Surin, K. 1995. "Raymond Williams on Tragedy and Revolution." In *Cultural Materialism: On Raymond Williams,* 143-72. Minneapolis: University of Minnesota.

Thompson, C. 1995. "In Space, Everyone Can Hear You Scream." *This Magazine,* August, 14-18.

Thompson, E.P. 1977. *William Morris: Romantic to Revolutionary.* 1955. Reprint, New York: Pantheon.

———. 1993. *Witness against the Beast: William Blake and the Moral Law.* New York: New Press.

Thompson, J. 1990. *Ideology and Modern Culture: Critical Social Theory in the Era of Mass Communication.* Cambridge: Polity Press.

———. 1995. *The Media and Modernity.* Stanford: Stanford University Press.

Tirykian, E.A. 1991. "Modernisation: Exhumetur in Pace (Rethinking Macrosociology in the 1990s)." *International Sociology* 6, 2: 165-80.

———. 1992. "Dialectics of Modernity: Reenchantment and Dedifferentiation as Counterprocesses." In *Social Change and Modernity,* edited by H. Haferkamp and N.J. Smelser, 78-94. Berkeley: University of California Press.

Tomlinson, J. 1991. *Cultural Imperialism.* London: Pinter.

Turkle, S. 1984. *The Second Self: Computers and the Human Spirit.* New York: Simon and Schuster.

———. 1995. *Life on the Screen: Identity in the Age of the Internet.* New York: Simon and Schuster.

Turner, G. 1990. *British Cultural Studies: An Introduction.* New York: Unwin Hyman.

Venturi, Robert. 1972. *Learning from Las Vegas.* Cambridge: MIT Press.

Volosinov, V.N. 1986. *Marxism and the Philosophy of Language.* Translated by L. Matejka and I.R. Titunik. 1929. Reprint, Cambridge: Harvard University Press.

Wang, O.N.C. 1996. *Fantastic Modernity: Dialectical Readings in Romanticism and Theory.* Baltimore: Johns Hopkins University Press.

Weber, M. 1958. *From Max Weber: Essays in Sociology.* Edited and translated by H.H. Gerth and C. Wright Mills. New York: Oxford University Press.

Webster, F. 1995. *Theories of the Information Society.* New York: Routledge.

Webster, F., and K. Robins. 1986. *Information Technology: A Luddite Analysis.* Norwood, NJ: Ablex.

Wheeler, K. 1993. *Romanticism, Pragmatism and Deconstruction.* Oxford: Blackwell.

White, D.E. 1999. Introduction to *Irony and Clerisy.* Romantic Circles Praxis Series. www.rc.umd.edu/praxis/irony/white/ironyintro.html

Wiener, N. 1954. *The Human Use of Human Beings: Cybernetics and Society.* New York: Doubleday.

Wills, G. 1987. *Reagan's America: Innocents at Home.* Garden City, NJ: Doubleday.

Williams, R. 1958. *Culture and Society: 1780-1950.* London: Chatto and Windus.

——. 1962. *Communications.* 3rd ed. Harmondsworth: Penguin.

——. 1961. *The Long Revolution.* Middlesex: Penguin.

——. 1966. *Modern Tragedy.* Stanford: Stanford University Press.

——. 1968. *Drama from Ibsen to Brecht.* London: Chatto and Windus.

——. 1973. *The Country and the City.* Oxford: Oxford University Press.

——. 1974. *Television: Technology and Cultural Form.* New York: Schocken Books.

——. 1977. *Marxism and Literature.* Oxford: Oxford University Press.

——. 1979. *Politics and Letters: Interviews with New Left Review.* London: Verso.

——. 1980. *Problems in Materialism and Culture.* London: Verso.

——. 1981. *Culture.* Glasgow: Fontana.

——. 1983a. *The Year 2000.* New York: Pantheon.

——. 1983b. *Keywords: A Vocabulary of Culture and Society.* Rev. ed. New York: Oxford University Press.

——. 1989. *The Politics of Modernism: Against the New Conformists.* London: Verso.

Zuboff, S. 1988. *In the Age of the Smart Machine: The Future of Work and Power.* New York: Basic.

Index

aesthetics: in capitalism, 35; critical
 resistance to, 29-34, 56; fascist, 31-32;
 and language, 67-69; in Marxism, 68;
 as model, 174; modern, 50, 117; and
 morality, 118; postmodern 30, 31;
 romantic view of, 2, 3, 24, 69
Agger, B., 109
Alexander, J., 109, 100, 179n. 1
Althusser, L., 51, 52, 57, 59, 61, 127
Arnold, M., 43, 44, 46, 50, 84
art, 24, 27
articulation, 60, 150-51
audience, 56-58, 61, 79, 81, 83, 85-88,
 152, 177n. 7. *See also* media: effects
 model, encoding/decoding

Barthes, R., 18, 73
Baudrillard, J., 8, 114, 123, 124, 157
beauty. *See* aesthetics
Bell, D., 12, 89-90, 92, 94, 98-103, 107,
 174-75n. 6; and postmodernism,
 178-80n. 1; and technological
 determinism, 181n. 7
Benjamin, W., 9, 31
Berland, J., 87, 140
Birmingham, Centre for Contemporary
 Cultural Studies, 4, 6, 12, 17, 57, 148;
 and cultural studies, 172n. 1; theory at
 72, 73
body, 61, 123-25, 128-29, 183n. 8
Bowie, A., 19, 33, 34, 67, 68, 109, 119

Calhoun, C., 139-40, 179n. 1
Campbell, C., 153, 154
capitalism, 89, 98, 99, 154, 162, 175n. 6;
 romanticism as critique of, 1, 111, 146,
 155-56. *See also* political economy
Carey, J., 62, 76
Christensen, J., 11, 19, 171n. 3
communication, 24, 77, 114, 142; and
 culture, 79, 80, 82, 138, 140, 165; gap
 in, 139, 141-42
community: class basis of, 84; discursive,
 84, 113, 136, 137; knowable, 83, 84,
 138; virtual, 136, 138; vs. global
 village, 85; pragmatism and, 76
complexity, 40, 92, 132
computers, 96, 107, 112, 122, 132, 138.
 See also Internet
consumerism, 153-54, 156
cultural: imperialism, 157; materialism,
 163-66, 185n. 5; populism, 145, 152-53
cultural studies: critiques of, 37, 46, 132,
 145, 147, 148, 152, 153; and
 economics, 152-53, 165; and effects
 model, 78, 79; issues in, 3-4, 7, 98,
 168, 181n. 9; and political economy,
 146, 149, 151-52; and romanticism, 6,
 9, 17, 18, 20, 22, 171n. 2, 184-85n. 3;
 UK vs. USA, 12, 79, 80, 82, 176n. 3
culturalism, 17, 18, 45, 47, 130, 172n. 1
culture, 45-47, 49, 83, 102; and economy,
 151, 164-65, and information, 101-103,